Portland
Public Library

In grateful recognition of a contribution by

Richard F. Libby

PAT

Also by Douglas Schoen

ENOCH POWELL AND THE POWELLITES

PAT

A Biography of Daniel Patrick Moynihan

DOUGLAS SCHOEN

Harper & Row, Publishers
New York, Hagerstown, San Francisco, London

This book is dedicated to the memory of my late grandparents Harry Bronston and Louise Collier Schoen and to their spouses Yetta Bronston and Lawrence Schoen. I owe them all a great deal and I am profoundly grateful.

FIRST EDITION

Designed by Gloria Adelson

Library of Congress Cataloging in Publication Data

Schoen, Douglas E., D.Phil.
   Pat.
   1. Moynihan, Daniel Patrick. 2. Statesmen—United States—Biography. 3. United States. Congress. Senate—Biography. 4. Sociologists—United States—Biography.
E840.8.M68S35   973.92′092′4[B]   78-20184
ISBN 0-06-013998-6

79 80 81 82 83 10 9 8 7 6 5 4 3 2 1

Contents

Acknowledgments vii

Introduction: Hell's Kitchen xi

1. A Sociological Phenomenon! 1
2. The College Years and London Life 31
3. The Return to New York 49
4. We'll Never Be Young Again 68
5. Moynihan for Mayor 93
6. The Family 103
7. Fulfilling a Dream: A Harvard Professorship 118
8. Switching Sides 144
9. A Retreat to India 187
10. Turtle Bay 208
11. The Big Gamble 246
12. A New Year in the Senate 263
13. Moynihan in Opposition? 276

Notes 296

Index 313

(Photographs follow page 210)

Acknowledgments

Writing a biography of Pat Moynihan has been a pleasure. More than 275 people contributed their recollections, memorabilia, and insights to this study. It was rare for an individual to decline to participate; people at the highest levels of government and private industry almost uniformly made themselves accessible to me and to the researchers who worked on the project. To everyone who was interviewed I owe a debt of gratitude.

A number of people deserve specific thanks for their help. Daniel Patrick Moynihan, despite a crowded schedule as senator from New York, made himself liberally available for interviews and responded to questions on any subject. In all, I conducted some eighteen hours of interviews with him in four separate sessions. Senator Moynihan's brother Michael supplied much of the chronology of the early Moynihan family history. Senator Moynihan's mother Margaret contributed specific recollections and a number of photographs. The cooperation of the entire Moynihan family has helped in many ways to make this book what it is.

In the course of my travels a number of people around the country were particularly hospitable. Ernestine and Fred Tangeman in Bluffton, Indiana; Julia Noe and Judy Rose in Louisville, Kentucky; Josh Gotbaum and Robert Gage in Washington, D.C.; and Joe and Marie Reisler all went out of their way to accommodate me, and I appreciate their kindness. On numerous occasions Congressman Stephen Solarz and his wife, Nina, welcomed me into their home in Washington, D.C., as though I were a member of their family, and I value both their hospitality and their insights into American politics.

Harry Hall, a friend of Pat Moynihan since 1939, provided me with copies of letters Moynihan had written between 1942 and 1953, and these were invaluable in writing about the early years. John Barry, a roommate of Moynihan in London, gave me a copy of his diary of that period, which contained a number of useful stories. And Dr. William Haddon, Jr., director of the Insurance Institute for Highway Safety, offered a mass of material on his field and additional material on Senator Moynihan.

Many people helped on the project by conducting interviews. John Elder in New Delhi, India; Marla Miller in London, England; and Diane Wallerstein in New York all contributed informative material. Frances Oliver, Kathleen Gleason, Janet Sabel, and Melinda Lande provided research assistance during the formative period of the book.

My principal research assistants were Melanie Dorsey and Lee Greenhouse. Ms. Dorsey had the unenviable task of tracking down every newspaper and magazine article on Pat Moynihan that appeared during the last twenty years, and she performed this task with precision, skill, insight—and most of all good humor. Mr. Greenhouse conducted many interviews in Washington, D.C., during the summer of 1977 and made a number of trips to track down people who knew Moynihan from particular periods.

I am grateful for the comments of those who read portions of the manuscript at various stages. Paula Newburg, George Miller, and Professor Abram Chayes of the Harvard Law School all made useful suggestions for the chapter on the United Nations. Nancy Derene read the entire manuscript and made a number of helpful suggestions. Finally, David Remes proofread the entire manuscript meticulously.

I must also thank those who excused me from my normal duties so that I might finish the book. Mark Penn was especially kind in assuming a large part of the burden of our opinion research firm. David Garth was charitable in allowing me the freedom needed to complete the work on schedule (and he has taught me a great deal). Richie and Debbie Lazarus gave considerable encouragement during the writing of the book.

I have been fortuante indeed to have had Erwin Glikes as editor. He and his assistant Barbara Grossman helped shape the book and refine the analysis. A young writer considers himself lucky to be in such capable hands. My literary agent Maxine Groffsky worked tirelessly to keep the project on schedule, and she, too, gave the manuscript a careful reading.

If I have learned anything from the process of writing this book, it is that there is a great repository of good and kindness in most people. I have benefited from the generosity of many.

Douglas Schoen

Introduction: Hell's Kitchen

> I was raised here [in Hell's Kitchen] during the Depression. We were poor. Our prospects were few.
>
> —Pat Moynihan, 1965

There aren't many families left now on 42nd Street between Tenth and Eleventh avenues on Manhattan's West Side, a block that used to be a principal meeting place for residents of the Hell's Kitchen neighborhood. The once bustling Irish working class neighborhood has largely been destroyed by redevelopment; the few residential buildings that remain on the block today are populated by poor blacks and Latin immigrants, with only a scattering of the elderly old-time residents. Where it used to be safe to walk the streets at most hours of the day or night young mothers now pull their children indoors at dusk for fear they might wander into the netherworld of Times Square only two blocks away on 42nd Street.

Most of the family stores have long since closed, the proprietors having moved to New Jersey or Long Island. A liquor store on Tenth Avenue between 41st and 42nd streets caters to local residents—only after they have proven to the great German shepherd who sits atop the counter that they do in fact plan to pay for their merchandise. In place

of many of the tenements that once lined the street are the headquarters
of Millar Elevator Industries. The occasional people to be seen on the
street are mostly tourists staying at the Travelodge Motel, and they can
be heard complaining loudly about the tour operator who booked them
into this out-of-the-way location.

In the 1930s and 1940s Hell's Kitchen was a virtual Irish village in
the middle of Manhattan, a tightly knit neighborhood populated by first-
and second-generation families who had displaced a large black community at the turn of the century. That had been a hard fight, and those
who finally won out sent down deep roots. Social life centered around
the home and such local bars as Margaret Moynihan's, which opened
in 1947 at 558 West 42nd Street.

The Moynihans, newcomers to an area in which acceptance was often
difficult to attain, quickly won over their new neighbors. During the day,
while the neighborhood people were at work, the local slaughterhouse
workers would stop in for lunch and a beer. If a meatcutter happened
to have wandered off with a side of beef, he knew that Margaret would
be happy to store it for safekeeping in the bar's refrigerator. Margaret
spent much of the day in the kitchen making corned beef and cabbage
while her often unreliable bartenders attended to the clientele.

Margaret Moynihan had two trustworthy bartenders in her sons Pat
and Mike, who were often called in to settle disputes and to resolve the
problems that arose in running a bar in a tough neighborhood. Both Pat
and Mike were in college and then in the navy during the period their
mother owned the bar, but they were expected to return home during
summer vacations and in periodic crises to help keep things running
smoothly. If the bartenders all decided to quit—as happened during
Pat's senior year at Tufts—he could be counted on to miss graduation
week in order to keep the bar functioning. When a bartender left after
a truck driver threatened to wipe the floor with him, Pat was soon there
to take over.

Pat, fond of displaying his navy whites, was perhaps the only person
to walk West 42nd Street in navy bermuda shorts and white shoes. "He
was really a down-to-earth kid," Dominic November, a former neighbor
of the Moynihans, recalled. "He was very interested in the labor move-

ment and always wanted an introduction to the head of my local, Johnny O'Rourke of the Teamsters."

Moynihan's Bar was no place for people with refined tastes. Only after Catherine Whelan, a neighbor and regular patron, asked for vodka on four separate occasions could Pat produce a bottle for her. (When he did produce it, he offered everyone a glass on the house.) It was the sort of place where the customers all ordered beer. School friends of Pat's, used to seeing him in preppie Cambridge garb, were often amazed at the sight of him in a bartender's white apron in the dimly lit barroom.

Pat Moynihan has never talked much about his early years. Hell's Kitchen was in fact only one stop on a crazy-quilt journey that took him from Tulsa, Oklahoma, to New York City's suburbs, to some of Manhattan's worst slums, to rural Westchester, and then to a stable working class neighborhood in Queens before his mother acquired the bar in Hell's Kitchen. His formative years combined shining shoes on West 43rd Street, working on the West Side docks, escorting young ladies at debutante balls, and spending much of his free time with people educated at Andover and Exeter. Thus Pat Moynihan's story is much more complex than the simple Horatio Alger tale of a poor boy's making good; it involves many dislocations, disruptions, rises and falls, flirtations with affluence, and struggles with poverty.

1

A Sociological Phenomenon!

I've lived much of my life in a jungle of broken families, watching
them tear out each other's minds, watching them feasting on each
other's hearts.

—Pat Moynihan, 1949

In the first class meetings of Government 244, Pat Moynihan's graduate
seminar in ethnic politics at Harvard, students were asked routinely to
talk about their family backgrounds, where their grandparents had come
from, what their grandparents had done for a living, and what their
parents did. When in the spring of 1972 John Wong told how his family
had escaped from mainland China in 1962 and had managed to scrape
up the fare for passage to the United States, Moynihan's eyes lit up.
"Wong, you are a sociological phenomenon!" he exclaimed in delight.
"Only ten years off the boat and you're at Harvard. It takes most families
two generations to do what you've done." To understand fully a politician's motivation and thought processes, Moynihan would explain again
and again to his students, you have to know where he came from and
what intellectual tradition influenced him.

1

Daniel Patrick Moynihan is a third-generation American on his father's side. His great-grandfather Cornelius Moynihan was a farmer and breeder of horses in Headford Junction, County Kerry, Ireland. Cornelius Moynihan's life was that of a poor peasant farmer; his wife Norah Connors Moynihan spent much of her day cooking over a large pot in the center of the dirt floor of their cottage. Cornelius' son Daniel Connors Moynihan continued to farm the family land in County Kerry.

Another son, John C. (Jack) Moynihan, was more ambitious. He went to school in County Kerry, then grew restless in the mid 1880s. In 1886, when he was nineteen, Jack Moynihan left for America, where he sought work in Jamestown, New York. After a series of temporary jobs, Jack found regular work laying oil and gas lines across Pennsylvania, Ohio, Michigan, and Indiana for J. P. Morgan's Standard Oil Company. But three years of the itinerant life was all Jack could stand; then he settled down as a superintendent of construction for the Kerwin Brothers, contractors in Toledo, Ohio.

In that capacity Jack Moynihan helped lay the first gas line from the recently discovered gas wells in northern Indiana to a little town thirty miles from Fort Wayne called Bluffton. On completing the job Jack Moynihan settled in Bluffton, where he lived in a rooming house and worked as a laborer until he was hired in 1902 by the Fort Wayne Gas Company. Six years later, when the company became the Northern Indiana Public Service Company, Jack was made manager of the Bluffton division, a position he held until his retirement in 1940.[1]

The people of Bluffton were predominantly Protestant in the late nineteenth century, and the adjustment was a little difficult for Jack Moynihan. (As late as 1900 there were only three other Catholic families —the Kellys, the Tangemans, and the Belgers—in a population of between 4500 and 5000.) Jack soon became active in the small St. Joseph's Church, and in 1895 he married another Irish Catholic from a neighboring town, Mary Fitzpatrick. Mary bore two children, John and Cornelius, then both Mary and Cornelius died of tuberculosis in 1905. In 1910 Jack married Elizabeth Effinger, a member of an old Bluffton family, and their union produced one daughter, Mary.

Despite his having come to Bluffton as a laborer and having spent his first years in town living in a rather rundown rooming house, Jack Moynihan rose to a position of some prominence in Bluffton. He was an organizing member of the Rotary and he belonged to the Moose club. As an active Democrat, he helped to get out the vote at election time —a process that involved visiting the Moose hall just before election day and buying beer for the regulars in exchange for their promises to vote the straight party ticket.

Jack Moynihan is remembered fondly in Bluffton. Violet Studgill, his secretary at the gas company, recalls that he always had a kind word for her and frequently told folksy Irish stories. Fred Tangeman, who during his teenage years worked for Jack Moynihan, pointed out in an interview that "the first thing people would say about Jack Moynihan was how much they liked him. You'd never hear a bad word about him. His kindness was well known, and people in Bluffton still remember how during the Depression he bought the farm his first wife's family owned so that they would have enough money to survive."

The Northern Indiana Public Service Company thought so well of Jack Moynihan that they spoke of him at length in their advertisement in the centennial edition of the Bluffton *Evening Banner* in 1937.

> There is one man who has been the guiding influence in serving Bluffton with gas. He is J. C. Moynihan, Bluffton manager of the gas company, a dean of the gas industry. Jack Moynihan has been closely identified with utility service here from its inception. For forty-eight years the town of Bluffton has enjoyed gas service, and for all but seven of those years, Mr. Moynihan has been actively engaged in seeing that its residents have the best service possible.
>
> The gas company takes this occasion, not only to congratulate Wells County on its centennial, but also to pay public tribute to Jack Moynihan, the oldest employee in point of service in the 12,000 miles it serves.[2]

When Jack Moynihan died in 1952, twelve years after his retirement from the gas company, the *News Banner* said in a front-page obituary that "for a long period of time [he] was one of Bluffton's most prominent and public spirited citizens."[3] There was a large crowd at the funeral; one of the mourners, who had not been in Bluffton for more than twenty-five years, was Jack's surviving son, John.

Throughout his childhood John had been a constant source of pride and concern to his father because of his powerful intellect and his almost total lack of responsibility. John Moynihan was considered one of the smartest boys in Bluffton. Neither he nor his best friend, Dean Reynolds, had to work hard to do well in school. Ernestine Baumgartner, a cousin of Jack Moynihan, remembers that Blanche Kaus, the principal of Bluffton High School in the early years of the century, told her repeatedly that John and Dean had scored in the ninety-ninth percentile on intelligence tests.

But John and Dean were not satisfied with studying and doing well in school; they were pranksters and hustlers who often incurred the wrath of the more staid residents of Bluffton. In high school the two were once put in charge of stacking piles of books, and when they grew tired of this they tried seeing how far they could throw them out the window. On another occasion they were caught swimming naked in a quarry where they had been forbidden to go at all. When they grew older they became dance promoters, recruiting local bands to play in Sturgis Hall for the teenagers.

John Moynihan was recognized as a leader by his classmates; he was president of his eighth-grade class and of the transition class between grammar school and high school. With Dean Reynolds, John Moynihan founded the Bluffton High School *Comet* during his senior year and served as the newspaper's first sports editor. World War I dominated young Moynihan's life in high school; in his junior year he served as a second lieutenant in the High School Volunteers of America, and in the school's Christmas play he portrayed an American soldier fighting in France. It was considered fashionable for boys from Bluffton to attend Culver Military Academy for training during the summer, and Jack Moynihan made certain that John went between his junior and senior years.

In the *Retrospect,* the 1919 Bluffton High School yearbook, John Moynihan was described as "the very image of Socrates, cut in mahogany." The mildly facetious prophecy that the yearbook editors composed made him a staunchly Republican midwestern newspaper editor in 1924, mobbed by a group of angry radical Democrats. Despite the attack, Moynihan refused to bend his principles. "Poor John," the prophecy read, "always had the habit of sticking by his own ideas no matter what happened."

One of John's very definite ideas was that he had no real use for school. Violet Studgill remembers her boss Jack Moynihan's worrying whether John would go to college. Ultimately John did spend some time at Notre Dame, but he was never a serious student. Instead he yearned to get into journalism.

On leaving Notre Dame he took a job as a reporter for the Huntington (Indiana) *Press* and there struck up what proved to be a lifelong friendship with author and humorist H. Allen Smith. Following a brief stint as city editor of the Bluffton *Evening Banner,* John Moynihan traveled across the state to take a job on a new newspaper in Jeffersonville on the Kentucky-Indiana border. When he was made city editor of the Jeffersonville *Bulletin* late in 1924, he wired his friend H. Allen Smith, inviting him to accept a job on the paper. The inducement was not working conditions; Monnie—as he had come to be known—went into great detail about the quality of the women in the nearby roadhouses and the large number of gambling dens in the area. Smith quickly accepted and found that Moynihan had not been exaggerating. Smith and Monnie devoted most of their evenings to prowling the local gambling dens and houses of ill repute. The two had a temporary breach when Smith fell in with a local high school girl and began spending much of his free time in soda shops. If you were a man, Monnie maintained, you spent your time gambling, boozing, and shacking up with women, not drinking milkshakes.

John Moynihan's attitude changed shortly after Frank (Daddy) Rager, a Louisville reporter, introduced him to Margaret Phipps, a recent high school graduate and nursing student. Margaret Phipps was the eldest of three sisters and was almost as brash as John Moynihan. Not one to hide her intelligence, Margaret had made it clear at an early age that she was smarter than most. She also liked to be different; once when all the other girls in town were planning to wear white satin dresses to a dance, Margaret chose black gingham. Nor was she deferential or retiring; longtime residents of Jeffersonville recall that Margaret told people exactly what she thought—at a time when women were expected to sit quietly and merely look attractive. Margaret is said to have actually kicked a man under the table of a restaurant in which they were dining when she did not like something he had said. And that was remarkable behavior for a woman in Jeffersonville, Indiana, in 1925.

Margaret Phipps came from a very good family in Jeffersonville. Her father, H. Willard (Harry) Phipps, a successful trial lawyer in partnership with another Jeffersonville man, Jack Sweeney, had a reputation for kindliness. At Christmas he sent his nephews to Quick's Store to pick up Christmas baskets for distribution in Clagsberg, the less affluent part of town. A family that had been burned out could count on Phipps to contribute at least some clothing. Phipps would generally defend anyone in need of legal representation, regardless of the person's race or ability to pay. When Phipps defended a black man accused of murder, a local druggist asked him privately if he didn't really believe that "they should hang the black bastard." Phipps's face reddened, and he asked the druggist if he owed him any money. When the druggist said no, Phipps left the store, indicating that he would not be returning.

While both Harry Phipps and Jack Moynihan were respected in their home communities, Phipps came from the more established family. His father, Daniel Phipps, had been a successful farmer, and his mother, Julia Grayson, had come from an old Kentucky family. Harry Phipps was well regarded by lawyers in both Jeffersonville, Indiana, and Louisville, Kentucky—the two cities in which he maintained offices during his career. His obituary described him as a leading member of the Clark County bar and called him a "highly proficient trial lawyer."[4]

Phipps counted Clarence Darrow among his colleagues; on Margaret's fifth birthday Darrow gave her a clothbound copy of *Black Beauty*. Like Jack Moynihan, Harry Phipps was an active Democrat. His brother Isaac was the longtime Democratic sheriff of Clark County, and Harry once ran for prosecuting attorney there. His daughter Julia remembers that her father used to say, "Any man who is too good to be a Democrat should die and go to heaven."

Harry Phipps's wife, Margaret Bickell, was from a German family in Louisville who owned a grocery store and brought her up rigidly. Consequently she was the sort of mother with whom children did not argue. Margaret, Lucille, and Julia Phipps knew they had much more leeway with their somewhat indulgent father than they had with their mother.

Margaret and Harry Phipps found John Moynihan an attractive prospect for their daughter. Although John was Catholic and the Phippses were Protestant, the family had no qualms about Margaret's converting and being married in St. Augustine Catholic Church in Jeffersonville in 1925. The newlyweds set off for Sebring, Florida, where Moynihan took a job as a real estate salesman.

On arriving in Florida Moynihan called H. Allen Smith, described the opportunities there, and urged him to join them. Smith drove all night to Sebring and managed to land a job as a reporter on the local paper (where he met the woman he would later marry). Unfortunately, the real estate business in Sebring went bust at just about the time John Moynihan arrived. And with a habit of living beyond his means, he had purchased a green Studebaker on credit and now couldn't pay for it. Undaunted, he arranged one morning late in 1925 to present Smith with the car, which he said would be repossessed within the month. Given his debts, Moynihan had to leave town quickly, and he and Margaret headed back to the midwest. In Tulsa, Oklahoma, he found a job as a reporter on the *Tribune*. A few months later Smith joined him again, Moynihan getting him a job on the paper.

John and Margaret Moynihan's first child, Daniel Patrick, was born March 16, 1927. There were complications; the baby was sickly and there was some concern at first about his chances for survival. When Pat was healthy and growing, the family moved to New York City, where John Moynihan had taken a job as an advertising copywriter for RKO.

John Moynihan's only acquaintance in New York was his old friend from Bluffton, Dean Reynolds, who met the family at the Pennsylvania Hotel, opposite Penn Station. Reynolds was then dating Winnie Winckler, and she accompanied him to greet the Moynihan family. While Reynolds and Moynihan remained friends in New York, Winnie Winckler soon parted company with Reynolds. However, she became a close friend of Margaret's, and the Moynihan children always called her and her husband, Tony Avellina, aunt and uncle.

The Moynihans spent a few months in Greenwich Village before moving to Ridgefield Park, New Jersey, where Michael Moynihan was born in 1928. There the Moynihans enjoyed a comfortable suburban life,

John taking the ferry across the Hudson River to his job at RKO and Margaret devoting herself to raising their two sons. They enjoyed a degree of affluence at first; Margaret had charge accounts at a number of Fifth Avenue department stores, and Pat and Mike were always well dressed. It was clear that Margaret Phipps had married well. Her sister Julia, married to a golf professional and living near the Moynihans, had to work for a doctor in New York City to supplement the family income.

Being the mother of Pat Moynihan when he was two or three years old was a full-time job. A precocious and active child, Pat found numerous ways to introduce chaos into the Moynihan family life. Once when the family planned a dinner party, Margaret and John found that all their good silverware was missing. Afraid that it might have been stolen, Margaret nevertheless asked Pat if he had any idea what had happened to it—and Pat took her into the backyard to show her where he had buried it. On another occasion Pat traded a bottle of his father's home-brewed alcohol to a neighbor for a bottle of root beer.

Aunt Julia Noe was caring for Pat one day when he got into a fight with a child who was bigger and stronger. The boy had been taunting Pat for some weeks, but Julia told him that he had to stand up to the bully. Pat went back into the street and took more punishment than he gave. When he returned to the house, Julia told him that while he was bruised and bloodied, he had managed to get in a few good punches. And Aunt Julia offered to buy him a pair of boxing gloves.

In 1931, after Pat's sister, Ellen, was born, John Moynihan moved his family to a larger house in Stewart Manor in Nassau County, just outside New York City. The children remember their father reading them bedtime stories and poems in those days and taking them to his office on Saturday mornings.

During the early 1930s the Moynihans spent half their summers at their parents' homes in Indiana and the other half with the Irish colony in New York City's Far Rockaway, where John Moynihan's cousin John and his wife, Hannah, had a house. The Moynihans divided their time in the midwest between the Phippses' farm in Kentucky and their house in Jeffersonville and Grandpa Moynihan's house in Bluffton. Pat and his brother (and later their sister) usually headed for Indiana on the Broadway Limited as soon as school was out in June, often traveling unaccompanied. On one such occasion when Pat was six years old, he returned from Indiana alone on the overnight train. On the first day he spent all the money his grandparents had given him for food on lemon pie, but he was able to persuade a couple of nuns on the train to buy him breakfast the next morning. Along with his suitcase, Pat was carrying an old banjo and a copy of *Time*. The sight of him wandering around Grand Central Station attracted an Associated Press reporter who wrote a short item about him that appeared in the *New York Times* in July 1933.[5]

In Indiana the Moynihans and the Phippses lavished attention on their grandchildren. Margaret Moynihan remembers her father-in-law feeding the children candy before meals and letting them gamble at the Moose hall. The early summers in Indiana were happy times that contrasted sharply with what was becoming an increasingly unhappy home life for the Moynihan family in New York.

John Moynihan had soon found that the quiet family life of the suburbs was not to his liking, and he began spending periods of time away from home. He was attracted to the life of the New York journalists of the day, a life that emphasized boozing, gambling, and carousing. Joel Sayre, a contemporary of Moynihan's, has described his generation of journalists as being part of the "nothing's sacred school of newspapering."

> The newspapermen of [this day] were, in cold fact, much as newspapermen were pictured on stage and screen—hard-drinking, irreverent, girl-chasing, iconoclastic young men wearing snap-brim hats with cigarettes dangling from their whisky-wet lips and bent on insulting any and all individuals who stood in their path, no matter how celebrated or sacrosanct. There were some who complained at times about this popular depiction, insisting that it was not a true portrait, that the gin-soaked reprobates were few in number. They lied in their teeth.[6]

John Moynihan earned extra income by coming up with titles for new RKO movie releases, and in doing this he was drawn further into the show business world. He spent many nights in speakeasies with Reynolds and Smith and in all-night bridge games in the *New York Times* office on West 43rd Street. He and Smith would regularly stay out late, and sometimes Moynihan would not be home for weeks at a time. Next-door neighbor Nell Smith even blamed Margaret for corrupting Nell's husband, Allen. Margaret wanted to keep her own marriage together, yet she found her husband, John, to be irresponsible and apparently unconcerned with the family's welfare. Meanwhile, Moynihan was seeing another woman, had begun to drink excessively, and had lost a lot of money at the racetrack. He found Margaret overbearing and demanding, and in the middle and late 1930s he spent less and less time with the family. He also managed to get himself into trouble.

John Moynihan's way of life required a substantial supply of money —much more than publicists were paid during the Depression—and he began to borrow heavily from loan sharks. By 1935 his debts were large and he was unable to come up with the money he needed to pay off a loan. One night he found himself being chased across tenement roofs by gangsters wielding gun and knife. The next morning he was discovered lying face down in an alley, severely bruised and battered. The injuries were not serious, but the incident appeared to put a damper on Moynihan's behavior. Julia Noe suspects that the beating may have affected John's mental stability; he seemed to act differently thereafter, and she recalls his doing uncharacteristic things such as shadow boxing before the bedroom mirror, as though he were a fighter.

While John Moynihan's life may have been somewhat erratic, that of the rest of the family certainly was not. They now lived in a comfortable neighborhood in Crystal Gardens, Queens, where Pat, Mike, and Ellen played in the street and carved their initials in freshly laid cement pavement. They attended the local Catholic grammar school and quickly showed intellectual promise. During the 1936 election campaign Pat and Mike distributed Roosevelt pamphlets and fliers in their neighborhood, marking the first political involvement of the Moynihan brothers.

In the fall of 1937 John Moynihan left home for good, leaving behind a family bewildered by his behavior. Initial efforts to locate him failed; ultimately he moved to San Jose, California, where he remarried and took a job on a local newspaper. He never again saw his son Pat, and he had only one brief meeting with his son Mike, who visited him in the early 1950s.

Suddenly the Moynihan family was plunged into poverty. Jack Moynihan, aghast at his son's abandoning his wife, had little money to spare but sent what he could to Margaret. The situation was still worse because the Phipps family had also suffered a reversal: Margaret's father had died in 1935, and in 1937 the family home in Jeffersonville was largely destroyed in a flood. That summer Pat's family shared a summer home in Huntington, Long Island, with a number of temporarily destitute relatives from Indiana.

Jack Moynihan's assistance was not enough to keep the family from undergoing a drastic change in circumstances. Margaret Moynihan was forced to move her family from their comfortable middle class neighborhood in Crystal Gardens to a cold-water flat on East 88th Street. Margaret was by then under great emotional strain, and Julia Noe, who had moved back to Louisville, returned to Manhattan to help move the family. The apartment on East 88th Street was anything but luxurious. John Moynihan never provided a penny for support, and the family was on welfare for a brief period. Mike and Pat shared a double bed in one room, and Ellen and her mother shared another room. The only heat in the apartment was generated by the stove in the kitchen; it circulated through the flat only because the previous tenants had knocked a hole in the wall of Margaret's bedroom.

While there may have been a good deal of confusion, the family was not disorganized. The children continued to attend local Catholic grammar schools. Margaret taught English in the Women's House of Detention and took on whatever part-time work she could find as a practical nurse. There were always books and magazines around the house. (When asked some years later about the presence of reading material, Margaret Moynihan seemed surprised and even somewhat insulted that an interviewer would even ask whether there were many books in her home.)

The Moynihans spent little time on East 88th Street. In the course of the following year or so they moved into a succession of apartments on the upper West Side, taking advantage of landlords' offers of free rent for signing new leases. The children attended Holy Name School at West 97th Street and Amsterdam Avenue, and in the afternoons Mike and Pat shined shoes in Times Square. Pat was very businesslike; he was out there to do a job, and he was loud and boisterous in order to make his presence known. Mike was more mischievous; he often spent the money he made on candy and sweets. At Christmastime Pat would put on heavy clothes and boots and take the D train to Brooklyn to sell

Christmas trees for Tony and Winnie Avellina, warming up with glasses of whiskey during the eight-hour days of hawking pine bushes.

At about this time Margaret Moynihan instituted a sort of communal arrangement in the household. All money earned was to be deposited in an old sugar bowl in the kitchen, and each member of the family was entitled to draw on it according to his or her needs. While the family always had enough to eat, the constant moving and the dislocations took their toll. Margaret, needing time to make herself more secure financially, sent her children in the winter of 1939 to live with Aunt Julia in Louisville through the spring and summer.

Pat went to Jeffersonville High School, where he was immediately identified as a character. (Mike still recalls the time Pat shocked the locals by taking a racy magazine to school.) Pat became an avid boy scout who won merit badges in firemanship, pioneering, and reading. His scout leader, Orville Holmes, recalled that a short time after Moynihan arrived in Jeffersonville he was selected a patrol leader. On one occasion, starring in a boy scout show, Pat forgot his part and proceeded to do a solo skit in which he portrayed a screaming woman. The performance scared and amazed his fellow scouts, and Pat won the prize for the best skit.

Margaret Moynihan continued to work while her children were away, all the while seeking to marry someone with the financial means to support her and the three children. One candidate was Henry Stapelfeld, sixty-five years old and a friend of Winnie Winckler's mother. If Margaret Moynihan was somewhat flamboyant and outspoken, Henry Stapelfeld was just the opposite; he was not terribly bright or engaging, and he had never been married. Winnie advised Margaret not to marry him, but the promise of financial security persuaded her to do it. For Stapelfeld owned a substantial amount of Standard Brands stock and a fourteen-room house on thirteen acres in rural Westchester. If there was no emotional attraction between the two, at least Stapelfeld could be counted on to provide for Pat, Mike, and Ellen. Stapelfeld seemed to offer her security, and on that basis she agreed to marry him.

It was clear from the outset that the marriage was not going to be a success. They bickered constantly over money, and Stapelfeld reneged on his promise to provide for Margaret's children. The fourteen-room house was a source of pride to Margaret (who used a picture of it on her

Christmas cards in 1940 and 1941), but the house and grounds were rarely well kept. Stapelfeld had no gardener and would have a maid only one day a week. He became stingier and stingier as time went on, and in the winter of 1940 he was telling Margaret to keep the lights in the house turned off while the sun was shining. Mike and Pat disliked him, teased him, and pulled such pranks as slashing the tires on his automobile.

Pat Moynihan was twelve when the family moved to the town of Kitchewan, and he went into the ninth grade at Yorktown Heights High School. He was then a tall and painfully thin figure whose lack of coordination and exaggerated features quickly made him someone to be picked on. One boy cracked an egg over Pat's head in the schoolyard. Moynihan was not a fighter, but neither was he the sort who would walk away from a fight. He often succeeded in talking his way out of trouble —while his brother, it seemed, was always involved in a scrap.

Pat's few friends were an odd mixture. John Anders was a local tough who spent much of his time in the woods trapping skunks. Anders once rescued Pat from a group of kids who had him up against a brick wall on a fire escape. Harry Hall's family owned a large farm on Baptist Church Road in Yorktown Heights. Moynihan and Hall were probably the best students in their class, and the two spent a good deal of time together working on the Hall farm, a tall glass of iced tea their only compensation at the end of the day.

Moynihan's friends from this period recall that the two brothers appeared uncomfortable about their home life. The bickering and arguing that had marked Margaret's marriage to John Moynihan had returned. Pat's response to the fighting was to withdraw from the family, to spend more of his time hunting with Anders or working on the Hall farm. He could also be found at the secondhand store of his neighbor Patricia Coote. Mrs. Coote lived in a small cottage next to Stapelfeld's house and kept some of her personal effects in Stapelfeld's barn. A very literary New England Christian Scientist, she helped make a difficult living situation marginally better by engaging Pat in conversation on a wide range of subjects.

While Moynihan may have appeared somewhat uncoordinated and immature in those days, he was beginning to show signs of the ambition and the concern with style that would be characteristic of later years. In the fall of 1940 Moynihan accompanied the Hall family when they drove their younger daughter to a prep school in Connecticut. In Greenwich they passed a number of mansions that everyone admired, and the Halls recall Pat's maintaining that some day he would have property like that. Pat made it a point to dress "properly" for social events—he was the only boy in the school to wear a tuxedo to the junior prom.

The Avellinas spent virtually every weekend in Kitchewan trying to help Margaret make a go of her marriage to Stapelfeld, and they were always available to take the children for day trips to such events as the 1939 World's Fair. In the spring of 1941 Margaret separated permanently from Stapelfeld; in the summer, staying with her sister Julia Noe in Louisville, she gave birth to his son, Tommie. That summer Pat had a job at the golf course where Courtland Noe worked, and he saved $36 to buy himself a suit.

In the fall of 1941 Margaret, her children, and the new baby moved back to Manhattan to an apartment on West 92nd Street. Mike went to Joan of Arc Junior High School on West 93rd Street, and Pat started the eleventh grade at Benjamin Franklin High School in East Harlem. While Moynihan would later complain about the academic quality of Benjamin Franklin—telling a reporter that it was "no Bronx High School of Science"—he was enthusiastic while he was there. His initial reaction was that "the teachers are swell," though as virtually the only Irish youngster in a student body that was heavily black, Italian, and Puerto Rican, he felt somewhat isolated.

The principal was Leonard Covello, an educator of some prominence because of his work with working class children; the teachers were a mixed lot who paid special attention to the very bright students like Moynihan. But Pat found Franklin to be easier academically than Yorktown Heights High School had been. In French, for example, Miss Damon at Yorktown had consistently given him 70s while at Franklin he was at the top of his class with a 90 average.

Perhaps the most difficult aspect of attending Franklin was fitting in socially. Moynihan wasn't from East Harlem and hadn't even spent much time in Manhattan. Yet he fell in quickly with an intellectually pugnacious boy, Bob Tenenbaum, who fancied himself an actor. Together they worked on the school newspaper and the yearbook.

Classes lasted only from 8 A.M. to noon, and Moynihan, like his father more than twenty years earlier, quickly became involved in journalism. After only five months at Franklin he was editing the school newspaper, the *Almanac*, and helping to edit and dummy a local community newspaper, the East Harlem *News*. Putting out both papers meant that Moynihan would often be in his office, the Journalism and Publications Room, until 6 P.M.

And then Moynihan still had to work. The divorce from Stapelfeld had left Margaret Moynihan in financial straits, and she needed the help of Pat and Mike. Again Pat took to shining shoes in Times Square, opposite the old Paramount Theatre on 43rd Street. In December 1941 he wrote a friend that he was making a "luxurious" living of about fifty cents an hour. Occasionally a customer would pay him a dollar for a shine, but this was an unusual occurrence. Shining shoes was a novel, almost romantic experience for the increasingly worldly Pat Moynihan, and he invited his old friends from Westchester to visit him whenever they were in an exploratory mood and wanted to see how the other half lived.

Social life was difficult for Moynihan, still a gangly, awkward boy who was ill at ease with girls. Franklin was not a coeducational school, so Moynihan met girls only when he attended citywide conferences on public affairs topics. His interest in a couple of girls at Yorktown Heights High School had been cut off by the move to New York City.

At the age of fourteen or fifteen Pat Moynihan began to show serious interest in politics. As one of the better students at Franklin, he was invited to attend a special political science class for two hours a week, and he enjoyed it tremendously. His views were staunchly on the left but were by no means doctrinaire. He once urged a friend to read a section of Erskine Caldwell's *Some American People;* it would convince him, Pat said, to become at least a mild socialist. He believed it important that he read *Das Kapital,* and he told his mother so. But he was skeptical of zealots and fanatics. In a letter in 1941 he rhetorically asked a friend whether he was still convinced about the inevitability of the revolution. Moynihan assured him it was coming, citing facetiously as authority a speaker on a soapbox in Union Square.

When Harry Hall was sent to Andover for his last two years of high school, Moynihan wrote to him mocking the revolutionary fervor of the privileged students in private schools. When Hall seemed to be moving away from a dedication to leftist politics and toward a more active interest in baseball, Moynihan elaborated on his latest thesis, that sportswriters and ballplayers were paid large sums of money by the vested interests to keep American boys ignorant of everything but the batting averages of the Brooklyn Dodgers. Yet the mocking tone of some of Moynihan's comments on the left belied an ambivalence that at least some of his classmates and friends detected. Thus, when the editors of his high school yearbook looked into their crystal ball, they saw Pat Moynihan as a bank president "cussing out the labor unions and durn radicals."

His family life was something Moynihan spoke about only reluctantly, and most of his friends knew nothing of his life outside school. "It was something Pat just didn't talk about," one friend recalled some twenty-five years later. "We sort of vaguely knew that his father had left some years before, and that's about all we knew."

A job in a defense plant provided steady income and some security for Margaret Moynihan, and she moved her family from the tenements of the West Side to Astoria. The Moynihans rented a large apartment in a converted mansion—the Mary Blackwell House on 27th Avenue— then owned by a family that had converted it into apartments. The Moynihans' quarters were not spacious; Pat and Mike shared a bedroom, so did Margaret and Ellen. But the house itself was quite elegant, so much so that one friend of the family recalls that he thought of the Moynihans as living in a mansion. The family's time in Astoria was one of the happier, more stable periods in their lives—even though Bob Tenenbaum remembers a good deal of hollering and carrying on.

Life was hard for Margaret. She came home dead tired from her job at 4 P.M. or 5 P.M. and had to cope with an infant son, a pre-teenage daughter, and two active teenage boys. For Pat Moynihan the difference between life in Astoria and life in Manhattan was striking: he no longer woke up to holes in the walls and paint flaking from the ceiling; his new house was cheerful and had a large porch where on weekends the family could sit and drink beer with friends and neighbors.

Improved financial circumstances did not permit Pat Moynihan to quit working, but he graduated from shoeshining to other, more profitable ventures. For a time he was a stock boy at Gimbels, a job that paid him better than any other job he had had. And it offered additional benefits: it provided him with stationery for writing friends and it gave him the opportunity to liberate stray merchandise from his capitalist bosses. Need I say more?

The job at Gimbels allowed Pat to buy new books and a wardrobe. Having a good wardrobe—which became of central importance to Moynihan when he discovered London's Savile Row tailors—was something he could not then afford. And Moynihan was of at least two minds on how he wanted to dress. On the one hand, he believed that certain events called for "proper" dress, and he always had a suit for formal occasions. On the other hand, he often tried to affect a working class look, the appearance of having just come from a blue-collar job.

To make money was the constant and principal challenge, and the Moynihan brothers developed a scam to supplement their income. They went out to the Rockaways and rented a bungalow or stayed in one rented by their cousins Hannah and John Moynihan. In the evening Pat and Mike would pick up a bundle of the next morning's newspapers to sell in the local gin mills. The smaller Mike took the papers into a bar and began to hawk them. After a few minutes Pat would amble in, knock the papers out of Mike's hand, announce in a loud voice that the bar was his territory, and then stalk out of the bar with a flourish, leaving his brother and the newspapers scattered on the floor. Sympathetic customers, taking pity on Mike, would buy all his papers, and he would go home and split the money with Pat.

Holding a wide variety of jobs did not affect Moynihan's academic performance; he was elected to Arista, Franklin's honor society, in the spring of his junior year (1942), and he finished first in his class. Pat was also elected secretary of his class—an exceptional tribute in that he did not come from the neighborhood and had attended the school less than two years. At that time admission to City College was based on academic performance in high school, and Moynihan's grades qualified him for a place in the class that would enter City in the fall of 1943.

During the summer of 1943 Moynihan again sought exciting work.

Too old for shoeshining and wanting something more lucrative, he headed for the docks, where he was hired as a day worker on Piers 48 and 49 at West 11th Street in Manhattan.

As marine freight handlers, the dock workers unloaded freight cars that had been brought over from New Jersey, piling the goods on the docks where longshoremen would later carry it into ships. Dockers worked in gangs of seven, each gang having a freight car to unload and a section of the dock to work on. Two of the seven men worked as stevedores, one in the car and the other on the bulkhead, unloading the goods. Three or four men carried whatever the stevedores had unloaded from the car to the dock on hand trucks. A boss or checker directed the men and made sure the job was done properly. For his first six months on the docks, Moynihan worked almost exclusively as a stevedore.

Dock workers were hired at two hours in the morning—8:30 and 10:30—and anyone who showed up at the earlier hour was virtually guaranteed a job. The pay was 78¢ an hour. Moynihan worked at a feverish clip that summer—to such an extent that some of the older workers nicknamed him Young Blood for his tenacity. The boss on Pier 49, a black man named Claude, took a particular liking to Moynihan and treated him well. After establishing himself on the docks, Moynihan persuaded Bob Tenenbaum to join him. Tenenbaum worked periodically, Moynihan fairly steadily through the summer.

Moynihan enjoyed talking of work on the docks with his friends from Westchester, who lived in a very different world. For Harry Hall, who had just gone off to Andover, Moynihan delighted in providing a particularly detailed account—after all, it was something about which preppies knew nothing. The summer of 1943 was largely a success.

But there was one embarrassing moment. One night in July he had stayed up late reading Thomas Wolfe's *You Can't Go Home Again.* When he arrived at the docks the next morning, he was not particularly tired, but by midday he was beginning to feel groggy. At 2:15 P.M. his gang had finished their boxcar and the checker told them to take a short break. Moynihan climbed to the top of a freight car and took a nap.

Two hours later the foreman wakened Moynihan from his slumber and fired him. Moynihan was shocked and disillusioned—but not so much that he couldn't write a rather elaborate description of the event for Harry Hall, in the hope that a writer friend of Hall's, Bill Maxwell, would see it, recognize Moynihan's literary skill, and give him a job.

Soon rehired, Moynihan continued working on and off as a stevedore until January 1944. That month the U.S. Employment Service sent over twenty men who had never worked on the docks before. Not having the skill to work as stevedores or checkers, they were put to work as truckers. Then, to fill the need for new checkers, the dock boss made Moynihan a checker. While Moynihan acknowledged privately that he did not feel equipped to handle the job, he ordered the new men to put some snap into their work and enjoyed pushing around the college students who were working during their vacation. One Saturday Moynihan told the three men from New York University in his gang that Pier 48 was no damn college campus. They would have to work to survive, he said; that was what *he* had to do. Pat Moynihan might have been going to City College, but he was a working man before he was a student. He *had* to be there; *he* was no rich college kid slumming on the docks.

There are differing accounts of how Pat Moynihan actually got into City College. His transcript from his first year there reveals that he was admitted on the basis of his high school record. Officers of the alumni association recall now that an entrance examination was not required until after World War II. (Prior to 1945 the only students who had to take tests for admission were those whose high school grade-point averages did not qualify them for the day session.) But Moynihan remembered the facts differently. He had never had plans to go to college, he told a reporter in the mid 1960s. College "was something for rich kids. Anyhow, the only college I'd ever heard of was Notre Dame, and that was because of their football team." There was an admissions test for City College, and he took it only to prove he was "as smart as I thought I was." On the day of the test, Moynihan said, he "played it very tough" and swaggered into the room with his longshoreman's loading hook jutting out of his back pocket. According to his account, he passed the test and then decided to go to college in the fall.[7]

Moynihan may have confused his admission to City College with his entrance into the navy's officer training program (V-12). Apparently that exam was more traumatic for him than he has been willing to admit. Pat was afraid he would fail the test, and Harry Hall had to spend a good part of the fall and spring of 1944 persuading him to take it. When Moynihan did pass, he sent a telegram to Hall at Andover: MOYNIHAN IN NAVY, SECRETARY KNOX DROPS DEAD.

Before Moynihan entered the navy in June 1944 he spent one year at City College. In recent years Moynihan has spoken of the influence of the institution on his political ideology,[8] but early in his freshman year he wrote that "it is extremely disappointing, filthy, colorless, and hard." His early disillusionment with CCNY might have been in part because a watch his mother had given him for his high school graduation was stolen from his gym locker while he was taking a shower. He found his French and Spanish courses so difficult that he doubted he would pass. He had more confidence in economics and history, but passing trigonometry was touch and go. At midsemester he was reported to be failing both language courses, and in the end he just managed to pass them with Ds. He got another D in basic hygiene (the required health and physical education course). Trigonometry continued to be a problem, but he finished with a C. His confidence in his ability in European history and introductory economics was well placed; he earned an A in both. Moynihan also passed a remedial speech course he was required to take, because of a minor speech impediment (which can still be noticed today when he becomes excited).

In the fall of 1943 Moynihan stopped working for the first time in a long while. Not working made him feel out of sorts, and he claimed to be unable to sleep or to digest his food. In fact his real concern was flunking out of college; he indicated that if he failed four-fifths of his courses, he would return to the docks. About all that Moynihan expressed much enthusiasm for late in 1943 was his social life—and he delighted in recounting to his friends his successes with women.

Partying took up a good portion of Moynihan's Christmas vacation and the 1943–44 intersession recess. Harry Hall had been invited to a number of debutante balls around town, and he knew several women who attended exclusive New York City women's schools who needed escorts. Mrs. Samuel Ordway of Kitchewan was looking for just such a companion for her daughter Ellen. Moynihan filled the role perfectly. Mrs. Ordway remembers that, unlike many of the available young men, Moynihan was talkative and entertaining. While Moynihan did not feel comfortable in the role—dancing at the Plaza with prep school women was not taught on Pier 48—he apparently carried it off with aplomb.

Moynihan's real passion at that time was jazz, and he spent hours at such events as Leadbelly concerts and at jazz halls like Nick's in Greenwich Village. He acquired a reputation as a real aficionado and won the nickname Jellyroll (an old black jazz singer's term for sexual intercourse). By the fall of 1943 Moynihan had taken to signing his letters with his name followed by a drawing of a jelly roll cake.

If any group of people aroused Pat Moynihan's ire during the late 1960s, it was upper middle class students who demonstrated on college campuses. To be sure, there was much that students did that was irrational and even counterproductive; but what was most interesting about Moynihan's reaction was its vehemence. Not surprisingly, if Moynihan had little patience with students who protested the Vietnam War, he had even less thirty-five years ago with students who tried to avoid service in World War II.

One night in February 1944 he went drinking in Greenwich Village with a group of bohemians. One young man—Moynihan described him in a letter as a "curlyhaired young darling from NYU"—was up for military classification the next morning and "the poor soulful lad just couldn't bear the thought of associating with vulgar proletarians, or of digging ditches, or of being ordered about by a brutish sergeant." The fellow's solution to the problem ("like a hundred other sensitive misunderstood illtreated young artists") was to get a deferral on psychological grounds. Moynihan told him pointedly that the army would be wise to his scheme—and he added "a few personal comments which were shocking to all concerned." The young man was ultimately inducted, and to nobody's surprise Moynihan was not invited to his send-off party.

The school break allowed Moynihan to return to "his docks," and it was then that he was promoted to checker. It was a moment of great pride for him; he wrote only half facetiously that the promotion marked "another step in his stairway to the stars."

For reasons that are not entirely clear, Moynihan now cast aside socialism to become a devoted capitalist. Perhaps his conversion was a result of his entering college or of his newfound authority on the docks.

He wrote Harry Hall that the conversion was as if "a new life has come to me and the glorys of the Capitalist system and the American way have burst into my life like the sun on Easter Morn." His new credo was "Long live the American way of life—down with the reds and the labor unions." He also advised that if Hall had preserved any letters of his containing remarks that might be construed as radical, he should burn them. The direction was of course facetious, but it suggests some sense on his part that what he thought might well be important someday.

The spring of 1944 was much like the previous fall: Moynihan spent long hours worrying whether he would pass his courses and even longer hours hanging out at Nick's. He found it hard to discipline himself to study French and Spanish, and often he dedicated a whole weekend to study only to pass the entire time sleeping and drinking Pepsi and beer. At Nick's he became quite well known—to the extent that the bartenders bought him drinks and jazz musicians played "Indiana" for him on the eve of his departure to visit relatives there.

Much of the year Moynihan was in debt, scraping along from day to day, often borrowing from his mother and his friends. He lost so much in one dice game that spring that he had to return to the docks (where he now earned about $1.50 an hour) to extricate himself from a precarious financial position. He spent one Saturday working thirteen hours, rolling coal tar, for about $20, and he sold some of his spare clothing to a friend.

In the spring of 1944 Moynihan got As in English composition and European history and again had real trouble with French and second-year Spanish. He got another D in French, but he managed to pull his Spanish grade up to a C. While his high school yearbook had predicted that he would be a great soapbox orator—and many now feel that he has more than lived up to that notice—his speech teacher was apparently less sanguine, and he got a C in public speaking. And once again he received a D in hygiene. In June 1944 Moynihan was told that he would lose all credit for his year of Spanish if he did not continue taking the language for another year.

School ended for Moynihan in June 1944; less than a month later he was assigned to Middlebury College in Vermont for the start of his navy training. The application process for the V-12 program had been nerve-wracking, but Moynihan soon fell in love with Middlebury, a lovely old New England town that provided a vivid contrast to Benjamin Franklin High School and City College.

Moynihan now came in contact with a class of people he had previously had little to do with—upper middle class white Protestants with preparatory school educations. The people he saw from day to day no longer had names like Italo Di Geronomo or Robert Tenenbaum but now had names like Emmett Van Allen Murray III. Of the group Moynihan associated with, only Angus Deming could have been considered affluent, yet they were preppies and he was not. Joe Reisler (who went to Andover) and Story Zartman (who went to Exeter) sensed no great differences between them and Moynihan—except that Moynihan was a bit more of a character than either one of them was. "We didn't see Moynihan as a poor boy from New York among rich prep school boys," Reisler recalled. "We were just a group of guys thrown together. Those sorts of differences weren't really important." But there was a sense that Moynihan was someone out of the ordinary. "Moynihan was definitely an oddity," Deming remembers. "You really didn't know what to make of him."

The differences, perhaps unimportant to his prep school friends, were of critical importance to Moynihan, and he never really felt comfortable with Murray, Reisler, and Deming. Moynihan was a strongly partisan Democrat who supported Franklin Roosevelt enthusiastically in 1944; most of his Andover friends supported Thomas Dewey and gave Moynihan a hard time for his backing Roosevelt for a fourth term. (Moynihan ribbed them back, and Reisler retaliated by putting up Dewey posters in Moynihan's room.) The cultural and economic differences made the deepest impact on Moynihan. He could visit Deming's estate in Spring Valley, play tennis, and impress Deming's father with his wide range of knowledge—without ever feeling comfortable.

He summed up his feelings about the group in a letter he wrote Harry Hall in 1945, shortly after leaving Middlebury. Murray, Reisler, and Deming were the three Moynihan felt closest to, yet he "would never recognize or accept their position." They were "good guys" who "know a lot more about raising hell and making love than most people," yet he was "very jealous in a way about how satisfied and happy they are with themselves and things as they are." It was their attitude toward life that Moynihan could not accept. "Nothing phases them. They get my ass by the way they sit there and wallow in every kind of economic and social advantage our society has to offer and remain completely spiritually and mentally mediocre, while people who really could learn go stewing away at CCNY." Moynihan concluded that all three needed "a good swift kick in their blue blood asses. They need to get hurt once in a while. They need to get some feeling in them." Yet, while his resentment was strong, Moynihan had to admit that he genuinely liked them. And, he wrote, "If I abstained from having anything to do with anybody I thought could use a kick in the ass, I wouldn't have many drinking companions." If he were to break off contact with Murray, Reisler, and Deming, "I might even go so far as to say I'd have to do a lot of rationalizing before I could manage living with myself."

Originally the navy had hoped to send the recruits to midshipmen's school for ninety days after six months at Middlebury. But with no pressing need for new navy officers, the six months became a year and then stretched to sixteen months. The routine was not very militarily oriented, and the war seemed far distant from the placid Vermont campus. No guns were used; the only martial activity that the V-5 and V-12 trainees engaged in was marching.

Surprisingly, life at Middlebury was much like that at a very regi-mented New England prep school. In the beginning Moynihan and the other prospective officers were subjected to a harsh routine. They were awakened at 6 A.M. for twenty minutes of calisthenics followed by a twenty-minute run through the obstacle course. Moynihan's lack of coordination made the obstacle course difficult for him, but what he lacked in ability he made up in desire. His friends remember him strug-gling through the course, his arms and legs flailing, often trailing the rest of the group. The run was followed by a quick shower and then breakfast. Classes began at 8 A.M. and continued until 4 P.M. Then there were usually team sports and games like killer ball (a combination of tackle football and basketball).

Moynihan stayed away from most of the team sports, but one night he was induced to enter a boxing match. There were ten matches on the card; in the final bout Moynihan was pitted against a fellow who was three inches shorter, thirty pounds heavier, and heavily favored. In the first round Moynihan came out with both arms swinging windmill style and promptly knocked the man down. However, the opponent's superior boxing skill overcame Moynihan's aggressiveness, and Moynihan lost a close decision.

At Middlebury the emphasis was on naval training rather than on liberal arts, and in his first term Moynihan took engineering drawing, naval organizations, physics, mathematics, English, and psychology. Again his grades were undistinguished: he could only manage Cs in the navy courses, but he got Bs in psychology, math, and physics. The only true intellectual stimulation came when Moynihan and the fellows took a professor to dinner on Sunday nights.

Lights had to be out at 10 P.M., and the rules were strictly enforced. As might have been expected, Moynihan had a number of run-ins with the authorities. One of his nemeses was Chief John Acropolis, a 5'4" physical education instructor (and later a Teamster union official). One night Acropolis was on duty when Moynihan and the other third-floor residents of the dormitory had been confined for some violation. Entering Moynihan's room, he said in a loud voice, "Stand at attention when I come in the room, Moynihan."

Moynihan jumped quickly to his feet, knocking over his chair, which he didn't dare pick up. Acropolis looked at Moynihan standing at attention and the chair lying in the middle of the floor and turned and walked out of the room, shaking his head. Moynihan, befuddled, remained unmoving in the middle of the room. Acropolis, annoyed that Moynihan had been unable to come to attention quickly, returned to the room to find Moynihan still standing, gazing vaguely at him.

"Moynihan, I thought I told you to stand at attention when I come in the room."

"Chief," Moynihan responded, "I'm still at attention from the last time you came in."

There were many more women than men at Middlebury in 1944, and Moynihan found this to his liking. In the first months he would go to as many as five different parties or dances in a weekend.

One football weekend in the fall of 1944 he lacked the fifty cents for admission and stayed home to do his laundry. Late in the afternoon he went to a postgame buffet at one of the women's dorms, spotted an attractive woman, and learned from a friend that her name was Cathy Brittain. Moynihan approached her. "Cathy, why haven't I seen you since that cocktail party in Newport?" Cathy asked if he didn't mean Rockport. "Of course, Rockport," Moynihan replied. "How have you been?" It was the beginning of a romance—until Moynihan fell in love with her roommate.

Moynihan's major romantic involvement at Middlebury was with Gloria Greenley, whom he met at the French club ball early in January 1945. Greenley, who had spent time in France and Switzerland during her high school years because her mother was involved in the theatre in Europe, found Moynihan brilliant and enjoyed his stories about New York City.

The routine at Middlebury left little time for fraternizing, and Moynihan had to make the most of what time he had. On Saturdays there was inspection until noon, and then the men would hitchhike north to the Vergennes liquor store, hoping to reach it before the 3 P.M. closing. Liquor was cheap in Vergennes, and the men usually spent much of Saturday afternoon drinking in preparation for the Saturday night dance.

On St. Patrick's Day, a Saturday in March 1945, Moynihan had had rather too much to drink (his birthday had been the day before) by the time he was to pick up Gloria Greenley. It had snowed that day in Middlebury, and Moynihan crawled across the drifts in his sailor's cap, bell-bottom trousers, and pea jacket until he reached the women's residence hall. Covered with snow, he entered the hall and told the house mother to "send down Greenley." Greenley arrived and tolerated a somewhat soused Moynihan for the weekend, giving him cake with pink, chocolate, and green icing and taking him to Sunday dinner at the Middlebury Inn. Their relationship grew stronger; they would spend a part of each day together, and each of them decided not to go out with anyone else.

It quickly became known on the small campus that Greenley was Moynihan's girl. Moynihan enjoyed the relationship—though she was on the dean's list and he was afraid she might be smarter than he—but he was not ready to settle down with her. At the age of eighteen he still enjoyed going drinking with the boys—when he could rustle up the money. He saw Greenley steadily until he left Middlebury in July 1945.

Moynihan came to like life at Middlebury, and his grades went up during the winter of 1944–45. He got three Bs in math courses, a B in naval history, and Cs only in physics and naval organizations. The math and science courses were particularly difficult because of his intense dislike for the subject matter. While Moynihan wanted very much to be a navy officer, the subjects so bored him that he had a difficult time concentrating on them.

He was made a squad leader in February 1945, which eased his workload and gave him more time in the afternoons and evenings for Greenley and for occasional extended visits to New York. In New York Moynihan continued to go to debutante balls with Ellen Ordway. On one trip Gloria Greenley joined him, and they sampled jazz at Nick's. Meanwhile, Moynihan was having trouble again with the naval courses, managing only a D in thermodynamics and a C in math while getting Bs and As in history and English.

When it was all over, Moynihan and company had not seen much of navy life at Middlebury. The V-12 program ended in June 1945, and Moynihan decided to go into ROTC. His first choice was Columbia, but he was sent to Tufts, just outside Boston, while his friends Reisler, Zartman, and Deming were sent to Brown.

Moynihan had to adjust to a more rigorous life at Tufts, which was much more like the navy than Middlebury had been. The students were constantly drilled, and they had to march wherever they went. The captain of the Tufts ROTC unit had been the skipper of the *Astoria* at Pearl Harbor and was still bitter about the experience; consequently he was rather ill-tempered during his tenure at Tufts.

The academic work was definitely not to Moynihan's liking. In his first term he had four naval science courses—seamanship, damage control, coastal piloting, and celestial navigation—and it was understood that one could not flunk a course and still get a degree in naval science. Moreover, the answers to examination questions were either right or wrong; if you didn't know something, there was no way to bluff with a theoretical answer. Moynihan got 20 percent on his first celestial navigation exam, but he was able to pull up his grade on subsequent tests.

Money continued to be a problem. Moynihan's social life was limited

by the amount of cash he had on hand. Dates were often arranged for
7 P.M. in order to miss the dinner hour, but on one occasion Moynihan
was outfoxed. When he showed up at the Statler in Boston at 7:30 P.M.
to meet a blind date from Auburn, the woman told him she hadn't eaten.
After a $14 dinner Moynihan suggested going to a local dance hall. The
southern belle said she would just love to see a floor show. One floor show
and eight drinks later the check arrived, and it came to more than $14.
After considering a disappearance through the men's room, Moynihan
told his date he had only $10 left, and she loaned him $5.

On evenings when Moynihan had no date he would go drinking with
a new friend, Dick Meryman, a preppie (Andover) who had an old model
A Ford. Moynihan enjoyed going with him from bar to bar in downtown
Boston, looking for women to pick up. There were also weekends in New
York City with Bob Tenenbaum and Harry Hall that invariably involved
much storytelling and drinking.

Despite the hard work, Moynihan apparently had little trouble adjust-
ing to life at Tufts. He earned only one demerit in his first three months
—for failing to wear his rubbers during inclement weather. In early
September 1945 he was made a squad leader and a mail orderly as well.
The naval science courses became more manageable, and his grades
improved. Life was easy, Moynihan realized, if one did exactly as one
was told.

Moynihan's one real problem then was his vision, for naval officers
needed almost 20/20 vision to qualify. Like many young people at that
time, Moynihan did eye exercises and memorized eye charts in order to
pass the periodic eye examinations. Moynihan also hurt his ankle late in
the year, but this actually worked to his advantage, for he was able to
miss physical training and marching for a couple of months.

During his first year at Tufts Moynihan began thinking seriously
about his future. At eighteen, with only a few months of ROTC left,
what was he going to do? By nature Pat Moynihan has never been very
confident about his prospects. But in the fall of 1945 there was a hint
of optimism, a sense that maybe, if he could get through his naval
training, he could also get a B.A. Moynihan learned that even as a
commissioned officer he would be eligible for the GI bill. And he realized
that with the credits he had accumulated he might earn a B.A. and even

a master's degree in one or two years following his required naval service.

The initial optimism faded when Moynihan sorted through his courses, trying to choose a major. He began to doubt that he would ever get a B.A. through the GI bill. Again there were severe economic problems; late in 1945 he was faced with the possibility of having to accept a loan from Gus Deming's father—something he was resolutely opposed to doing—in order to finish the ROTC program. He had an average of only $1.75 a week for socializing, which put a great cramp in his style. His response to this state of affairs early in 1946 was to economize, to borrow from friends, and to travel to Indiana and Kentucky in the hope of getting some money from his grandfather Jack Moynihan and his grandmother Margaret Phipps.

In 1946 Moynihan showed signs of a serious interest in politics. He was one of three Tufts delegates to a four-day conference of the Student League for World Government in Concord, Massachusetts, where eighty-five colleges in twenty-six states were represented. Moynihan returned from the conference with a renewed desire to have some impact on political affairs. But beyond having an impact, Moynihan came to believe that it was important to have some perspective on what he was doing. Much of the satisfaction to be derived from political activism came from his awareness of having played a central role in effecting change.

The other event of note early in 1946 came in January, when he hitchhiked to Middlebury for Winter Carnival. He had wanted to re-create the previous winter, found that he couldn't, and grew sad. He saw faces he recognized, but he could not remember the names; his return rekindled memories he had wanted to extinguish. Moynihan had been happy at Middlebury, largely because of Gloria Greenley, but that relationship had ended. The weekend left him shaken.

Moynihan graduated from Tufts in June 1946 with a bachelor of naval science degree and an ensign's commission. He was assigned to a repair ship in Norfolk, Virginia, and later spent part of 1947 as a seagoing communications officer on the USS *Quirinus*.

Dick Meryman was also assigned to a ship in Norfolk, and the two friends spent a good deal of their time together. They found Norfolk a dull town and would often go to the movie theatres to see three different films in one day. There were no public bars; each tavern was organized as a private club, and admission meant paying a $10 membership fee. The $10 was usually good for just about a month, the saloons changed ownership so frequently. The bars were raunchy and the clientele worse.

With his adventurous spirit, Moynihan decided he'd like to learn how to sail during his stay in Norfolk. His crew had built a sailboat for their captain, but the captain had been transferred and the boat was just sitting in the navy yard. Moynihan claimed the boat temporarily and persuaded Meryman to sail with him upriver to a yacht club. As soon as they got out of the harbor the wind died down, and they had to row all night to reach the yacht club. They hitchhiked back to their ships, vowing to return the next weekend and sail home.

The following Sunday they found that a big race was being held, but they expected to be able to maneuver around it. Moynihan's navigational ability proved to be less than perfect: they drifted across the starting line just as the race was to begin. The race organizers had Moynihan and Meryman towed to shore. Their embarrassment may have been even more acute in that Moynihan and Meryman were dressed in old work shirts and dungarees while the men and women watching the race wore blazers and sun dresses.

The *Quirinus* left port late in 1946 and traveled through the Caribbean, making stops in Trinidad and St. Thomas. In the spring of 1947 Moynihan returned to the States, where he received his discharge in July and decided to spend the summer with his mother, who had just gone into a new business venture—running a saloon in Hell's Kitchen.

2

The College Years
and London Life

I've changed. How many times have you seen me come home in
one crisis or another, patch it up, and leave feeling that things might
somehow work out? They never will, and I am stronger for the
knowledge.

—Pat Moynihan, 1948

If growing up without a father was difficult for Pat, Mike, and Ellen
Moynihan, Margaret Moynihan bore the burden of bringing up a family
alone, in a poverty for which her early life had not prepared her. She was
sometimes overwhelmed with cares, the experience of having gone
through two bad marriages before she was thirty-five having drained her
psychologically. To support four children on the salary of a practical
nurse was a constant struggle.

The work of a practical nurse in a defense plant was trying too, and
in 1945 Margaret Moynihan jumped at the opportunity to run the
chicken concession in a bar in the Rockaways operated by her husband's
cousin John Moynihan. Unfortunately, while the bar was a great success,

the chicken concession barely broke even. Yet the sight of her relatives successfully operating a tavern excited Margaret Moynihan, and she decided to do the same when another cousin of her husband, Dan O'Riordan, offered her a saloon on West 42nd Street.

Moynihan's Bar was dimly lit and smelled of stale whiskey. There were old-fashioned shades on the lights and a few tables in the back where food was served. The family lived upstairs in a railroad flat that Margaret decorated with furnishings from the family farm in Kentucky. The apartment was by no means elegant, but Margaret added her own touches, such as exposing a brick wall behind the stove. She quickly made friends of her neighbors (the Whelans, the Lambs, the Novembers), cooking hams on Sunday evenings and caring for Margie November's mother, who was dying of cancer. (Her generosity is remembered; the Novembers still have the four-poster bed Margaret gave them.) And during this period Margaret remarried again. Her third husband was a truck driver from the neighborhood, Scotty Dolan.

When Pat returned from the navy in the summer of 1947, he walked the neighborhood proudly in his long white trousers and white shoes. During the summer he tended bar and tried to keep things together in the family. There was an unsettled feeling in the house, and Pat spent a fair amount of time away from the bar. When crises developed—as they invariably did—he had to return to pick up the pieces. At the end of the summer Moynihan went up to Dublin, New Hampshire, with Dick Meryman. After a peaceful week he returned to find that the bartender Margaret had hired to take his place had just quit—and Moynihan went behind the bar again until classes resumed.

Taking advantage of the GI bill, Moynihan returned to Tufts in the fall of 1947 to complete work on his B.A. With his credits from City College and Middlebury, Moynihan needed only one year more to earn his degree. He rented a room on College Avenue in Medford for $3 a week and settled down to study, devoting most of his attention to a political theory course and the history of Europe in the nineteenth century.

Moynihan tried his hand at lacrosse only to find that he was too tall and awkward to play for the college. He also returned briefly to journalism, writing a column for the Tufts *Weekly* with a new friend, Larsh

Mewhinny. The column was called Cerberus, after the three-headed dog in Greek mythology who guarded the gate of hell. In the column Moynihan explained that his concern was with "the preoccupation with trivia, the passion for mediocrity, the bland complacency of ignorance and indifference that has robbed the student body of any semblance of the intellectual climate of a university." Moynihan was prepared to "destroy, to humiliate and to disrespect. We were so because we are part of it; because it matters to us."

The administration drew sarcastic and vitriolic criticism because, according to Cerberus, it had failed to lobby vigorously enough against Communist control legislation (which Cerberus felt threatened academic freedom) and it overemphasized social and recreational activities to the detriment of support for the library. At first the column was taken seriously, and in a signed article the president refuted Cerberus' allegations with respect to Tufts' apathy on anti-Communist legislation.

But Moynihan's career as a college journalist was short-lived. After writing three columns he and Mewhinny resigned in dissatisfaction with the way in which their efforts were edited. In a letter to the editor of the Tufts *Weekly* upon their resignation, they said that their material was edited "in what we believe to be an unimaginative, unsympathetic manner, and to censor or distort our ideas to the extent that we can no longer feel our presence on the staff is desired."[1]

If Moynihan could afford to be sarcastic in print, he had less freedom once he left Tufts' cloistered halls. For Moynihan was becoming something of a wise guy, and this got him into trouble late in the term. A couple of weeks before graduation on May 13, Moynihan and Mewhinny were out drinking and stopped for a hamburger and coffee at the Jumbo Diner in Somerville. Parking the car, Mewhinny backed into another car parked behind him. A policeman who saw the incident asked to see Mewhinny's license and registration.

This enraged Moynihan, who felt that no offense had been committed, and he began lecturing the cop on the basis of his authority, citing among other things Max Weber's theory of charismatic leadership. The policeman, unimpressed with Moynihan's knowledge of social theory, arrested him, and when Moynihan resisted, he began hitting him with his nightstick in the legs and in the back. The injured Moynihan was forced to spend the night in jail. Later he decided not to pursue the incident because it was so close to graduation. He had been accepted for graduate study in international law and politics at the Fletcher School the following year, and he did not want to jeopardize that opportunity. Moreover, he had been nominated for Phi Beta Kappa, and he suspected that the report of an arrest would not sit well with the selection committee.

Graduation in 1948 did not go smoothly for Moynihan. He was turned down for Phi Beta Kappa, which left him bitter. And after having worked himself into a state of nervous exhaustion over his studies (he felt he had never been so ill in his life) Moynihan had to forgo the graduation week festivities in order to settle a dispute at the bar. The family was desperately short of money, so Moynihan had been sending everything he had to his mother, leaving him low on money for food. Again he borrowed from friends. It had been a difficult spring for Moynihan, and he had to spend a good part of the summer trying to keep Moynihan's Bar running smoothly.

Before he could begin work on a graduate degree at Tufts, Moynihan had to do two weeks of reserve duty with the navy. He was assigned to an old destroyer, the *McDougall,* and shipped out to Bermuda for war games. The ship made it to Bermuda quickly on the heels of a hurricane, and it looked as though Moynihan would have to spend a full week in navy maneuvers. Then, the day before the first exercise, he developed a discomfiture in a wisdom tooth that apparently necessitated constant dental attention. So before the *McDougall* left port each day, Moynihan and the ship's doctor went ashore, ostensibly to get him dental care. In fact the two retired to the Coral Beach Club, where they were entertained by a Major Cookson who had served with the British in India. They drank stingers and swam all day and returned to the ship at night.

The voyage home was considerably less pleasant. The ship encountered the hurricane again, and Moynihan spent the last hours of the trip on deck in a wild gale, being brought steak, potatoes, and coffee every two hours to keep him going. The day after his return Moynihan went to the Fletcher School at Tufts to begin work on an M.A.

Moynihan became increasingly interested in politics in 1948. He was a strong supporter of Harry Truman and an equally strong opponent of

Henry Wallace. Moynihan's views on politics and foreign policy then were very much in accord with the position he espoused in the 1960s and 1970s. Wallace himself was not a Communist; but Moynihan felt that the movement for Wallace's third party had "from the first come under the Communist Party aegis," Moynihan wrote Harry Hall. The Communists supported Wallace because they expected him to divert enough votes from Truman to elect a reactionary Republican president and Congress. And such a Republican administration could presumably be counted on both to withdraw from Europe and to bring on a depression. As he would in the 1960s and 1970s, Moynihan advocated an aggressive anti-Communist foreign policy as well as an interventionist domestic policy.

Moynihan found the M.A. program somewhat intimidating at first, and he was glad it was not competitive, for he believed that his classmates were smarter than he was. He hoped they would assist him with his work if he had trouble, and he vowed to work as hard as he could during the year.

He lived in Wilson House, the graduate student residence, and he quickly became friendly with many of his classmates. Despite his self-professed nervousness, his classmates remember him as an easygoing, seemingly carefree student. George Wallis remembers that Moynihan always seemed to be playing touch football on the lawn. William Bowdler, now U.S. ambassador to South Africa, recalls that Moynihan joked frequently with other students and got himself into embarrassing situations. One evening Moynihan appeared in the dining room in a tuxedo, a bunch of Phi Beta Kappa keys hung around his neck and a towel on his arm, posing as a waiter during the meal. On another occasion, while the cook was on vacation, Moynihan had trouble lighting the stove. Trying to find the pilot light, he turned the gas up high. Everyone in the dining room heard the big whoosh as Moynihan was blown across the room, later to emerge with singed eyebrows and hair.

While Moynihan may have seemed carefree, the school year was difficult for him, and late in the spring term he found he had to cram three months of work into the remaining four weeks. Nor was it an easy year at home. Margaret fell far behind with her bills, and Mike and Pat had to pawn their watches and hit every available friend for loans in order to raise money. And Moynihan's social life ground to a halt as he devoted himself to his studies.

Whenever Moynihan worked hard, his nerves tortured him. Long hours of study produced a constant tension through the left side of his body that made sleeping and eating almost impossible. Often the pain was so persistent that he had difficulty concentrating on his studies. Moynihan believed that the pain was psychosomatic and that a summer away from studying would help him to relax—but first he had to make it through his exams.

The hard work paid off. While Moynihan did not do terribly well on the written exams, his verbal acuity acquitted him well on the orals, and he ended up the valedictorian of his graduate group. Moynihan felt that being named valedictorian served to establish his candidacy for a Ph.D. and would more or less help to get him a job teaching in the fall. But most important was the renewal of confidence and spirit this honor provided him.

Early in the spring of 1949 Moynihan had decided to get away from the tensions of his academic and family lives and do something with Dick Meryman in the summer—something that would serve no end other than that of a good time. To this end Meryman purchased a 1935 Packard hearse that he called the Pleasure Dome. And in June 1949 he, Moynihan, and two Harvard Law School students, Roberts B. Owen and Robert Fisher, met in Albany for a cross-country trip to Alaska in search of their fortunes.

The group ran into trouble almost immediately. By 9 P.M. on the first day there was a leak in the gas line that held them up for a couple of days. Then an axle broke in a small town in Michigan. Not having the money to buy a new axle for the Pleasure Dome, they had to go to a junk yard and pull an old axle out of an abandoned car.

En route again, they headed into Montana and then decided to cross the border into Canada. However, the Canadian immigration officers took one look at the motley crew and decided they would have to have $1000 in cash with them before they could enter the country, given the high unemployment rates there. With only $200 among them, the travelers had to make other plans. On hearing that a dam was being built in the Rockies, they headed for Hungry Horse, Montana, where hiring was said to be going on. As they entered Hungry Horse, the brakes gave out on the Pleasure Dome; they had to coast to a stop, and doing so took them through three red lights.

The available work in Hungry Horse was not terribly inviting. One job entailed clearing brush from the basin behind the dam. For the street-wise Moynihan—who had shined shoes in Times Square, hustled news-papers, and worked on the docks—the job proved to be too much. Meryman recalled that the field boss kept the men working at a pace that "only the Indians and Canadian lumberjacks could endure." Moyni-han lasted one day.

There were other jobs in Hungry Horse. The four picked strawberries, and they sang (Fisher played the guitar) in saloons, seeking mugs of beer as compensation. They did not need much money; their campsite was on a bluff overlooking a stream that offered plenty of large trout. The problem was catching them. For Moynihan, whom Fisher described as "marvellously innocent of anything west of the Gowanus Canal," fishing was no simple task. Eschewing rod and reel, Moynihan tried to trap the trout with a floppy hat that had holes in it. When they had no fish and money was low, the group subsisted on lettuce and ketchup sandwiches.

Meryman and Moynihan were the gamblers in the group, and they made a few dollars hustling the natives with three-card monte. They also got into a few games of twenty-one, which relieved them of any cash they had made.

When a carnival came through Hungry Horse, the group gravitated toward it in search of entertainment and money. On the carnival's last night they went to a skin show where for fifty cents each they heard a comedian tell dirty jokes. This exhausted their funds. When Moynihan struck up a conversation with the madam who ran the show, she invited the group to stay for the second show, which offered erotic dancing, but would not let them stay for the third show, which included audience participation. The madam also invited Moynihan and Co. to help her and the other concessioners take down the carnival after the night's festivities were ended. They jumped at the chance, and they ended up getting paid twice when both concessioners and carnival manager gave them a few dollars.

After three weeks their money had run low and Moynihan separated

from the group and headed for a lumber camp fifty miles up river. There
the work was hard, the food was bad, and the pay was low. He had
probably never handled an ax before, and given his awkwardness, he
probably had difficulty maneuvering around the logs, but he claimed he
would have stuck it out had it not been for another attack of nerves.
After having been laid off for a couple of days he decided to head back
to New York. He convinced Meryman (who by pulling the wrong cord
had already blown out all the lights on the dam) to go with him, and
the two hopped a freight train. The ride was not without drama; the pair
were periodically kicked off trains or chased out of stations by yard cops,
and eventually they separated, Moynihan returning alone to New York.

Moynihan spent a couple of days at the bar, then checked into a
hospital to have his back examined. Some fifteen doctors stuck pins into
him and twisted his back in various directions in an effort to determine
the cause of the pain. Moynihan found the situation frustrating; it was
as if the fifteen doctors gathered every day "in an ill-concealed attempt
to scare off the evil spirits with an incantation of medical jargon accompanied by the tappings of hammers and swishing of needles." Nothing
wrong was found and Moynihan was released shortly thereafter.

Moynihan suffered one disappointment in the summer of 1949.
When he returned to Fletcher following his trip, he took the foreign
service exam. He was relatively confident about his ability in the history
and political science sections of the exam, and he could, after all, write
well. But the economics section worried him; he had had only a rudimen-
tary course and he remembered only the basic concepts. Yet on the exam
Moynihan scored in the high 80s on economics and in the mid 30s on
the social science and English sections. His overall score was below the
cutoff point. Receiving notification of his failure, Moynihan decided
that if the exam was so strangely graded, he wanted nothing to do with
the foreign service. Nevertheless his career would be marked by confrontations with it.

Moynihan returned to Tufts in the fall of 1949 and began the research
for his doctorate, having decided to write about the United States and
the International Labor Organization. For the first time in his academic
career Moynihan occupied more than a single room, and he was able to
relax a bit. He now taught for the first time, lecturing in the introductory

government course at Tufts. Moynihan wrote Harry Hall that he had mixed feelings about his teaching ability, but was pleased to have students who listened so intently to him.

In the spring Margaret exhausted herself running the bar and Pat returned home once more to take over. He sent his mother to Kentucky to recuperate, telling her he wanted to sell the saloon, but she returned before he could do so. Moynihan was working sixteen-hour days in an attempt to keep the business solvent, and he vowed that when the crisis was over he would leave Hell's Kitchen for good—it was time for him to lead his own life. He expected that in the next couple of years he would settle down and marry. His obligations then would be to other people in other environments—away from Hell's Kitchen. His feelings toward the neighborhood were ambivalent. He felt both powerful hatred and a strong attachment to the neighborhood. But most of all he felt he had to get away.

In the summer of 1950 Moynihan convinced his mother to sell the bar. Then he went to Cambridge for the summer session at Harvard, hoping to complete his course work for his Ph.D. so that he could continue teaching in the fall. The backache that he had thought was psychosomatic grew worse, and his doctors finally diagnosed it as a herniated intervertebral lumbar disc and decided not to operate. Eager to get away from Cambridge, Moynihan spent a few days speaking in Washington in order to explore employment opportunities in the field of international labor. Afterward he was satisfied that he had made a number of contacts that might be useful and pleased that he had friends whom he could count on to put him up and entertain him.

Moynihan's plans to spend the next few years in Medford or Washington were altered drastically in August 1950 when he was awarded a Fulbright scholarship for graduate study at the London School of Economics.

Reflecting on his life in the summer of 1950, Moynihan felt satisfied that his mother had at last sold the bar, his brother Mike had apparently found a woman to marry, and his sister Ellen was engaged. His only concern was that at twenty-three he had not yet married. Financially he had never been in better shape. His Fulbright grant gave him transportation to England on the *America,* his tuition and books, and £50 a month. His benefits from the GI bill brought the total to the equivalent of almost $300 a month. Since the average British wage of the period was about a third of that, and since Moynihan had no formal obligations in terms of courses or exams, his prospects for a comfortable life were ideal.

His one problem before leaving for England concerned Korea. But as soon as he had resolved that it was more important for him to go to England than to fight in the war, the navy decided it did not need him. His thinking then was not totally unlike the line he has articulated in his recent writings on the United States' posture in world politics.[2] In both instances he argued for the importance of ideological competition along with strategic concerns. The critical battle for the United States in 1948, as in 1975, involved concepts of freedom and liberty.

> The crucial battles are at present being fought round and about the world not with guns, but with ideas—specifically with symbols—and not amongst the high aristocracy or the parliamentarians, but amongst the sprawling, plodding, stupid, sluggish, ugly, beautiful working people of the world who like some great giant are awakening from the nightmare of the 19th century, thrashing about, and demolishing the world that was built on their backs.

Given his analysis, Moynihan could certainly do more for America by learning about the European labor movement than he could by working in a navy laundry office in San Diego.

Moynihan sailed for England on the *America* on September 9, 1950, planning to spend ten months abroad and in the end staying two and a half years. During the crossing he shared a cabin with another Fulbright scholar, John Barry from Tulsa, Oklahoma. In manner Barry was just the opposite of Moynihan—quiet, serious, somewhat taciturn. Nevertheless Moynihan asked him to share a flat in London. Barry, however, had made arrangements for a room in a house near Paddington Station and had to decline. But Barry later found his room poorly heated and the environment unpleasant, and when Moynihan called him on returning from a couple of weeks in Paris, Barry was glad to reconsider.

The two lived for six months in a flat at 25 Queen's Gardens, then early in 1951 moved to 36 Edwardes Square. The house was owned by an eccentric soldier, Colonel Campbell, who had seen service in India and who took a liking to Moynihan and Barry. Immediately after they had moved into the house, Mrs. Campbell brought them up a Wedgwood china service for twelve so that the two gentlemen from America would be able to give a proper tea.

Moynihan's initial reaction to England was one of sheer delight. He found it wonderful that he would be attending the finest graduate program in the world, making excellent money, and was required to do nothing in return—class attendance and exams were optional—but sign his checks.

As Moynihan soon realized, research students at the London School of Economics led a pretty easy life by American standards. With no required courses to attend, they were free to pursue their interests to whatever degree they chose. For the first time in his life Moynihan had an ample sum of money to live on and a world to explore in England and the rest of Europe. A nagging sense that he was a little old to be wandering around unmarried and careerless could not be allowed to interfere with his falling in love with his new life.

One night early in November he and Barry had a drink with Dr. Alan McPhee of the University of London, who had a special interest in United States labor history. For close to an hour and a half Moynihan kept up a running commentary on American books on the subject, thereby intimidating Barry, who had not read any of them and who felt he knew something about the field. Barry felt somewhat better when Moynihan admitted later that he had not read most of them either. Barry made a note of the incident in his diary and concluded, "There was a point for me to learn."

The two of them went on frequent pub crawls, and Moynihan studiously avoided settling down to serious work. He told himself he couldn't finish anything in the allotted time even if he worked assiduously, and besides he was a little tired of academic life; he had been in college since the fall of 1943, and he needed some time off.

London was the perfect place to take time off. But first Moynihan had to dress for it. With the money for quality clothing for the first time in his life, Moynihan indulged himself. He took to wearing a bowler hat. His shoes were made for him by a bootmaker. The Savile Row firm of

Taylor and Solash made his suits. Moynihan enjoyed introducing his newfound American friends to his tailor, taking them in to be fitted for clothing.

One of these friends was Sander Vanocur, later a network newscaster; he and Moynihan explored London and the English countryside together. Another was the CBS bureau chief in London, Howard K. Smith, whose wife was also a student at LSE. The Smiths occasionally had Moynihan to dinner, along with other bright young American graduate students. But they took little note of him then; he was so rarely serious that they never thought of him as a potential national politician. Today Howard Smith remembers Moynihan then as "just a pleasant person to have to dinner."

Moynihan relished the constant round of parties, the meetings with political and labor leaders, the evenings in the pubs or at the theatre. As he wrote home to America, he was keeping "well stuffed with sausage and beer, staying up till dawn reading irrelevant books and talking to unlikely people." It was as though Moynihan were able, if only for a short time, to forget life in New York City. And in that relatively short period of time he was trying to reshape his image.

One of the "unlikely" persons Moynihan met was Joanna Gollogly, the former mayor of Greenwich. Mrs. Gollogly invited Moynihan to tea one afternoon and introduced him to her daughter Mary, another LSE student. The two quickly became close friends, Moynihan seeing Mary steadily for two years. Like Moynihan, the Golloglys were of working class Irish origin. Mr. Gollogly was a boilermaker who had been active in politics.

Mary was also involved in politics and served as an alderman on the Greenwich Council. Her personality was very different from that of Moynihan; she was far more serious than he, and she wondered whether he would ever make anything of himself. Yet she sensed that Moynihan had a definite presence. When she took him to a reception at the Greenwich City Hall, she was struck by the way the waitresses catered to him and made it a special point to bring him a glass of sherry. The Golloglys virtually adopted Moynihan, inviting him and his friends to spend vacations and holidays at their home and entertaining his mother when she came to visit in 1952.

Moynihan did occasionally visit LSE to do research and to meet fellow students, but he was not very productive. His supervisor, William Pickles, now reader emeritus at LSE, reports, "I don't remember seeing a line in writing from him." Still he regarded Moynihan as an "articulate, intelligent person, with a wide range of knowledge and interests. He worked hard but completely unsystematically." Pickles' most vivid recollection is of the attractiveness of Mary Gollogly at a dinner party given by Moynihan and Barry.

Paul Niven, the late CBS journalist, and Robert McKenzie, a professor of sociology at LSE, were other friends of the period who spent long hours in pubs arguing politics with Moynihan and Vanocur. "We were all about five years older than the average graduate student then because of the war," McKenzie explained. "This meant we had a more experienced eye—you'd lived a bit. We were more interested in the politics of the country than the campus."

Many of those who met Moynihan in London did not regard him as an intellectual. He was bright, to be sure, yet he was so rarely serious about anything that people tended to discount him. But beneath the cheerful, fun-loving exterior, Moynihan thought quite intently about contemporary international politics and America's role in the world.

While he would later become involved in the discussion of morality and human rights in foreign policy, he was somewhat more pragmatic in 1951. His major concern then was to help prevent a third world war from developing out of the Korean conflict, not to advance an argument that would demonstrate the moral superiority of the American position. America's allies did not demand that the United States demonstrate its moral virtue by condemning the Chinese Communists as aggressors; rather they wanted the United States to do everything it could to maintain the peace for the overriding practical objective of preventing mass annihilation in another world war. To this end, they held that it was important to the United States to stop its constant attacks on the Chinese and instead begin to work for peace.

Certainly Moynihan did not urge capitulation to Communism. It was alarming that British socialists like G. D. H. Cole seemed to be more sympathetic toward China than toward the United States; after all, the British were a democratic people and the Chinese were not. Moynihan believed it important that he and his fellow students refute all efforts by intellectuals in Britain to criticize the United States unfairly. Thus, when an article by Cole appeared in the *New Statesman* in February 1951, claiming that America was using South Korea as a base for an attack on Communist China, Moynihan responded bitterly.

Cole wrote that a free Korea was of no use to the United States unless the United States was planning aggressive action against China. Moynihan labeled this view "an evasion of the truth and a slander on the moral sense of the American people." Cole also hypothesized that the United States was in fact building up its position in Asia for an attack on China. Moynihan responded that "such a priori deductions concerning American motives and intentions derive from a wild, almost mythological conception of American society and are inexcusable and irresponsible." And he mocked Cole's contention that the United States offered no more hope to the world than the Russians did.[3] Reflecting on the exchange, Moynihan wrote home:

> I get the impression Americans are not generally aware of just how fundamentally we are being opposed by a small but enormously vital element in British society or just how much we are being disagreed with by British society in general. I respectfully submit that we had damned sure better get off our intellectual asses but quick.

Moynihan's proselytizing on behalf of the American position was not limited to the columns of the *New Statesman*. He and Sander Vanocur often sat in the refectory at LSE, trying to explain the racial situation in the United States to Africans and Indians who were bitterly critical of America. (The Africans and Indians were hypocrites, Moynihan and Vanocur argued; there was just as much racism in their countries as there was in America.) The appearance of his letter in the *New Statesman* also brought Moynihan a number of requests to speak on the United States' position in Asia. These experiences were an introduction to what Moynihan would be trying to do at the United Nations twenty-five years later, when he would meet much the same hostility and fight many of the same battles.

Perhaps the most exciting part of going abroad for graduate study is taking advantage of the travel opportunities. College vacations in

Europe may last six weeks and travel can be very inexpensive. On his arrival in Europe Moynihan spent a couple of weeks in Paris, and during his first months in England he took a number of day trips with Vanocur, Barry, and Mary Gollogly. In January 1951 he and Barry took an overnight train and bicycle journey to Canterbury to see the cathedral and monastery. A week later they went to Greenhithe to see the *Cutty Sark*, the only clipper ship then still in existence. The ship was closed to tourists, but Moynihan said that he and Barry were officers in the U.S. armed forces, and consequently they were treated as visiting foreign officers and assigned a longboat and crew to show them around. In the spring Moynihan and Barry traveled together through France, stopping in Paris for a wedding and drinking through the night on the Left Bank before heading for the Loire Valley to see the châteaux.

That winter Moynihan was recalled to the navy and sent to Germany to help set up what proved to be an abortive North Sea command. When the plan fell through, Moynihan was sent on tour to Hamburg and Berlin. He was struck by the emptiness and desolation of East Berlin, and the economic depression of West Berlin and Hamburg made a lasting impression. After dark, Moynihan wrote, both cities "lurched into a kind of frenzied Brechtian caricature." Sad people with even sadder looking children sat in bars and nightclubs, drinking through the night. It was an unsettling experience, one that emphasized for him "the impermanence of things."

The rest of the trip was very pleasant. Moynihan's diet consisted of rye whisky and sirloin steak. When he and the other fourteen reservists arrived in Berlin, they were met by a commander with a fleet of limousines and taken to a cocktail party in their honor. Moynihan was promoted to lieutenant, had a car available to him, and had no trouble getting cash advances. (With one such advance he bought an elaborate camera.)

The trip that meant the most to Moynihan was probably the one he and Barry took to Ireland in June 1951. They traveled first to Dublin, where they had tea with a Moynihan cousin, Cornelius Moynihan. The next morning they went by bicycle and bus to Nenagh in search of Barry's roots. They could find no trace of Barry's grandfather, but they did meet a pub owner who was also named John Barry.

In Headford Junction in County Kerry, where Pat's grandfather Jack Moynihan was born, they stayed with Dan Conn Moynihan, a son of a Moynihan who had remained in Headford Junction when Jack left for America in 1886. The Moynihan name adorned all the stores in Headford Junction, but Dan lived a spartan life as a peasant farmer. His cottage had a dirt floor, and the bed Moynihan slept in had a corn-shuck mattress. The visit was not allowed to disrupt Dan's normal routine; he had the two Americans up early digging peat before they were given breakfast. The cooking was done over a fireplace, and Moynihan and Barry were fed a steady diet of boiled eggs and bacon. A little wary of their American relative at first, the Headford Junction Moynihans after a couple of days treated him as a member of their own family.

Perhaps to supplement his income when his fellowship expired in June, Moynihan took an administrative job at an air force base. The job was not taxing, it allowed him the luxury of a midday nap in the infirmary, and he could buy inexpensive liquor by the case at the post exchange. Moynihan took all the English daily newspapers to work with him. Occasionally the Communist *Daily Worker* was among them, and when this was noticed, the air force investigated him for Communist sympathies. Moynihan was cleared.

When his fellowship ran out in June 1951, Moynihan decided to remain in England another year. He lived alone at Edwardes Square after John Barry left for the United States, and he maintained his usual habits. He was moved by the death of King George VI in February 1952, and he attended the funeral by Green Park.

In 1952 Moynihan moved to a flat at 41 Emperor's Gate in South Kensington, which he shared with two British graduates. Frank Fenton had earned highest honors at Oxford, receiving a double first in classics and philosophy, and Dante Campailla had a law degree from Cambridge. Through Fenton and Campailla Moynihan became friendly with J. H. Plumb, the historian and professor of history at Cambridge.

Two old Middlebury friends, Joe Reisler and Story Zartman, came to visit in the spring of 1952. They found Moynihan entirely at ease and seemingly unconcerned with his work. Impressed at first with his elaborate file cabinet full of index cards, they found that most of the cards were recipes for drinks rather than notes on the International Labor Organization. Reisler and Moynihan went to the Continent for a couple of weeks and spent a particularly memorable time in Copenhagen. In England Moynihan treated Reisler and Zartman to a constant round of parties and entertainment. One of their calls was made at Mary Gollogly's house in Greenwich. It was a fortuitous meeting for Reisler; a year later, when Marie and Pat had broken up, Reisler looked her up in New York, and they were subsequently married.

Pat contributed $1800 to the cost of the trip his mother and her friend Winnie Avellina made to England in the autumn of 1952. Margaret was delighted to visit Pat, and she fell in love with the Gollogly family. Moynihan gave his mother the grand tour of London, and to this day Margaret still speaks of her trip.

Mike Moynihan also stopped in London on his way to Burma, where he was to be a Fulbright scholar for 1952–53. Pat was convinced then that Mike would be the success of the family, and he predicted that his brother would become a high-ranking foreign service officer. Pat told Mike that their father had shown up at their grandfather's funeral in Bluffton during the summer, and there was word that he was now living in San Jose, California. Mike was deputized to call on him on his way home from Burma the following year. Mike paid the visit, spent an hour or two in awkward conversation, and after a moment's hesitation took the $200 the elder Moynihan offered him. On leaving his father, Mike went to a YMCA, rented a typewriter for an hour, and wrote out an account of the conversation for Pat. It was the last the family would see of John Moynihan; he died about a year later.

By early 1953 Moynihan was ready to leave England. The cold, wet English winters were beginning to affect him, and he had completed the research for his doctoral dissertation. Moreover, he was anxious to return to America and to become involved. But while politics was his first love, he decided to avoid government service at first and to give teaching a try. He wrote to Harry Hall, "I have come to feel that people like myself who profess to care what goes on should of all things and of all times not cut their political balls off at this juncture and become neutral observers and impartial servants." Electoral politics fascinated him, but he doubted that he could win an election; he feared that he would constantly take positions that the majority opposed.

Moynihan came away from England dissatisfied with his personal development. He saw himself as having an "almost first class critical intelligence" and "second class abilities." This left Moynihan feeling that he would always be dissatisfied with his own accomplishments and envious of those more skilled than he. Even a Ph.D. would not make him happy, for he felt he knew only too well how much better he could really be. In a certain sense, however, he was satisfied: "I'm as good as some and better than most, and if I get me a good woman I shall like as not be content."

3

The Return to New York

In the early 1950s I had to get my transcript from City College and when I got it I realized my name was listed as Patrick Daniel rather than Daniel Patrick. Until then, I didn't think it was important whether I was listed correctly or not. But I had finally grown up. Very late it came to me, I could say my name was *this* and not that. I had started to take myself more seriously.
—Pat Moynihan, 1978

Just before leaving England, Pat Moynihan heard on the BBC an interview with an American who had been head of the Oxford Union and was confident that he would return to Ohio and become a senator. Moynihan, unable to see very far beyond finishing his own dissertation, was amazed that someone his age would be thinking that far ahead.

As it happened, Moynihan got his start on a political career on the voyage back to America. After stopping in Berlin to see Paul Niven, Moynihan traveled through Austria, Yugoslavia, and Italy before sailing from Genoa on the *Andrea Doria*. One day, sitting in the second class lounge busily typing a part of his thesis, he was approached by a longtime activist in New York Democratic politics, Paul Riley. The two talked, and Riley offered to provide him with introductions in the city. Back in

New York, Riley called Adrian Burke, later associate judge of the New York State Court of Appeals, and Burke directed Moynihan to Robert Wagner's campaign for mayor.

In retrospect, the Wagner campaign seems to have been the perfect point of entry into city politics for Moynihan. Then the Manhattan borough president, Wagner was supported by the de facto head of the Democratic party in New York, Carmine DeSapio, who was trying to end a period of corrupt and inefficient government. Wagner appeared to be the ideal candidate. The son of the late Senator Robert F. Wagner, Sr., he was half German and half Irish, had been educated at Yale, and was popular with ordinary New Yorkers as well as with the business establishment.

Wagner's broad appeal made him attractive to Moynihan. Moynihan was never really comfortable with either of the major factions in the Democratic party in Manhattan—the Tammany Hall regulars or the insurgent reform Democrats—and for him the Wagner candidacy was the perfect bridge between the two wings of the party. The reform Democrats were largely upper middle class Ivy League Protestants and Jews who were trying to organize at the grass roots to destroy the "bossism" of Tammany Hall. Moynihan nominally allied himself with this reform movement, joining the Tilden Democratic Club in the Gramercy Park area.

But Moynihan had greater sympathy for DeSapio and the regular Democrats. They were his people; they came from the same neighborhoods and they knew what it meant to have to go out and earn a living. Irish Catholic politicians had made New York perhaps the first major American city to be ruled largely by "men of the people"—no small achievement, in Moynihan's view. Moynihan did not hide his admiration for DeSapio: he considered him "incomparably the most able politician the New York Democrats have produced since [Jim] Farley."[1] What disturbed Moynihan about DeSapio (and provided the basis for his affiliation with the reformers) was that the Tammany leader did not think much about issues. It was not that DeSapio was conservative; if anything, his inclinations were centrist. DeSapio simply had little sense of what he wanted to do *after* he won power. In Britain Moynihan had met Labour politicians with strong working class ties who also had a clear ideological framework; at home he found political leaders of similar background whose interest in government did not go beyond handing out jobs to the boys.

Moynihan could not bring himself to throw in his lot entirely with the reform Democrats. For they had gone to private schools and Ivy League universities,[2] and although they thought about issues, their interests often did not coincide with those of working class Catholics. Worse, they had little real understanding of how ordinary people lived—something Moynihan believed was essential for effective political service. Moynihan thought of himself as a product of the working class, but his education precluded total identification with it; at the same time he could never really feel comfortable with upper middle class liberals, even though they had gone to the same or similar universities. Yet Pat Moynihan believed he understood how working class people lived in a way that the upper middle class never could, and ultimately he came to resent them for presuming to speak for that stratum of society. In 1953, when his resentment was still being formulated, Moynihan found himself viewed quizzically by both working class machine Democrats and upper-middle-class reformers.

With his roots in the city's neighborhoods and his issue orientation, Wagner was the sort of candidate with whom Moynihan had few problems. So, armed with Adrian Burke's introduction, Moynihan went to Wagner headquarters and volunteered his services to Jonathan Bingham, then a campaign aide and now a congressman. Bingham has few clear recollections of Moynihan's activities in 1953, but he kept Moynihan's name on file as that of a bright young man who could be useful in future campaigns.

Moynihan's volunteer work on the campaign ended with the election in November, and he went looking for a job. After a number of fruitless interviews with advertising agencies, he took a position with the International Rescue Committee, a nonsectarian volunteer agency that assisted refugees forced to leave their own countries through persecution. The IRC was trying to relocate refugees from East Berlin in the West, and Moynihan had been in Berlin in 1953 and had observed the refugee situation firsthand. The organization was both anti-Communist and anti-fascist, thereby fitting well with Moynihan's ideological posture.

The IRC involved Moynihan at an early age in what later came to be called human rights activity, and undoubtedly it helped to reinforce his belief in the importance of protecting civil liberties in world politics. The job was not terribly difficult; Moynihan spent much of his time drafting press releases. (IRC officials believe he was vastly overqualified for the post.) The job paid $8000 a year, which allowed him to take an apartment on 14th Street—one large, cluttered room at the back of an old brownstone. But Moynihan was rarely there; he spent his free time drinking in local bars such as the White Horse Tavern (a pub that had been frequented by the poet Dylan Thomas in his later years).

An officer of the IRC, Dick Saltzman, remembers an occasion when Moynihan differed with the leadership. After the Communists took power in North Vietnam in 1954, there was a large flow of refugees from North Vietnam to South Vietnam. Leo Cherne, director of the IRC, returned from a trip to South Vietnam with a plan for assisting North Vietnamese intellectuals who had fled to the South. Moynihan argued against such a move, contending that Vietnam was no place for the organization to be involved—the problem was too great and the IRC too small to make an impact. Despite Moynihan's protestations, the IRC became involved in Vietnam.

Neither Saltzman nor Cherne expected that Moynihan would stay with the IRC for long, and neither was surprised when he told them in the fall of 1954 that he would be taking a leave of absence to work on the Averell Harriman campaign for governor of New York State. Earlier Moynihan had joined Jonathan Bingham in supporting Franklin Roosevelt, Jr., for governor, but Roosevelt had withdrawn in favor of Harriman and was running for attorney general on the Harriman slate. Bingham, who had agreed to be research director for the Harriman campaign, asked Moynihan to work on the campaign, and Moynihan leapt at the chance. Harriman had an international reputation as a diplomat and could have been a potential presidential candidate if he won the race. His campaign could provide the break Moynihan needed.

Moynihan jumped right into the fall campaign as a speechwriter, traveling with Harriman on his campaign trail throughout the state. He worked hard, and when Harriman won, Bingham asked Moynihan to go to Albany as his one of his assistants. Bingham was to be secretary to the governor, which effectively made him Harriman's executive assistant. Moynihan's post would give him contact with Governor Harriman and provide the opportunity to work on a number of state issues. On the last day of 1954 Pat's sister, Ellen, and her husband Addison Parris drove the excited Moynihan to Albany.

His first assignment was to help organize the inaugural, taking on any problem that arose in the course of the preparations. (When the wife of a staff member asked Moynihan precisely what he did, Moynihan answered, "Anything they tell me to do.") He moved furniture in the governor's office, worked on the transition with Milton Stewart, Harriman's patronage dispenser, handled routine correspondence, and supervised the distribution of state cars. In his early days in Albany Moynihan acted as a sort of gatekeeper for Harriman, entertaining people who were waiting to see the governor. One of those whom Harriman routinely kept waiting was Republican Attorney General Jacob Javits, who often had to wait forty minutes to see him, and during these delays Javits and Moynihan struck up a friendship that would later serve as the underpinning of their close working relationship in Washington.

When the new administration settled in, Moynihan was placed in an office outside Harriman's with two other people, Jean McDonald and Elizabeth Brennan. Brennan had worked tirelessly on the Harriman campaign and had come to Albany as Bingham's secretary. She had become friendly with Moynihan during the campaign, for they had similar Irish Catholic backgrounds and had developed an easy rapport. Working in the same office, spending the better part of each day together, they grew progressively more friendly during the winter of 1955, yet they had never really had a formal date when Moynihan proposed to her.

In February 1955 Elizabeth went skiing in New Hampshire with friends and returned to Albany on a Sunday night with a broken leg. Since her apartment was on the second floor of a building without an elevator, Harriman's secretary, Bernice McCrae, offered to let Elizabeth use her room at the Ten Eyck Hotel, a few blocks from the capitol. That night there was a reception at the hotel that was attended by most of the Harriman staff, including Moynihan. After the reception Moynihan went upstairs to look in on Elizabeth Brennan. It was only a short visit;

Pat walked into the room, told Elizabeth that he was going to marry her, and promptly left, leaving his future wife stunned.

Liz Moynihan has said that she married Pat because he was the funniest man she had ever met. And it was precisely for this reason that a number of friends cautioned her about rushing into a marriage with him. Some asked whether Moynihan was responsible enough. After all, wasn't he always posturing and pontificating, rarely showing a serious side? Elizabeth apparently saw behind the seeming lack of seriousness, the bragging about understanding the workings of Tammany Hall, and the exaggerated tales of his adventures in Hungry Horse, Montana, to the ambitious—if unfocused—person that Moynihan was in Albany. In spite of her friends' lingering sense that she was too good for him, Liz Brennan married Pat Moynihan in Cohasset, Massachusetts, at the end of May 1955. After a short residence in Liz's apartment, they purchased a house in Coeyman's Hollow, some thirty miles outside Albany, and Liz stopped working full time.

Moynihan wrote speeches for the governor on a wide variety of subjects and helped Bingham draft the governor's annual message to the legislature and various phases of the legislative program. He traveled with Harriman to speaking engagements in various parts of the state and often served as an advance man. His strong suit in his first year or two were "mood speeches" for such events as St. Patrick's Day and the annual Al Smith dinner in October.

Moynihan was well liked by the staff but for the most part was viewed as a character, someone who was great fun to drink with, and he and other Harriman staff members often went to Yezzi's, a bar near the capitol, for drinks at the end of the day. Few knew him well, however, and he made a different impression on different types of people. To a number of the more intellectual members of the administration Moynihan was someone who had worked his way up from the streets of New York and claimed to understand better than they how the system worked. Those with roots in the party organization saw him as another intellectual reformer and were annoyed that he bragged about his education and occasionally wore his LSE blazer to the office. A number of the party regulars were suspicious of him at first, and Milton Stewart had to reassure Tammany leader and Secretary of State Carmine DeSapio that Moynihan was reliable.

His reputation then was one of conviviality and an ability to talk on any subject. Staff members remember Moynihan as the hit of the annual Christmas party, famed for his fishbowl punch. At one staff party in the country Moynihan amazed everyone by delivering an extemporaneous ten-minute speech while standing on a tree stump—after someone had remarked that the stump looked like a wonderful place for an old-fashioned political speech.

That Moynihan did not develop a reputation as a serious thinker during the early years of the Harriman administration was in part because he did not have permanent responsibilities. "Pat had a hard time finding his niche," one staff member from the period recalls. "He also procrastinated a good deal; speeches were always finished at the last minute." Another staff member was put off by Moynihan's seeming nonchalance. "He'd say 'no sweat' to anything I asked him to do, even when he hadn't any idea how he was going to handle the problem."

One of Moynihan's notable contributions in the early years of the administration concerned license plates. Traditionally, VIPs in New York State were given plates with their initials on them. Each of the plates bore a unique combination of two letters, so there was a maximum of 676 "vanity plates" available. There were many demands for the vanity plates after Harriman took office, but because so many had already been distributed by the previous Republican administration, only a few letter combinations remained. Moynihan proposed, and the governor accepted, a plan to change vanity license plates in New York State from two-letter to three-letter combinations, which made 17,576 vanity plates available for distribution. Control over the distribution of the plates was given to the county chairmen, who now had a new form of patronage to distribute to the party faithful.

Another Moynihan specialty was the history of the capitol; he knew every nook and cranny of the building and gave tours to distinguished visitors. Moynihan also developed a gimmick to promote interest in politics throughout the state: people who had voted in fifty consecutive elections would receive a special certificate from the State Board of Elections.

In 1956 Moynihan became assistant secretary for reports, a post that carried a $10,500 salary. He was required to obtain reports on their operations from all the state departments—with a view toward publicizing those programs that were newsworthy. To monitor the various agencies Moynihan set up an elaborate chart room and developed a systematic reporting system that he relished showing off to visitors. The Harriman administration was a creative place to be in the mid 1950s, a time when there was little activism in government nationally. Harriman anticipated many of the initiatives of the Kennedy-Johnson era, and as assistant secretary for reports Moynihan kept abreast of much of what was happening. He worked with Industrial Commissioner Isidor Lubin on developing the poverty program and with men like Mark McCloskey on the problems of juvenile delinquency.

Moynihan was chairman of the Governor's Traffic Safety Policy Coordinating Committee, which under his direction at the end of 1958 issued a report advocating a shift of government attention from the behavior of individual drivers to the design of the automobiles. At that time the auto industry had succeeded in convincing America that accidents were due to careless drivers rather than to faulty car design; Moynihan was one of the first to popularize the notion that government should instead concentrate its attention on the construction of the vehicle. The work on auto safety was in an early stage during the Harriman administration, and Moynihan returned to it after the governor's term had ended.

In June 1958 Jonathan Bingham took a leave of absence from his post as secretary to the governor to run for the State Senate from the Bronx, and Moynihan became acting secretary. Moynihan was then one of Harriman's most important aides, responsible for running the government and coordinating state agencies on a day-to-day basis during the remaining months of the administration.

As more a governmental than a political aide to Governor Harriman, Moynihan did not have a major role at the New York State Democratic nominating convention in 1958, where the statewide slate of candidates was selected. Nevertheless the convention had a profound effect on his career, for it marked the first serious clash between the largely Manhattan-based reform Democrats and the regular Democrats now firmly under the control of Carmine DeSapio (Harriman's secretary of state and the state Democratic national committeeman).

There was no question about the renomination of Harriman as the Democratic candidate for governor. The battle took place over the choice of a Senate candidate to oppose Republican Kenneth Keating. DeSapio supported Manhattan District Attorney Frank Hogan, a prosecutor with an impeccable record and close ties to the party organization. Harriman believed the party needed a candidate less closely identified with New York City and Tammany and more experienced in foreign affairs; his candidate was Thomas Murray, a member of the Atomic Energy Commission. The Manhattan reformers, who held only a small number of votes at the convention, were passionately committed to Thomas Finletter, a patron of their movement and a former secretary of the air force. While the reformers made the most noise, the real dispute was between Harriman and DeSapio, who controlled the bulk of the votes. The ensuing floor fight could have been averted had DeSapio and Harriman been able to settle on a compromise candidate who would agree to make the race. (Their choice, Mayor Wagner of New York, refused to run, and last-minute efforts to settle the issue privately failed.) The reformers, who had not even been admitted to the party inner sanctum, held out for Finletter, and a three-way fight developed. Hogan ultimately won the nomination, but by then the damage to the state ticket had been done. The electorate had seen a party ripped apart by dissension—a dissension that did not end after Hogan and Harriman were nominated.

Until the convention had been called into session, Moynihan paid little attention to the political machinations, assuming that a compromise would eventually be reached. When he arrived in Buffalo, the matter had not been settled. He played no role in mediating the dispute, but he was privy to most of the private negotiating sessions. He then considered himself nominally part of the reform faction, but at the time he was "appalled" by their behavior and attitude. It was understandable that regulars and reformers would differ on their choice of candidates, "but I was startled by the contempt in which the liberals, almost exclusively a middle- and upper-class group, many new to Democratic politics, held the judgment of party leaders who had spent their lives working at such politics." The reformers refused to give Hogan any credit for his record in law enforcement, believing him unqualified because he knew only the cities and did not share their internationalist perspective. In nominating a man whose experience was in the cities, the regulars were in fact anticipating the concern with urban problems that developed in the 1960s.[3]

Despite the facts that Finletter had no visible support outside one section of Manhattan and that Hogan was chosen by the same method that all previous Democratic nominees for statewide office had been chosen, the reformers charged that the nomination was a product of DeSapio's "bossism" and refused to campaign with the regulars for Hogan and Harriman against their Republican opposition—even after DeSapio named Finletter honorary co-chairman of a citizen's committee. The lack of political coordination hurt the Democrats in the November election. Liberals deserted the ticket in droves, giving the Republican Nelson Rockefeller a half-million-vote victory and Keating a much smaller 100,000-vote margin. The defeat left Moynihan out of a job and somewhat bitter at the liberal upper middle class reformers who he believed had cost Harriman the election.

Moynihan continued to serve as the governor's secretary until Harriman's term ran out at the end of December. Late one afternoon the governor's personal secretary, Bernice McCrae, entered Moynihan's office and asked of him and the two other aides present, Bob McManus and Bob Kasmire, "Which of you would like to write a book about what it was like to be in a Democratic administration after twelve years of Republican rule?" Governor Harriman had plans to donate his papers to Syracuse University and was eager that a book be written about his administration. Moynihan, who had no serious job prospects, was interested.

Moynihan had long assumed that he would return to New York City to work when his time in Albany came to an end, but now he decided that he really wanted to be a college professor, and he told his wife that he wanted to take the job working on the Harriman papers at Syracuse. It was a difficult decision. It meant making what might be the final decision about what he wanted to do with his life —a decision that he had put off since his graduation from college. It also meant that he would be settling down, if only for a short period of time. But he now had a son, Timothy, born in 1956, and a daughter, Maura, born in 1958, and it was important that his life have greater stability than a job in government provided. The Syracuse job would not pay very well, but Moynihan determined that he could manage on the salary.

In January 1959 Harriman met with Moynihan and Harlan Cleveland, dean of the Maxwell School of Citizenship and Public Affairs at Syracuse University, and arranged for his papers to be donated to the school and for Moynihan to head a New York State government research project that would culminate in a book on the administration. Harriman also made a bequest to the school that would pay Moynihan's salary. The Maxwell School then had a rule that all assistant professors had to have completed their doctorates, but Cleveland persuaded the faculty to make an exception. Cleveland also encouraged Moynihan to finish his thesis on the International Labor Organization.

The doctorate had been low on Moynihan's list of priorities. After working hard on it in his last year in England, he had almost totally forgotten it during his years in Albany. In fact, when he married Liz Brennan and moved into her apartment, he left his only copy of the manuscript outside his apartment to be thrown away. Fortunately, a neighbor who looked at the manuscript called to ask if he had really intended to get rid of it, and Moynihan reclaimed it.

With the appointment at Syracuse, Moynihan's attitude toward the Ph.D. changed. No longer the relatively carefree young man out to build a name for himself in politics, Moynihan now saw that the Ph.D. meant security for his family, and he determined to finish his thesis in his spare time. Moynihan had begun to mature. More, his self-image had improved to the point that he began to feel that what he said mattered, that "there was properly a place for me in this world." Feeling more secure about himself made it easier for him to devote relatively long stretches to writing—in a prose style that had been quite elegant since he was fourteen. And now, perhaps for the first time, Moynihan began to believe that he was someone who should be taken seriously; and this sense of self-worth helped provide the discipline that had previously been absent.

Discipline was essential if Moynihan was to complete the other principal requirement for a Ph.D. from the Fletcher School: the mastery of two foreign languages. He had yet to pass qualifying exams in French and Spanish, and given his low aptitude for the languages this was quite a problem. With the help of his wife, Moynihan studied vocabulary words on flash cards, and on one occasion he devoted his time on a long cruise to Miami almost exclusively to French and Spanish.

Moynihan still had not learned how to concentrate on one project for a sustained period. He continued to procrastinate, jumping from subject to subject. "I wasn't really at the point where I could write books then," Moynihan admits. "I was just happy to be able to turn out articles." In retrospect, Moynihan believes that he did not then have a clear understanding of what good scholarship was. His training in international law at the Fletcher School left him unprepared to be a professor of government or sociology. But while Moynihan may have lacked the discipline to do a sustained piece of work, his articles won him prominence in New York as a journalist of broad intellectual range.

At a meeting of the Governor's Traffic Safety Policy Coordinating Committee Moynihan had been struck by the questions of Dr. William Haddon, Jr., then director of the Driver Research Center of the New York State Department of Health. Haddon asked repeatedly whether there was any evidence that the state's point system (under which a driver lost his license after amassing a specified number of points awarded for traffic violations) had any appreciable effect on lowering the accident rate. The responsible officials persistently told Haddon that the evidence existed, but on further investigation Haddon found that this was not true. Moynihan believed Haddon was on the right track in questioning the state procedure, and the two soon formed a working relationship on auto safety matters, Moynihan handling the political and journalistic side and Haddon handling the professional and scientific end. Haddon's questions made Moynihan realize that the traffic safety people in Albany did not have a productive approach to the traffic safety program. While Haddon and others recognized that it was more important to concentrate attention on what could be done to reduce injuries due to impact in collisions, little had been done to publicize this notion. The point had been made by Hugh DeHaven as early as 1942, but the debate was being conducted largely in technical journals by experts, and if anything were to be done about car design, the issue would have to be popularized.

"Epidemic on the Highways," Moynihan's article in *The Reporter* of

April 30, 1959, popularized for the first time the research findings of Haddon and his predecessors. It argued that traffic safety was fundamentally a public health problem, that accidents resulted from the concentration of a large number of vehicles in a small area rather than from a nation of careless drivers. The article pointed out that lowering the speed limit in Connecticut had not significantly reduced the number of accidents or the number of injuries caused by accidents. (And even if it could be shown that human factors were responsible for many accidents, what could the government do to influence the personal traits of individual drivers?) However, the article said, research had shown that injuries received in accidents were caused in large part by faulty automobile design, the improvement of which could eliminate 75 percent of the nation's auto fatalities each year. There was evidence that automobile design had a direct impact on the accident rate, that certain model cars were more prone to accidents than others. The article concluded that since the auto industry has traditionally been resistant to the introduction of such safety features as padded dashboards and seat belts (on the assumption that they would be costly and hurt sales), it was important that an independent federal body regulate the auto industry and develop safety standards for cars.[4]

The article created a stir. Moynihan devoted three weeks to answering the correspondence it generated. He wrote Haddon that he had done the article to get the subject out of his system so that he could return to his work on the Harriman administration, yet the response was such that he wondered whether "the subject was going to ruin his life." Moynihan was pleased that little in the piece had been questioned—and disappointed that the auto industry had ignored it altogether.

Part of the reason for the considerable response to the article was Moynihan's skill as a journalist. He aroused public interest with his colorful approach to an essentially dry subject and his suggestion that the profits of the industry were "drenched in blood" because more than one in three cars produced in Detroit ended up in an accident. Such rhetoric helped to create a degree of popular concern that had hitherto been missing from the discussion of auto safety.[5]

The auto safety article, Moynihan's first major publication, won him a reputation in New York publishing circles as an incisive social critic, and the editor of *The Reporter,* Irving Kristol, encouraged Moynihan to do more writing. Over the next two years Moynihan spent a fair amount of time writing for the magazine. The content of virtually all his nine published articles between 1959 and 1961 placed him within the broad New Deal Democratic consensus. The auto safety pieces were decidedly hostile to the industry; in criticizing its greed and stupidity Moynihan was echoing the sentiments of many liberals on the nature of corporate America. Democrats have traditionally criticized the narrowness and venality of big business, and Moynihan's attack on the auto industry placed him squarely in that tradition.

His other writings reflected a similar bias and demonstrated a commitment to increased federal spending as a means of solving domestic problems. In an article on federal highway policy he criticized President Dwight Eisenhower for cuts in aid to housing, hospital construction, and the fight against water pollution at a time when funds for highway construction were freely available. New roads were being built with little attention being given to how highway construction would affect population growth and distribution. Nor was proper attention being paid to mass transit.[6] (In time Moynihan's view changed. Later he would conclude that in the Eisenhower years he had "overestimated his own ability at government, while Eisenhower encouraged others to underestimate him." Eisenhower was a "great politician" who maintained a strong domestic and international position by not exposing his presidency to damage and criticism it could not withstand. During his time in the Nixon administration, Moynihan tried to get the president to set up as a memorial to Eisenhower an institute for the study of the military-industrial complex.[7])

While Moynihan did not write extensively on foreign policy and defense at this time, what he did write placed him in the mainstream of liberal anti-Communism—the position he had taken in England. He shared the government's concern for keeping pace with the Russians, especially after *Sputnik* was launched in 1957. In a letter to the *New York Times* in March 1959 he wrote that "the Sputnik failure was entirely a political failure. The Republican executive and the Democratic legislature failed to allocate sufficient resources to provide for the national defense."[8] He called for a strengthening of ROTC on university campuses and suggested (while reviewing a book on the interaction between education and the military) that the secretary of defense take an interest in the matter.[9]

Moynihan's concern over *Sputnik*, while related to his support for higher levels of defense spending, centered on another issue—that of academic freedom. He was disturbed by the link between defense and education that had been written into the National Defense Education Act of 1958. The legislation required that the federal government give assistance to universities working in fields related to programs that were important to the national defense. This bothered Moynihan precisely because it gave the federal government too great an interest in what the universities did. The bill also included a provision requiring that students receiving government loans take loyalty oaths. Even to apply for a loan, a student had to sign a statement that he or she did not believe in the overthrow of the government and was not a member of an organization that did. "This may be the first time that belief, rather than overt action, has become a criterion of loyalty," Moynihan wrote in *The Reporter* in June 1959. The article concluded with praise for Senator John Kennedy, who had shown "the courage he has written about in introducing legislation to get rid of all this."[10] Moynihan showed his concern for academic freedom in a mildly hostile review of a book on federal aid to education; he felt that the work made the mistake of overstating the degree of freedom that social scientists enjoyed.[11]

Moynihan's burgeoning career as a journalist took him away from his work on both the Harriman book and his thesis, thereby generating some resentment among his colleagues. At the end of his first year at Syracuse University, Moynihan wrote a friend that he was still "pound[ing] away here in the archives." He was then just beginning to think that a book was feasible. At the same time he was preoccupied with current problems of politics and government. His anger at the Harriman defeat had not subsided, and he referred to Governor Nelson Rockefeller in the most unflattering terms. Nationwide concern over the possible effects of a nuclear war had led Rockefeller to begin an ambitious program to encourage the construction of bomb shelters. Moynihan wrote, "If that [Rockefeller] doesn't stop, he's going to have half the population of the state hiding in their home-made bomb shelters and the other half in

State police uniforms looking for them." Moynihan still served the New York State Democratic Committee as secretary of its Public Affairs Committee, making speeches periodically to groups around the state. His work on traffic safety continued and brought him invitations to address such groups as the National District Attorneys' Association. He considered a contract offer for a book on the subject but couldn't see how to fit it into his schedule. Moynihan may have been a full-time academic, yet it was clear that many of his interests lay outside the halls of the Maxwell School.

In 1960 Moynihan's most important outside activity was probably the presidential campaign of Senator John Kennedy. Moynihan identified closely with Kennedy and was committed to his candidacy from the outset. He knew Kenneth O'Donnell, a member of Senator Kennedy's staff, from the days when Moynihan worked for Harriman. His work with the state Democratic committee had kept Moynihan involved in state politics, and he was selected as an alternate delegate to the 1960 convention in Los Angeles. He knew he had to convince Averell Harriman, a longtime antagonist of Joseph Kennedy, to support the Massachusetts senator. His first meeting with Kennedy was not particularly eventful, and must have left Moynihan somewhat disappointed. At one point Kennedy came walking through a hotel lobby where Harriman and Moynihan were standing and Harriman introduced Moynihan to the Senator. Moynihan mentioned that he taught at Syracuse and Kennedy told him in an off-the-cuff manner that he had an honorary degree from Syracuse before walking off. That was all that happened. There was no brilliant exchange, no recognition that Moynihan was someone to take note of. It rankled Moynihan that he was just another delegate, another person Kennedy could exchange pleasantries with and then walk by. But this first meeting, however brief it was, undoubtedly stimulated Moynihan to work even harder so Kennedy would have to take note of him. Moynihan's major role at the convention was to write a two-minute seconding speech for Kennedy that Harriman was persuaded to deliver.

The Los Angeles convention and the events surrounding it confirmed Moynihan's skepticism and distrust of the reform Democrats. The reformers, many of whom went to the convention supporting Adlai Stevenson, viewed Kennedy with "the same disdain" they had viewed Frank

Hogan—because Kennedy was not clearly identified with the liberal wing of the party and because he had close ties with machine politicians like Charles Buckley of the Bronx, who had endorsed Kennedy well before the convention. Moynihan left Los Angeles determined to work to help elect Kennedy.

Preoccupied with his research and teaching responsibilities and his preparation for the Ph.D. oral examinations, which came before the election, Moynihan was unable to do much for the Kennedy campaign in Syracuse. He wrote a position paper on traffic safety for the national campaign, which argued that automobile accidents were America's greatest public health problem. While the statement was issued in Kennedy's name and reflected a fundamental change in thinking on the issue, it is unlikely that the candidate ever saw it.

It was Liz Moynihan who did the grass roots organizing for Kennedy on a day-to-day basis, working in the Citizens for Kennedy organization run by former Maxwell School dean Harlan Cleveland. Liz could be counted on to arrange a reception for Pat Kennedy Lawford among Republican and Democratic women in Syracuse on short notice—and, at the request of the Kennedy organizers, to keep the local politicians away from the ladies' affair without offending them. Her success in such tactful undertakings made her one of the most effective organizers in the Syracuse area.

Pat's efforts at political campaigning were sporadic. He delivered a series of speeches across the Mohawk Valley, emphasizing to the largely Catholic organizations that Kennedy was Catholic. After one speech in a Polish hall in Rome he was greeted with five minutes of sustained hand-thumping applause. His other campaign efforts were less effective. (On one occasion he advised a local Kennedy organizer to use a sound truck to tell people to take Republican bribes and vote Democratic.) On election day Moynihan served as a poll watcher in one of the most disreputable districts in the city. Just after the polls opened in the morning Moynihan stormed in, wearing a tweed hat and a trench coat, in search of Republican chicanery. Finding a locked door inside, he began banging on it, screaming that people inside were up to no good. Someone finally located the keys to the door, opened it, and found the room within empty.

On election night the first call for returns that Robert Kennedy made to New York State was to Liz Moynihan. She had told him that if his brother carried Syracuse, he would win the entire state. When Robert called from Hyannis Port, Liz Moynihan was proud to report that Kennedy had won Syracuse.

The victory both elated and relieved the Moynihans. Pat was eager to take a job in the administration, and Liz—who generally disliked academic life—was eager to leave Syracuse. (By the end of the campaign she had been telling friends that Pat had better get a job in Washington because they were going to be thrown out of town for their single-minded devotion to the cause of John Kennedy.)

After two years in Syracuse, Moynihan too had grown weary of academic life. He hated the jealousies that existed among members of the faculty and believed that having colleagues speak ill of one was an occupational hazard that one had to put up with whether one was successful or not. Harriman, however, wanted him to remain at Syracuse and finish the book, and he discouraged talk of an administration post for Moynihan in 1960 by telling Kenneth O'Donnell that Moynihan wanted to complete the book before leaving Syracuse—after Moynihan made it clear he wanted to work for Kennedy. Moynihan succeeded in getting a post only after Sander Vanocur recommended him to Willard Wirtz, then an assistant to Secretary of Labor Arthur Goldberg. Goldberg interviewed Moynihan, liked him, and offered him a job as an executive assistant.

With great excitement, Moynihan prepared to go to Washington. He had secured a promising job in an activist administration under a man whose background was similar to his own. And he was working for John Kennedy, for whom he had almost boundless admiration. Moreover, he had finally completed the requirements for his doctorate, having passed the orals during the campaign, and he could now take pride in hearing himself called Dr. Moynihan. There remained only the matter of the book on the Harriman administration, less than one-third of which had been written. In the spring of 1961 Moynihan called on Stephen Bailey, then dean of the Maxwell School, to tell him that he was going to the Department of Labor and that he would finish the book in Washington. Bailey, who doubted that Moynihan would be able to work on it there, asked him to show the unfinished manuscript to Harriman, Clark Ahlberg, chancellor of the university, and Paul Appleby, director of the Bureau of the Budget in the Harriman administration and a former dean of the Maxwell School.

Neither Appleby nor Ahlberg liked the manuscript. They thought that it was unnecessarily critical of Harriman and that it was not an objective narrative history of his administration. Specifically, they said that Moynihan spent too much time dealing with such issues as the governor's inept handling of the meeting of the leaders of organized crime at Appalachia in 1957 instead of focusing on the substantive achievements of the administration. On the basis of these judgments Bailey decided not to publish the material Moynihan had written and relieved him from the project. He flew to Washington and took Moynihan to lunch at the Cosmos Club to explain the reasons for his decision.

Moynihan was relatively impassive at lunch, but later he sent Bailey a letter accusing him of knuckling under to Harriman's wishes. Harriman had also disliked the manuscript, and Moynihan believed that Harriman had used his influence to suppress its publication. The decision not to publish was a violation of academic freedom, Moynihan wrote. His account was fair; he could not change the fact that Harriman had lost the election. Bailey wrote back that in his opinion the manuscript was unsuitable for publication and that Harriman had exercised no influence.

Moynihan, stung by the affair, decided against completing and publishing the manuscript on his own, even though Harlan Cleveland read it and urged publication. Harriman doesn't like it, Moynihan told Cleveland, and I'm going to forget about it. Full of a strong desire to reshape American society, Moynihan—like so many other New Frontiersmen—had turned to the new challenges of Washington.

4

We'll Never Be Young Again

Kennedy had been my President in a way that happens only once.
... In a not altogether absurd sense it could be said I spent my whole
life preparing for his Presidency and had done so rather as he had
done. We had been officers in the same Navy, had learned something of that: he, obviously, more than I, but I had learned also.
—Pat Moynihan, 1972

One agency of the federal government that was not eager to have
Moynihan in the Kennedy administration was the FBI. When Moynihan's name was put forward as an assistant to Secretary of Labor Arthur
Goldberg, the Bureau told an administration official that Moynihan had
been arrested for drunk driving in 1952. When Richard Donahue, an
assistant to Kennedy aide Lawrence O'Brien, confronted Moynihan
with the report, Moynihan had little trouble clearing his name. "In
1952," Moynihan told Donahue, "I was in England and I did not even
have a driver's license."

Moynihan had further troubles with the FBI when his article "The
Private Government of Crime" appeared in *The Reporter* in July 1961.
The article chided the FBI for not having waged a vigorous enough
campaign against organized crime.[1] Moynihan was then just starting his
job with Goldberg, and it was not until August that the Bureau realized

that the author was now an official of the Department of Labor. When it did, an angry J. Edgar Hoover called Goldberg to protest the appointment on the ground that Moynihan's obvious anti-FBI bias would "slant" his viewpoint during the hearings on federal employee-management relations that Moynihan was then conducting. Goldberg defended Moynihan and suggested that he go to the Bureau and explain his position.

Moynihan sought a meeting with Hoover, but the director told his chief assistant, Cartha DeLoach, "I am not going to see this skunk." DeLoach gave Moynihan a tour of the Bureau and later described him in a memo to Hoover as an "egghead" who "talks in circles and constantly contradicts himself." The FBI then dropped their protest against his appointment but put his name on a special list of people whom the Bureau staff could contact only with the express approval of the director.

With his appointment finally secured, Moynihan had to find a place to live. Driving in northwest Washington, he saw a deserted cottage on the Davies estate, *Tregarin,* just off Macomb Street. The estate (now an international school) was a large wooded area that offered the seclusion of country life and the convenience of living within the District of Columbia. Moynihan made a deal with the owner of the estate to refurbish the cottage, repaint it, and put in a new stove in return for a relatively low rent. It proved a perfect location for bringing up children; Sander Vanocur, Fred Graham, and other friends frequently visited, bringing their children on weekends and wandering around the property with the Moynihans.

At the Labor Department Moynihan quickly developed a good working relationship with Arthur Goldberg and was appointed staff director of the President's Task Force on Employee-Management Relations in the Federal Service. The task force, established as a result of a presidential memorandum (June 22, 1961), consisted of Goldberg as chairman, the secretary of defense (Robert McNamara), the postmaster general (Edward Day), the director of the Bureau of the Budget (David Bell), the chairman of the Civil Service Commission (John Macy), and President Kennedy's special counsel, Theodore Sorensen. The presidential memorandum seemed to recognize the right of federal employees to join and participate in unions and to have their grievances resolved by man-

agement officials in federal agencies. It set out the broad parameters of
the study and gave the task force the power to recommend standards for
the recognition of employee organizations, the matters on which they
should be consulted, and the participation of employers and their representatives in resolving grievances. The memorandum represented an
attempt by the White House to circumvent Congress on the issue; there
a solid body of opinion was decidedly hostile to giving federal employees
the right to organize and bargain collectively. The Kennedy administration expected to use the task force's recommendations as the basis for
an executive order, thereby avoiding the possibility of congressional
disapproval.

Goldberg eased Moynihan's transition to federal service by telling the
task force at its first meeting that Moynihan had vast experience in
government despite the fact that he was new to Washington. As secretary of the committee and staff director, he had to keep meetings
running smoothly and to coordinate the hearings that would be held in
six cities. Moynihan also had an important behind-the-scenes role. The
Budget Bureau and the Defense Department were opposed to collective
bargaining at the outset, and Moynihan was to meet privately with their
representatives on the task force to try to persuade them to change their
views. One member of the task force, William Carey, who served as
David Bell's deputy, recalls that Moynihan presented a great deal of
research that demonstrated the success of collective bargaining experi-
ments. On one occasion Moynihan arrived at a meeting with Carey
armed with a massive amount of supporting material, prepared for a hard
negotiating session. Carey, who was already convinced, said, "Take it
easy, Pat, everything is going to be okay." Moynihan and Goldberg also
persuaded the Defense Department and the Civil Service Commission
to accept collective bargaining, successfully assuaging John Macy's fears
that his agency would lose influence. Day and Goldberg were staunchly
in favor of collective bargaining from the beginning, and by the end of
the summer a consensus had been reached.

The task force discovered that there was no general federal policy
regulating employee-employer relations. Some agencies (e.g., the Post
Office) were heavily unionized while others (e.g., the State Department)
had few—if any—employees who belonged to professional organiza-

tions. Opportunities for collective bargaining were generally limited, existing only where management allowed it.

As staff director, Moynihan summarized the task force's findings and presented its recommendations. He wrote much of the final report, which urged that the federal government give employees the right to organize and to have their organizations recognized for the purposes of collective bargaining. Moynihan suggested that the recommendation read that the government was "eager" to enter into collective bargaining relations, but some believed this went too far, and in the final report the government was said to be "affirmatively willing" to enter into such relations. The report did not recommend a specific type of organization that should be recognized in each department of government, but it presented suitable options for each. Other recommendations dealt with the scope of consultations and negotiations, grievances, appeals, and procedures to be adopted in the event of impasse.[2]

The report represented a small personal triumph for Moynihan. In his first major piece of work in Washington he had proved to be an able deputy to Goldberg and had drawn praise from virtually all the members of the task force. He and John Macy became friendly. (In the mid 1960s Moynihan suggested to Macy that the government establish a set of honors for civilians, patterned on the honors list in England. Macy liked the idea but did not want to have the awards take on the appearance of conferring nobility on the recipients. As a compromise, the Medal of Freedom became the Presidential Medal of Freedom, thereby elevating the award to a higher level.) Postmaster General Ed Day and Moynihan also became friendly. Moynihan tried to convince Day that one solution to the unemployment problem was to return to twice-a-day mail deliveries (largely discontinued in 1950) in order to employ more people.

Moynihan and Goldberg took the report to President Kennedy late in 1961, hoping he would issue an executive order that provided for union recognition and collective bargaining in the federal service. It was a critical moment for Moynihan, his first opportunity to talk privately with the president whom he admired so much. Kennedy, however, showed little interest in the subject and seemed not to remember that six months earlier he had agreed to provide for union recognition. Just as Moynihan and Goldberg were to present their report, Moynihan recalled in a *Playboy* interview some 16 years later, the president wandered out of the Cabinet room and into the Oval Office. He returned some minutes later with a poem that had appeared on the front page of the Dallas *Morning News* and contained an elliptical yet cutting reference to his brother Edward Kennedy (who was then just beginning his campaign to win the Senate seat the president had vacated). The first letter of each line of the poem spelled out the phrase, "Shit on Ted." The paper had used an acrostic to attack Ted Kennedy, and the president could not recall the term. He turned to Moynihan, searching for the word. But Moynihan also stumbled, unable to think of it. A trivial incident, but it had great significance for Moynihan. Had he only remembered the word *acrostic*, the president would have realized how clever he was, and his standing in the administration would have improved. The Washington gossip circuit might even have heard stories of how a young assistant to the secretary of labor had instructed the president!

While Kennedy may not have been impressed by Moynihan's abilities, he accepted the task force's recommendations almost exactly as they appeared in the report Moynihan had written. On January 17, 1962, Kennedy issued executive orders 10987 (on appeals) and 10988 (on employee-management cooperation), thereby giving formal executive approval to the task force's proposals.

In 1962 Moynihan was involved in three major projects in his capacity as Goldberg's special assistant. He wrote the introduction to Goldberg's report on the settlement of the New York City Metropolitan Opera musicians' strike, which the Department of Labor had arbitrated. He was a Labor Department representative at the negotiation of an International Textile Agreement in Geneva. The Amalgamated Clothing Workers of America and the International Ladies' Garment Workers Union had complained about the increasing flow of Japanese and Taiwanese goods onto the American market, encouraged by the restrictions placed on trade with East Asia by the European nations. Along with representatives of the State, Commerce, and Treasury departments, Moynihan hammered out an agreement designed to avoid strict import barriers by providing that all nations have a proportion of the expanding world market. Federal officials who worked with Moynihan in Geneva gave him high marks for his negotiating skill.

Finally, Moynihan developed "Guiding Principles for Federal Architecture," calling for the promotion of a form and style that would reflect positively the character of American government. Public buildings need not be monumental, Moynihan argued, but there was a need to return to the concepts of the City Beautiful Movement and specifically the plan Pierre L'Enfant formulated for Washington in the eighteenth century. The development of public buildings was critically important: "An era of great public works is as much needed in America as any other element in our public life," Moynihan wrote later.

Previous administrations had given little attention to architectural planning, and Moynihan became involved in the project by accident. The old Department of Labor building was located at 14th and Constitution. Additional offices were scattered throughout the environs of the District of Columbia, making it difficult to organize work in the department. Goldberg, wanting to do something about the Labor Department situation, got President Kennedy to appoint a committee on office space for the federal government. The labor secretary assigned Moynihan to the committee, and Moynihan joined with its members in suggesting to Goldberg that rather than argue with the General Services Administration about the location of a new building for the department, the committee should press for the redevelopment of all of Pennsylvania Avenue. The group interested Goldberg in the idea by bringing in such architects as I. M. Pei to discuss renovation plans. The statement of general architectural principles grew out of the more narrow office committee report.

The committee also prevailed on Goldberg to recommend to the president that he appoint a Commission on Pennsylvania Avenue, which he ultimately did. Its first chairman was architect Nathaniel Owings; its membership included Moynihan, Frederick Gutheim, Cloethill Woodward Smith, Charles Horsky, and Bill Walton (the latter two White House aides with responsibility for the arts). The commission began meeting late in 1962 with an eye toward making a report to the president about a year later.

While Moynihan had acquired a broad range of experience during his first year in Washington, he was particularly valuable to the Kennedy administration for his detailed knowledge of New York State politics. Governor Nelson Rockefeller then loomed as a serious political threat, and the Kennedys placed a high priority on trying to defeat him in the 1962 gubernatorial election. So, after New York State Democrats nominated Robert Morgenthau for governor in 1962, Robert Kennedy prevailed on Moynihan to resign his post and become the candidate's principal speechwriter and research director.

If the White House was optimistic about the prospects of defeating Rockefeller, Moynihan was decidedly pessimistic.[3] He believed that the internal party strife that had hurt Averell Harriman and Frank Hogan in 1958 would continue to damage the Democrats' chances in 1962, for the fight between reform and regular Democrats continued. Early in 1961 Moynihan had predicted that the Democratic nominee for governor in 1962 could lose to Rockefeller by one million votes if the party divisions were not eliminated. He had even suggested that the White House not contest the election actively. Nevertheless, when the decision was made to put the prestige of the president behind Morgenthau, Moynihan came to his aid. The results, however, tended to confirm Moynihan's suspicions. Morgenthau lost decisively, although not by the million-vote margin that Moynihan had predicted. Morgenthau proved to be an inept campaigner; the high level of support he held in pre-election opinion polls did not materialize on election day.

Before leaving the Labor Department, Moynihan had been offered a promotion to assistant secretary to replace Jerry Hollemen, who had resigned following disclosures that he had accepted a $1000 gift from Billie Sol Estes, the Texas financier. When Moynihan returned to Washington early in 1963, Willard Wirtz had replaced Arthur Goldberg as secretary of labor, following Goldberg's elevation to the Supreme Court. Wirtz and Moynihan were then close friends, and Wirtz asked Moynihan to take the still vacant post. Moynihan quickly agreed, eager to move up and to be working with a friend.

In March 1963 Wirtz asked Moynihan to head a new division of the department, an Office of Policy Planning and Research. He would have the general responsibility of assuring that the department's policies and programs were adequate to meet the problems within the responsibility of the department and to ensure that any research that was undertaken could be expected to furnish the necessary information to solve those problems. Moynihan's office would help coordinate policy on manpower, labor standards, and labor-management relations; it would be in a position to help "predict or to respond quickly to social and economic problems as they emerge."[4] A description of Moynihan's job, written just before he took the position, indicates that he was given relatively free rein to make policy suggestions, with few constraints on his areas of inquiry. His office was outside the daily flow of work in the Labor Department, and except for his responsibility for overseeing the operations of the Bureau of Labor Statistics, Moynihan was on his own.

Moynihan quickly recruited three assistants to work with him in his new post, and they were responsible for much of the substantive research that his office produced between 1963 and 1965. Phil Arnow, a creative researcher, became deputy assistant secretary, and he was joined on the staff by two people who over the years would come to do a great deal of legwork for Moynihan, Paul Barton and Ellen Broderick. It was clear that Moynihan expected considerably more than the traditional nine-to-five day from his staff. He drove them (and others in the Labor Department) hard and expected them to work the twelve to fourteen hours a day that he put in. The department librarian, Margaret Brickett, recalls that Moynihan made extensive use of the facility for his research on a wide range of subjects. He sought materials on the English honors list, research relating to his work on the President's Commission on Pennsylvania Avenue, and evidence to support his idea for providing compensation to crime victims. He was constantly seeking out officials at various levels of the bureaucracy in search of data to support his hypotheses, and he had a reputation for being impatient and demanding at times. There were those in the Labor Department who believed he made a calculated effort to show how hard a worker he was by rousing his superiors on weekends to ask them supposedly urgent questions. Yet many of those who completed projects for him found him very appreciative. Moynihan was the sort of person who would send unsolicited letters of praise to the superiors of people with whom he had worked, and often he sent letters of congratulation to colleagues who were promoted. He expected much from his co-workers, and he stood behind them when they performed as he expected.

His appointment as assistant secretary of labor allowed him to return to his interest in auto safety. Just before entering the Labor Department in 1961, Moynihan told a conference on passenger car design and highway safety that a Federal Automotive Agency should be created with the responsibility for federal highway safety research and development—which presumably would coordinate research on automobile design.[5] No such agency existed when Moynihan joined the Labor Department, and Goldberg had appointed him the department's representative on the President's Committee on Traffic Safety, an industry-dominated group. He served for a year on the committee before learning that its chairman, who had the power to use the president's seal and to spend public moneys, was in fact paid by the industry. Moynihan found the situation outrageous—an "impartial" traffic safety spokesman was actually working for the people he was supposed to watch—and he lobbied strongly for greater control on the chairman's power. He won a small victory in 1962 when a White House meeting chaired by the secretary to the Cabinet agreed that the seal was being abused—but there was no resolution as to what should be done.

No serious attempts were made to regulate the auto industry in the early 1960s, though Moynihan and others in the government had begun work on legislation to develop standards of safety in the design of cars. There simply was not enough reliable data on how accidents occur, Moynihan concluded. Just after his appointment in 1963 he testified at some length on the subject of accident statistics before the Subcommittee on Public Health and Safety of the House Commerce Committee. He argued that past efforts to collect useful statistics had been "almost wholly useless" to accident researchers. What was needed was a federally funded National Accident Prevention Center that would conduct research on the subject. Moynihan believed that his testimony was important, yet little note was taken of it. The proposed legislation did not pass, his statement was not reprinted in any traffic safety publication, and no reporter questioned him further after the hearing. It was as if he had not spoken at all.[6]

Despite the reluctance of Congress to act, Moynihan's research continued. He contemplated writing a book on auto safety with Dr. William Haddon, but a young part-time consultant whom he had hired, Ralph Nader, published his now classic *Unsafe at Any Speed* in 1966. The book drew on Labor Department files and made a number of the same points that Moynihan had made in his 1959 article in *The Reporter*. It angered Moynihan that Nader had written his book before him; he said nothing publicly, but he believed he could have written a better book, and he was miffed that Nader had used Labor Department material.[7]

While the scope of Moynihan's activities broadened considerably in his new post, he was still used on special government and political projects in New York State. In the summer of 1963 the Labor Department sent him to Brooklyn to confer with the sponsors of a civil rights demonstration that protested the paucity of jobs for minorities on federal projects. He continued to be a political operative in state politics on behalf of the president, and he addressed the state convention of the AFL-CIO late in October, at a time when Rockefeller was being seriously touted for the 1964 Republican presidential nomination. Rockefeller was wooing New York trade unionists during the 1960s (he finally won the AFL-CIO endorsement in 1970), but in 1963 any alliance between Rockefeller and the unions was tenuous, and Moynihan did what he could to dissolve it. His speech was openly partisan; it attempted to link Rockefeller with those right-wing Republicans who were avowedly anti-union. Rockefeller, Moynihan charged, was trying to build an image pleasing to conservative Republicans. The Republican party was falling into the hands of "radical revisionists" who were allied with those running the John Birch Society. Under Rockefeller New York had reached a point of fiscal stagnation and was dropping behind the rest of the states in rate of growth.[8]

Moynihan's appointment as assistant secretary of labor in 1963 marked an important, perhaps decisive step in his career. On the day his appointment was confirmed by the Senate he told an old friend that the post would guarantee him a college professorship—that he would never again have to worry about job security. In fact by this time Moynihan would probably have had little problem in finding a good position in a university or in the private sector. He had merely lacked confidence in himself, and now his new position represented "making it."

Then he was almost thrown into shock by the assassination of President Kennedy in November 1963. In some sense the assassination was the final step in his personal maturation process: he felt he would never be young again after the president's death, and he went about his work with renewed commitment in the months that followed.

Though he barely knew Kennedy, Moynihan felt as though he had lost a member of his own family. John Kennedy was his president, in a way that happens only once; he identified completely with Kennedy and his aspirations, sensing that he had spent his whole life preparing for his presidency. And now the recognition he had once sought from Kennedy would never come. There remained only memories of muffed chances; he had never really gotten to know the man for whom he had spent his life preparing to work.

At the hour of the assassination Moynihan was at a Georgetown house discussing the renovation of Pennsylvania Avenue. When the news came over the radio, Moynihan and White House aides Bill Walton and Charles Horsky left immediately for the White House. Settling back in the taxi, Moynihan reached for his wallet to find the map of roads leading to the cave in West Virginia where the subcabinet was to gather if there should be a nuclear attack. Who knew what might follow the assassination of the president!

Just after Moynihan and his party arrived at the White House it was learned that the president was dead. Moynihan had gone directly to Ralph Dungan's office in the southwest corner of the West Wing, and there he and a dozen others heard a shrieking Ted Sorensen come running in from the Rose Garden bellowing, "It's over, he's dead." Hubert Humphrey, who had just entered, reached for Dungan as Dungan cried out, "What have they done to us?" McGeorge Bundy reached out for Sorensen, then put through a call to Secretary of Defense Robert McNamara.[9]

The president's trip to Dallas had given the White House maintenance staff a chance to change the carpeting in the Oval Office, and at the time of the assassination all of the president's furniture was piled in the hall. His prized rocking chair now rested on top of the mass of furniture. Leaving the White House with Walton, Moynihan thought to himself that someone must have known that a new president would be coming in. After putting Walton in a taxi Moynihan wandered aimlessly toward the Department of Labor, then, seeing no point in going to his office, reversed his direction and walked back to the White House. He felt somehow that his time in government was over, and he wanted one more look at the Oval Office. After gazing at the new carpeting and the furniture stacked in the hallway, Moynihan turned to Mrs. Lincoln's (the president's secretary) desk and picked up a picture of Kennedy. He took the picture to the center door of the Oval Office, saluted it stoically, and then marched quickly off. When a guard stopped him and asked for his Secret Service pass, Moynihan replied sharply, "What difference does it make?"

Moynihan considered getting drunk, but after a few drinks with a friend he found that his mood was not affected. On the contrary, his mind was working remarkably well. At some point that afternoon Moynihan reasoned that there was at least a possibility that the Dallas police might try to kill Lee Harvey Oswald. Moynihan was not sure who Oswald was and had no idea whether Oswald had pulled the trigger of the gun that killed Kennedy; all he knew was that Oswald had been involved with an organization that purported to be friendly with Castro's Cuba. And Dallas was the sort of city that was likely to have incompetent police, a city located in a state where someone might try to avenge the murder of Kennedy in something akin to the style of the Old West. All this led to one inescapable conclusion: the federal government had to get custody of Lee Harvey Oswald.

Moynihan did not have the authority to *tell* someone that this had to be done; he could only cajole one of his superiors in the government to do it. It proved to be a futile task. He went to Andrews Air Force Base to meet the Cabinet plane that Friday night and arrived early. The other second-level officials there were no help; they had no power, and their attention had already turned to angling for appointments in the new administration. Before the plane landed Moynihan cornered Undersecretary of State George Ball. His argument was this:

We've got to get on top of the situation in Dallas. American cops are emotional. They don't believe in due process, and they are so involved in corruption that they overcompensate when they run into something big.

You can't depend on them. The most profound national interest can't be left in the hands of policemen. The facts here are so confused that if we don't move quickly there will be no trouble later establishing a case against the Communists, against fascists, against anybody. It might be an anti-Khrushchev faction, it might be a Chinese faction out of Cuba—you couldn't construct a wider range of possibilities. But you can be sure of one thing. Nobody can predict what the Dallas police will do, and their saying a man is a Commie doesn't make him one.[10]

It was a startling hypothesis, and Moynihan got no one to take him seriously that night in Washington. Ball said that Moynihan was right and that he would speak with Dean Rusk—but nothing came of that. Bob Wallace, in charge of the Secret Service for the Treasury, told Moynihan that the situation was under control and that there was nothing to worry about. When someone told Moynihan that his thinking was outlandish, Moynihan replied angrily, "You stupid son-of-a-bitch. The freely elected president of the United States is lying dead in a box, and you're telling me I'm far out. It's the far out events that make history. It's far out to say that Caesar is going to be stabbed in the forum today."[11]

Moynihan's efforts continued for two days. He had access to virtually everyone in Washington, but he could convince no one that it was essential that the federal government take custody of Oswald. Robert Kennedy was not available, and no one else would act on Moynihan's suggestion. Again Moynihan attributed the reluctance of the Kennedy liberals to act to their lack of knowledge about how the world really worked. None of them had ever been arrested and been forced to deal with hostile police. In such circumstances Moynihan knew that anything could happen; it was the sort of thing "ordinary" as opposed to "educated" people knew.

When I was standing with the Cabinet at Andrews Air Force Base, saying we had to get custody of Oswald, I was talking to overeducated people who had learned the word paranoid, and who had been taught that people who go around being suspicious are crazy. Because awful things don't happen. As a matter of fact, awful things do happen. And ordinary people know that.[12]

Saturday afternoon, November 23, Moynihan went to the house of his neighbor and friend Mary McGrory on Macomb Street, having already spent part of the day at the White House. He was joined by Elizabeth Acosta, an assistant of McGrory, and White House aide Fred Holborn. There was no food in the house, so Liz Moynihan went home to get a duck she had been cooking and some french bread. She finished cooking the duck at McGrory's and opened a can of peaches to go with it. There was a great deal of drinking that night; everyone was tired and worn from the events of the previous day. Moynihan kept repeating that it was important to keep Oswald alive in order to find out what had really happened. If Oswald were killed, the American people might never know how Kennedy had been killed. That evening McGrory told Moynihan that she felt as though she would never laugh again. He replied, "Heavens, Mary, we'll laugh again. We'll just never be young again."[13]

The next day Moynihan's worst fears were realized. Shortly before Oswald was shot, Moynihan concluded a widely heard and replayed interview in which he spoke philosophically about President Kennedy: "We all of us know down here that politics is a rough game. And I don't think there's any point in being Irish if you don't know that the world is going to break your heart eventually. I guess we thought we had a little more time. . . . So did he."[14]

If he was philosophical just before Jack Ruby shot Oswald, Moynihan's mood turned to one of uncontrollable anger when he learned the news from Liz, who called him at the office. Moynihan kicked the wall violently and began calling friends, screaming about what had just happened in Dallas.

Moynihan now believed it essential that there be a comprehensive investigation of the assassination; a failure to do this would weaken the legitimacy of the government for at least a generation. Again Moynihan made the rounds in Washington—this time joined by John Macy, chairman of the Civil Service Commission—arguing the need for a complete investigation. The response was unencouraging: "At best we encountered incomprehension; at worst, the suspicion that *we* thought there had been a conspiracy. We did not; we were merely convinced that significant portions of the public would believe there had been one unless the inquiry went forward with this pre-eminent concern in mind."

Moynihan again believed that his efforts were all for nothing. The Warren Commission report was not definitive; commissioners did not attend meetings, and even the deputies they sent often did not show up. Warren himself was a man of "vast self-importance and rather small competence" who was not up to the task.[15] The fundamental questions were never satisfactorily answered.

If the assassination left Moynihan emotionally distraught, he refused to let it interfere with his work. Kennedy, Moynihan felt, "had a right to expect that those of us alive would *think* about what had happened, and not simply in terms of what it meant to us as individuals. . . . Surely I had learned that one man's death does not bring an end to things."[16] The morning of the day Kennedy was shot Moynihan had been testifying before a Senate subcommittee on the work of a presidential task force whose job it was to develop a program of guidance and job training for men rejected by Selective Service. It was a study Moynihan had conceived himself, and his testimony that day won him his first front-page mention ever in a newspaper (the early afternoon edition of the Washington *Star*). The final report of the task force was due January 1, 1964, and Moynihan was determined to do the best job possible.

In late June 1963 the director of Selective Service had presented his annual report to the Congress and the president, indicating among other things that about half of those persons called for physicals were either medically or physically disqualified. The report got scant mention in the next day's newspapers, but to Moynihan it seemed a crucial finding. It struck him that the 50 percent figure was important for two related reasons. First, those people who were rejected comprised an identifiable group that was likely to have trouble finding employment and would probably need supportive services. By identifying these people, the government could anticipate their problems. Second, the large number of rejectees appeared to be a powerful argument in favor of the administration's Youth Employment Act, the Labor Department's most important bill, which was then languishing before the House Rules Committee. Armed with the 50 percent figure, Moynihan had proposed that a study of candidates rejected by the service be conducted, and with the support of Secretary Wirtz a President's Task Force on Manpower Conservation had been duly appointed on September 30. The task force included the director of Selective Service and the secretaries of Defense, Labor, and Health, Education and Welfare. Wirtz was chairman and Moynihan did most of the staff work on the project. The initial findings of the commission, made public by Moynihan on the day of the assassination, showed that one-third of draft-age men were likely to be rejected for one reason or another as unfit for military service.

Following the assassination, Moynihan worked feverishly on the final draft of the report, writing late into the night and on weekends to complete it by the January 1, 1964, deadline that President Kennedy had set. It was important that the proposal be as readable as possible, and Moynihan exhorted his subordinates to improve its prose. When the Budget Bureau staff complained that the proposals Moynihan and Wirtz advocated were too expensive, they went to Kermit Gordon, the head of the bureau, and persuaded him to support their recommendations. The task force report, appropriately titled *One Third of a Nation,* called on the president to announce a nationwide manpower conservation program that would give people who did not qualify for military service the needed training, education, and medical services that would enable them to become self-sufficient citizens.[17]

While Moynihan's proposal was never formally adopted, the study was used by both the Defense Department (for its Project 100,000) and the framers of the poverty program assembled early in 1964. The study of service rejectees reinforced Moynihan's belief that the poverty program, which was being discussed with increasing interest following the assassination, would be most useful if it concentrated on providing jobs for unemployed people instead of trying to stimulate the participation of poor people in politics through widely divergent (and often poorly conceived) community action programs. As a member of the task force that framed the initial antipoverty legislation, Moynihan pressed to make an employment program the focus of the legislation. But he lost. And in retrospect he felt that once again the liberals and the intellectuals had defeated him—with what he believed would be disastrous consequences for domestic policy and social reform.

During President Kennedy's review of economic conditions in 1962 he asked Walter Heller, the chairman of the Council of Economic

Advisers, to give him some data on the nature of poverty in America.[18] The data Heller provided, along with such books as Michael Harrington's *The Other America,* had convinced Kennedy by mid 1963 that a comprehensive attack on the problem was necessary. In October Kennedy asked Heller to put together a series of proposals for his 1964 legislative program. Only three days before his death Kennedy told Heller that poverty legislation would definitely be included in the 1964 legislative message. Then the war on poverty was declared by Lyndon Johnson, who felt he had a mandate to end deprivation and hatred in America. Meeting with Heller the day after Kennedy's death, President Johnson told him to draft a proposal.

It was difficult to translate President Johnson's enthusiasm into a concrete proposal because there were many different conceptions of how the war on poverty should be constructed. There was also the problem of distinguishing the Johnson program from the other domestic legislation conceived in the early 1960s. The joint task force of the Bureau of the Budget and the Council of Economic Advisers that was set up to design the legislation received some thirty-five separate proposals, and it found a unifying theme early in December 1963. Both the Ford Foundation (through its "gray areas" program) and the President's Commission on Juvenile Delinquency and Youth Crime had funded indigenous community organizations with the expectation that such groups would best be able to plan a coordinated attack on poverty for the particular areas in which they were located. William Cannon of the Budget Bureau staff became convinced of the potential benefits of the community action approach and proposed that a development corporation be created in each of ten communities. The development corporation would plan the programs for its particular area and submit its proposal to the government for approval. When the plan had been accepted, the development corporation would be responsible for administering and coordinating it.

Initially, aid to community organizations was not expected to be a major part of the war on poverty. But the idea took hold, and in December 1963 the Bureau of the Budget decided that most of the $500 million committed to the poverty program would be devoted to aiding community organizations. This decision having been reached, there remained the questions of how to spend the money and how to define precisely the meaning of "community action."

The Department of Labor—and Moynihan in particular—vigorously opposed the Bureau of the Budget and Council of Economic Advisers' plan to fund community action. Moynihan had been a member of the first group Heller set up to develop the poverty program, and he had argued that the most pressing need of the poor was jobs. Thus the task of the federal government as he saw it was to provide a massive employment program and specifically to effect the passage of the department's Youth Employment Act. At that stage Moynihan opposed the community action idea largely because it did not emanate from his department; as the fuzziness of the proposal became evident, his criticism of its merits grew sharper.

There were a number of competing ideas as to how the community organizations should function after receiving federal funding. One group (primarily those in the Bureau of the Budget) saw the community organizations coordinating existing federal programs on a local level. Another and more radical group, including those who had developed the President's Commission on Juvenile Delinquency and Youth Crime, saw the community groups organizing the poor to fight the power structure and molding them into a more powerful political force. A third approach placed its hope in the establishment of a sort of domestic peace corps working in the ghettoes, organizing the poor to win their rights. In fact the typologies were not as distinct as they appeared, but the foregoing description reflects accurately the difference of views as then perceived. In late 1963 no clear consensus had developed on which strategy to adopt.

President Johnson gave the as yet unformulated poverty program a prominent place in his 1964 State of the Union address, indicating that his administration was "declaring unconditional war" on poverty. Now the pressure was on the administration to formulate a workable plan. The Heller task force made some effort to resolve the problem late in January when Lee White, an assistant special counsel to the president, sent a memo to the secretaries of Labor, Agriculture, HEW, Commerce, and Interior, the attorney general, and the administration of the Housing and Home Finance Agency, outlining its plan. The proposal was surprisingly vague, suggesting only that each affected community should have an organization or an official to mesh private and public assistance programs. There was no indication of how the community action agency should be represented; there was emphasis on both planning and action; and it was unclear which view of community action the task force embraced.

Secretary of Labor Wirtz and his assistant secretary filed a vigorous dissent.[19] In a memo drafted for Wirtz, Moynihan asked rhetorically, "What do we know about poverty that would lead us to suppose that the first step to getting rid of it is to have poverty-stricken communities propose plans?" Community action was a middle class proposal designed to cure a problem that had been conceived entirely in middle class terms. If $50 million were to be spent on the program at the outset, it was possible that the entire sum would only enrich middle class planners. The implementation of the community action approach would virtually ensure that no part of the money would actually reach the poor.

The memo also outlined the conflicting approaches to community action and argued that social scientists like Lloyd Ohlin and Richard Cloward and the grass roots political activists had a very different view of community action from that of the Bureau of the Budget planners. The social scientists and political activists wanted to use the agencies to organize the poor and attack the system; the bureaucrats merely hoped to coordinate at the local level the myriad of existing federal programs. What was dangerous was that neither group was really aware of what the other was thinking. Alternatively, the Department of Labor proposed that community action be de-emphasized in favor of concentration on the creation of jobs and job training. Essentially the poverty problem was one of income, and the quickest and most effective way of providing people with income was to give them jobs. The Department of Labor wanted to extend minimum wage coverage to virtually all retail, service, and agricultural workers, to strengthen unemployment benefits, and to provide additional funding for the Manpower Development and Training Act. Most important, the Department of Labor wanted a massive adult employment program, to be funded by a five-cent cigarette tax.

The uncertainty about the makeup of the community action program led President Johnson to bring in an outsider, Sargent Shriver, to give the program focus. Shriver approached the poverty legislation with an open mind; the day after his appointment he invited Bureau of the Budget and Council of Economic Advisers officials to his house to explain their plan. Shriver was skeptical at first, neither understanding the theory behind the proposal nor comprehending how it would work in practice. Nevertheless he called another meeting two days later (February 4) of all those peripherally involved in formulating the program.

The meeting was large, and it began with community action advocates explaining the concept—but the emphasis had changed since December. Gone was the concern for careful planning and the establishment of only a limited number of experimental agencies. Shriver, still unsure about the idea, seemed receptive when Wirtz argued that community action was not enough, that more immediate evidence of the effects of the war on poverty was needed, and that this could come only from projects that created jobs and/or provided educational aid.

Shriver saw a need for a more broadly based poverty program than one that was based on community action alone. He had his deputy, Adam Yarmolinsky, assemble a working task force to prepare background papers reflecting the topics discussed at the February 4 meeting. Moynihan was eager to be the Labor Department representative (as was the department's legislative affairs representative, Sam Merrick), and Wirtz gave Moynihan the assignment. He drafted the paper on job creation and employment; Wilbur Cohen of HEW wrote the paper on education and child health programs; Richard Boone and Paul Ylvisaker prepared the paper on community action; and Charles Schultze drew up the plan for the agency that would administer the poverty program (later the Office of Economic Opportunity).

The meeting on February 4 had given Moynihan hope that the poverty program might shift its emphasis from a community action approach to an employment strategy. True, Shriver had trouble synthesizing the different approaches (Moynihan later wrote that Shriver had "no taste and little patience for abstractions" and "a singular lack of reflection"), but he shared the Department of Labor's uneasiness with the community action idea, and he saw the political need for President Johnson to have something concrete to present to the electorate in 1964.[20] Moynihan and Wirtz convinced Shriver that he should include a massive employment program in the poverty legislation, even though the $1.25 billion program that the Department of Labor wanted would have dwarfed the rest of the task force's proposal. The problem was that the president was planning a tax cut and the employment program was to be financed by a five-cent tax on cigarettes. With an election approaching, Johnson did not want to raise taxes—moreover, he had been advised that a tax cut would stimulate the economy and create jobs. Thus the Wirtz-Moynihan proposal was summarily rejected at a meeting of the Cabinet on February 18.

While many of those who worked on the Shriver task force believed that the Labor Department proposal was never seriously considered, its rejection was viewed by Moynihan as a major defeat. Again liberal Democrats had rejected a Moynihan proposal, and again he would come to believe that their rejection had doomed the program. This soured Moynihan on the enterprise, and his participation in formulating the program dwindled.

There was another reason for the lessening of Moynihan's role after the legislation had been drafted. Wirtz was furious that Moynihan had allowed the proposed Job Corps program to be placed under the administration of the Office of Economic Opportunity rather than under his department. Labor Department staff members had reported to Wirtz Moynihan's disparaging remarks about the department's administrative abilities at meetings of the Shriver task force. Moynihan's own operation lay outside the mainstream of Labor Department activity, and on the task force he took the wider responsibility of developing an effective program rather than be a narrow representative of Labor Department interests. In fact he had little respect for the department's administrative abilities and believed the program could be better run elsewhere.

The broad antipoverty legislation drafted late in February 1964 consisted of five titles. The most important sections were Title I, which provided for Youth Employment Programs, and Title II, which created the Community Action Programs (CAP). The CAPs were primarily service oriented and were to be "developed and conducted with the maximum feasible participation" of the residents of the areas affected.

Little thought had been given, either in the task forces or in the drafting of the legislation, to the significance of the maximum feasible participation clause. While some may have believed its inclusion meant that the task force was adopting the view that the agencies were to be used to stimulate the organization of the poor to press for social change, this was not the case with the majority of the participants. One task force member who has written extensively on the poverty program has indicated that the phrase was included as a means of ensuring that the poor would not be bypassed in the administration and direction of the program. Moreover, "the clause . . . was inserted with virtually no discussion in the task force and none at all on Capitol Hill. . . . I cannot say that I was aware of the implications of the clause. It just seemed to me like an idea that nobody could quarrel with."[21]

The legislation was not altered substantially by Congress. (A Senate amendment calling for comprehensive community planning was stricken from the bill by the House, again raising doubts in Moynihan's mind.) Moynihan's involvement in the poverty program was virtually at an end He had attended Shriver's presentation of the measure to Congress in March and thereafter abstained from participating in task force activities. His close friend and colleague Adam Yarmolinsky had been forced out of the task force by conservative southern Democratic congressmen as a condition for their support of the measure. Yarmolinsky's successor as Shriver's assistant was Jack Conway, a labor organizer committed to the idea of involving the poor directly in all phases of administering the CAPs. A reconstituted task force under Conway developed the CAPs further and emphasized the creation of new institutions and political organizing by the poor. Meanwhile Moynihan watched with foreboding from his post in the Department of Labor, doing nothing other than attending the bill-signing ceremony in the summer of 1964.

Moynihan had been set back on two accounts: his emphasis on job creation was almost totally ignored, and in working to develop the best possible program he had come into conflict with his boss, Willard Wirtz. Relations between the two men grew increasingly strained over the next year, and for Moynihan the Department of Labor became a difficult place to work.

Moynihan became aware of Wirtz's antipathy when the secretary left him out of the presentation of the One Third of a Nation report to President Johnson. Early in February Wirtz's anger flared again when the columnists Evans and Novak reported that Moynihan had prepared the report on service rejectees. Wirtz believed that Moynihan had made a self-serving leak to the columnists and—as Moynihan described it— completely lost his temper. Moynihan denied speaking to Evans and Novak, but he could do nothing to assuage Wirtz. Relations between the two were never again friendly. And there were other reasons for Wirtz's dislike and distrust of Moynihan. Moynihan often livened up dull staff meetings with his off-the-cuff monologues on a wide variety of subjects —but Wirtz preferred that assistant secretaries give short and to-the-point reports on their activities. Relations between Wirtz and Moynihan worsened late in 1964 when Moynihan began traveling to New York on weekends to help Robert Kennedy in his campaign for the Senate. President Johnson was paranoid about Kennedy, and anybody associated with him was suspect. When Wirtz learned what Moynihan was doing, he told Johnson, and Moynihan was forbidden to do any more work for Kennedy. Johnson never forgave Moynihan for working for Kennedy and never fully trusted him again.

After the election Wirtz decided to fire Moynihan and another high-ranking staff member, Undersecretary Jack Henning, a former AFL-CIO official from California. However, when Wirtz told AFL-CIO Secretary-Treasurer Lane Kirkland that he planned to fire Henning, Kirkland replied bluntly that the AFL-CIO had installed Henning, not Wirtz. The AFL-CIO then made it clear to the Johnson administration that if anyone were going to be fired, it would be Wirtz. His battle with the nation's labor leaders left Wirtz in a vulnerable position: he had to prove his ability to run the department effectively. Consequently, during Christmas week 1964, Wirtz invited Moynihan for drinks at the Federal City Club and asked him to stay on. Moynihan understood that Wirtz needed him in order to enhance his own position, and Moynihan agreed to remain for another year, while he finished his research for a study he had decided to make on the black family.

While Wirtz may have succeeded in keeping Moynihan out of New York during the Kennedy campaign, Moynihan spent considerable time on city affairs in the period of his service as assistant secretary of labor. He helped to implement the poverty program by writing and speaking frequently about its problems and politics. In late 1963, when New York

Mayor Robert Wagner went to Washington to meet with President Johnson, he had lunch with Secretary Wirtz, Moynihan, and two aides and discussed the implementation of the poverty program in New York. Six months later, after Congress had passed the poverty legislation, Moynihan met again with Wagner and New York City Council President Paul Screvane. He also conducted a study of Long Island's faltering defense industries and indicated that the department would try to develop a retraining program for workers who could no longer find employment in that field.

Any confidence in Moynihan's understanding of New York's problems was not misplaced. Late in 1964 he delivered a speech to a City Planning Commission symposium on the future of New York City that seems almost prophetic in light of what happened in the middle and late 1970s. Among the speakers Moynihan was virtually alone in sounding a pessimistic note. He anticipated the fiscal crisis eleven years before it actually hit the city. The city, he said, was undergoing a crisis in the employment of skilled labor that could doom all rational planning efforts. Of every 100 jobs created in America between 1960 and 1964, only 1.6 were in New York State (as compared to 18 in California). Manufacturing employment had been rising in the nation during this period but was dropping ominously in New York. If there continued to be a sharp decrease in available jobs in the metropolitan areas, "the result could be a form of social chaos that will make any idea of planning by design seem a quaint notion of the idyllic past."[22]

Moynihan had demonstrated his expertise in New York City affairs in 1963 in *Beyond the Melting Pot*, on which he collaborated with Nathan Glazer. A major study of ethnic group life in American society, the book is now considered one of the definitive works on the subject. The book's main contribution was to question the conventional conception of American society as a homogeneous society in which group differences have disappeared or were in the process of disappearing. Today ethnicity has become fashionable; television programs like *Bridget and Bernie, Welcome Back, Kotter,* and *Kojak* celebrate it. But in 1963 there had been little questioning of the myth of homogeneity.

The book also offered a new way of understanding the role of ethnic groups in American society. Ethnic groups were more than just a relic from the periods of mass immigration; they were "a new social form" that in effect behaved as interest groups do. Political battles are often fought through ethnic groups, the candidates articulating the perceived political interests of their constituent groups. The authors concluded:

> We have tried to show how deeply the pattern of ethnicity is impressed on the life of the city. Ethnicity is more than an influence on events; it is commonly the source of events. Social and political institutions do not merely respond to ethnic interests; a great number of institutions exist for the specific purpose of serving ethnic interests. This in turn tends to perpetuate them.[23]

Beyond the Melting Pot describes and analyzes the role of ethnicity in New York life and politics from the point of view of distant yet sympathetic and informed observers. In 1965 Moynihan would abandon his scholarly distance and throw himself into the caldron of ethnic politics.

5

Moynihan for Mayor

I am a New York Democrat. I live in New York. I love New York
and believe in party regularity. If anybody thinks I would make a
candidate [for Mayor] let him say so.
—Pat Moynihan, 1965

Wanting to be mayor of New York City is an ambition that most people
find difficult to understand. The job is almost impossible, no one is ever
satisfied, and the money to effect serious change is not really available.
Yet for a person growing up in New York City with an interest in politics
it is hard not to imagine yourself living in Gracie Mansion. New York,
after all, is the center of the world (even if not everybody realizes it),
and gaining influence in the city means making it in New York. For a
real New Yorker success comes only with proving yourself in your own
city.

For Pat Moynihan the chance to rise to the top in New York City
politics came in 1965 when Mayor Robert Wagner announced that he
would not be a candidate for re-election. Wagner had served three terms,
wanted to spend more time with his sons, and was tired of the job. His
withdrawal from the race left the Democratic party without a candidate

93

to oppose the Republican and Liberal parties' likely nominee, John Lindsay.

The cohesiveness of the city Democratic organization had been broken in 1961 when Mayor Wagner turned against Carmine DeSapio, the head of Tammany Hall, and the other four borough chieftains. Wagner ran as a reform Democrat and trounced State Comptroller Arthur Levitt, whom DeSapio and the other county leaders had backed. Following his primary victory and his subsequent general election triumph, Wagner was able to install county leaders in Manhattan, Queens, and Staten Island who were loyal to him. (He was unsuccessful in Brooklyn and the Bronx, where Stanley Steingut and Charles Buckley remained in power.) Wagner maintained some support among Manhattan reform Democrats, but his alliance with them was tenuous throughout his third term.

In 1965 each of the three factions sought its own candidate for mayor. Steingut and Buckley supported Comptroller Abraham Beame, a former election district captain in Steingut's Madison Democratic Club and a loyal member of the organization. Wagner and the Queens, Manhattan, and Staten Island organizations threw in their lot with Paul Screvane, a career sanitationman from Queens who had been elected City Council president in 1961. Some of the Manhattan reformers supported Screvane, but the majority of them endorsed Manhattan Congressman William F. Ryan, a liberal from the West Side.

The one man left out in the cold was the newly elected Democratic Senator Robert Kennedy. Kennedy had close ties to Buckley and Steingut, but Beame was hardly the sort of dynamic leader who could excite the heir to the New Frontier. Supporting Screvane was problematic because Kennedy had opposed Wagner's choices for leadership positions in the state legislature following the Democrats' sweep in 1964. When Wagner withdrew, Kennedy approached Manhattan District Attorney Frank Hogan and asked him to run again. Hogan, perhaps wary because of what had happened to him at the state Democratic convention in 1958, told Kennedy he would run only if he were not opposed in the Democratic primary. Kennedy, of course, could not guarantee this, and Hogan never entered the race.

Some of Kennedy's aides floated Moynihan's name as a potential candidate to learn whether he might deserve the senator's backing.

Moynihan had been an early supporter of Kennedy for the Senate seat, and Liz Moynihan had hosted a hospitality suite for him at the 1964 Democratic convention in Atlantic City. In June 1965 Kennedy aides leaked word to the *New York Times* that the White House might support Moynihan for mayor. The story, which made the top of page one, was prominently headlined, "Aides of Johnson Have Candidate for Mayor Here," and it went on to say that "Kennedy Administration holdovers" were backing Moynihan for mayor.[1]

Apparently there had been no consultation with Moynihan. When he was reached by telephone in Yugoslavia (where he was attending a UNESCO conference) and asked for his reaction, he gasped, "What?" Recovering quickly, he indicated that he would love to run for mayor of New York City. The subject, he said, had been proposed to him by "respectable people in New York politics" over the past six months, and he would welcome the opportunity to oppose Congressman John Lindsay. Would he enjoy running against Lindsay? "Good God, yes. Any decent man would oppose a candidate who knows little and cares less about New York."[2]

In retrospect it is not hard to see why Kennedy aides sought Moynihan for the mayoral race. Against either Screvane or Beame, Lindsay would appear to be fresh, articulate, and a political independent. However, in a head-to-head fight with Moynihan these advantages would largely disappear. For Moynihan was also young, tall, and good looking, and he was not affiliated closely with any of the post-1961 factions of the New York City Democratic party. It was not inconceivable that reformers and regulars could unite behind him. But Moynihan did lack exposure in city politics, and it is difficult to see how Kennedy believed that a person without a political base could defeat two such entrenched politicians as Screvane and Beame.

Despite Moynihan's lack of grass roots support, his potential candidacy was taken seriously. The Washington *Post* reported three days after the first hints of a Moynihan candidacy that he was the "hottest prospect" in the field.[3] Screvane and Ryan welcomed his entry into the race, and a fourth contender for the Democratic mayoral nomination, Manhattan City Councilman Paul O'Dwyer, said Moynihan "was a serious liberal" who "has earned the right to serious consideration."

Lindsay commented that Moynihan would certainly be a "formidable candidate." Nicholas Kisburg, the Teamsters' legislative representative in Albany, said that Moynihan would add a "breath of fresh air" to New York as mayor.

But President Johnson was certainly not going to support anyone backed by Senator Kennedy or his friends. Three days after the initial *Times* report he indicated that he would remain neutral in the primary contest.[4] He was said to be irritated by the report of White House support for Moynihan and would not support his assistant secretary of labor.

Less than a week after the initial *Times* report of his candidacy, Moynihan returned from Yugoslavia to assess his chances.[5] He soon found that he had little support, Senator Kennedy having in the interim sought an accommodation with Mayor Wagner and Screvane.

Once he had announced his candidacy, Screvane realized it was important that he at least try to neutralize Kennedy. To accomplish this he asked Kennedy's brother-in-law Stephen Smith to accept a place on his ticket. The plan fell through when Wagner indicated that Smith was not acceptable to him. Screvane then called an assistant secretary of labor, James Reynolds, who had roots in New York City, and asked him to run. When Reynolds declined, Screvane asked him about Moynihan. Reynolds said that Moynihan could be an asset politically, but he wondered whether Moynihan was disciplined enough to stand the rigors of a campaign. Despite Reynolds' hesitation, Screvane asked Moynihan to join his ticket. After the *Times* story on Moynihan appeared, Screvane had called Wagner to ask if Moynihan would be an acceptable running mate. Both men had worked with Moynihan in setting up the poverty program in New York, and they had gotten on well. Wagner had once asked Moynihan to be the city's labor commissioner, and Moynihan had expressed his regard for Wagner when he first discussed his potential candidacy: "No one appreciates how good a mayor he has been."[6] Moreover, Moynihan was clearly acceptable to Kennedy, and Moynihan's presence on the ticket might lead Kennedy to give it some help. Screvane completed his slate by selecting Orin Lehman to run for comptroller.

On paper the ticket appeared to be very strong. Ethnically it was perfectly balanced: an Italian for mayor, an Irishman for council president, and a Jew for comptroller. Politically the ticket reached across the spectrum, one candidate (Screvane) representing traditional machine interests, another (Moynihan) representing the New Frontier-Kennedy tradition, and a third (Lehman) representing both reform and traditional liberal New York Democrats.

For Kennedy the situation appeared to be ideal. If Beame won, he would have an ally in City Hall through his close relationship with the Brooklyn and Bronx organizations. If Screvane won, the number two man would be a close ally. Yet in the end the primary campaign was a disaster for all concerned.

There was little Moynihan could offer the ticket beside his intellect. He had no political base in the city and no money to contribute to the effort. Nor did he bring large numbers of people into the campaign; perhaps his most important recruit was Liz, who worked full time for the ticket during the summer. And Moynihan's opponent on Comptroller Beame's ticket, Queens District Attorney Frank O'Connor, was a well-regarded New York politician with a strong base in his home borough.

On being named to the Screvane ticket, Moynihan took pains to emphasize that he was not seeking individual backing but would ask voters to support the entire ticket. In 1965 each of the mayoral candidates had slates of citywide and local candidates who supported them and whose names appeared directly below theirs on the ballot. Each candidate hoped that attractive candidates on his slate would induce voters to support the full ticket. Early on Moynihan feared that some voters might be tempted to support him along with candidates from other slates for mayor and comptroller.[7] A month later he would panic on learning that voters in some parts of the city were planning to support Screvane for mayor and Frank O'Connor for council president.

In mid July Moynihan went to great lengths to emphasize Screvane's acceptability to liberals. Screvane, Moynihan said, was the one person who gave straight answers to the Shriver task force that had drafted the 1964 Economic Opportunity Act.[8] Moynihan also sought to tie his candidacy and Screvane's to the president, despite Johnson's express desire to remain neutral in the race. The 1964 victory had finally given Johnson and Congress a mandate to do something for the cities; electing

the Screvane ticket would be one way of ensuring that the Johnson
administration's policies were implemented in New York.

Finally, Moynihan stressed his own close ties to New York. New
Yorkers are something special; serving New York would be like trying
to repay a debt that could never really be repaid.

> I would like to say that I owe something to the City of New York. I was
> raised here during the depression. We were poor. Our prospects were few.
> Yet there was never a day of my life that I would have wished to be any
> other person. There was then, as now, a sense of building an even greater
> city . . . and there is none like us.[9]

While Moynihan may have had a strong desire to serve New York
City, he was a particularly inept campaigner. Screvane's advisers thought
he would make an attractive candidate in personal appearances around
New York, but Moynihan had little capacity for glad-handing voters. He
was often late to appointments, and he showed little patience with
crowds that expected him to eat blintzes and hot dogs and to act as
though he loved walking the boardwalk in Coney Island on a hot summer
afternoon. Screvane was so disturbed at Moynihan's behavior during the
campaign that eleven years later he made it a point of telling anyone who
would listen that Moynihan would make a bad Senate candidate because
of his erratic campaign manner.

Rhetorically, Moynihan was not much better. Before the Overseas
Press Club he delivered one detailed speech on the need for channeling
vast amounts of federal money into New York, arguing convincingly that
the city by itself could not generate sufficient revenue.[10] But by and large
his statements on social policy—which, given his stature as one of the
leading academic experts on New York affairs, should have received
prominent attention—largely went unnoticed. What did get attention
were his ad hominem attacks on the other candidates. Of John Lindsay,
Moynihan said, "I sometimes think the only address [he] knows in the
City of New York is the Yale Club."[11]

His most publicized dispute was with Paul Rao, Jr., the campaign
chairman for the Beame slate. It came after Rao charged that *Beyond
the Melting Pot* was more anti-Italian than the television series on the
Mafia in Chicago, *The Untouchables*. Rao further charged that the

section on Italians (which had been written by Glazer) was a "mass of twisted facts, contorted conclusions and hearsay statements."[12] It was a gutter attack, and Moynihan responded in kind. Rao, he said,

> is a small little man. His daddy is a judge, his daddy got him lots of nice soft political jobs all his life. He has too many wives, but not enough principles. I was a stevedore on the North River piers before Mr. Rao got his first jar of hair pomade and if he thinks he can run me out of town, he's wrong.[13]

The polemic might have made Moynihan feel better, but it hardly improved his standing with Italian voters. For many the attack on Rao only confirmed what the Beame chairman had said to begin with, that Moynihan was anti-Italian. Six weeks into the campaign Screvane called Reynolds in Washington to complain that Moynihan had "alienated the Jews and Italians and was working on the Poles and Irish."

The combination of Moynihan's rhetorical gaffes and his poor campaigning made him the weakest member of the Screvane ticket. Regular organization leaders in Queens who supported Moynihan only because he was a member of the Screvane ticket grew anxious as his ineptness became apparent. With their instinct for self-preservation, the Queens regulars wanted to support the likely winner, their District Attorney Frank O'Connor, who was running with Beame. Consequently, Democratic district leaders in two assembly districts in Queens began urging their supporters to support Screvane and then cross over into the Beame column to vote for O'Connor. When news of the defections reached Moynihan, he quickly enlisted the aid of Mayor Wagner to quell the rebellion. Wagner had installed Moses Weinstein, a Queens assemblyman, as county leader following the 1961 victory, and Weinstein owed it to Wagner to support his ticket. Wagner asked Weinstein and the maverick leaders in Queens to stay behind the entire Screvane ticket, even if they believed O'Connor was the stronger candidate. More seriously for Moynihan, Screvane's managers began de-emphasizing Moynihan in the campaign advertising. The council presidency was the second office to be voted for, but the Screvane ads listed Moynihan's name third —and sometimes not at all.

Relations between Moynihan and Screvane became increasingly

strained as the campaign drew to a close. Moynihan explained his frequent absences from the campaign by explaining that he had been
meeting with influential journalists who could be expected to write
favorable articles about the Screvane ticket. When just a few days before
the election Mary McGrory wrote a column almost exclusively about
Moynihan and barely mentioning the other members of the ticket,
Screvane exploded. The ticket's campaign coordinators were also angry
at what they thought were Moynihan's attempts to make informal tie-ins
with Beame supporters who were not supporting O'Connor; they believed that such actions were a betrayal of Screvane.

The results on the night of September 14 confirmed the worst fears
about the Moynihan candidacy. The entire Screvane ticket lost, and
Moynihan made the weakest showing of the three. He had 37 percent
of the vote to O'Connor's 49 percent. Screvane lost more narrowly, with
36 percent of the vote to Beame's 44 percent. In Manhattan Moynihan
ran ahead of Screvane, but in the other four boroughs he ran far behind.
In Brooklyn Steingut brought out a big vote for Beame, who carried his
home turf by 53 percent to 33 percent over Screvane. Yet O'Connor ran
ahead of him, with 56 percent to Moynihan's 33 percent of the vote.
The Queens results were the worst: O'Connor trounced Moynihan, 57
percent of the vote to 32 percent, while Screvane collected 36 percent
of the vote to Beame's 47 percent. A more detailed analysis showed that
O'Connor carried the Jews, the Irish, and the Italians; only the Manhattan reformers gave Moynihan plurality support.

While Liz Moynihan would recall years after the event that the best
thing that ever happened to her husband was losing the race, Moynihan
did not take the defeat lightly. He left his headquarters with tears in his
eyes and the next day was full of fight at a press conference. Instead of
being conciliatory Moynihan said that the Screvane ticket should have
attacked the organization more directly in Brooklyn. In the Bronx the
Screvane-backed reform candidates had deeply dented the Buckley machine by winning the borough presidency, two State Senate seats, and
five State Assembly posts. Screvane and his citywide running mates had
also done better in the Bronx than they had elsewhere in the city. In
Brooklyn Screvane had not supported a full slate against Steingut, and

his slate was trounced. Moynihan concluded that "our Screvane team should have insisted that every Brooklyn Assemblyman, Senator, and Councilman who opposed our slate should himself have been opposed in the primary. That's what we did in the Bronx and see what happened."[14]

The fall Democratic campaign was poorly run and served only to make Republican-Liberal candidate John Lindsay look better. The columnist William Buckley, running on the Conservative line, took traditionally Democratic Catholic votes away from Beame, and Lindsay capitalized on disenchantment with twenty uninterrupted years of Democratic control of City Hall. Beame, Lindsay charged, was a captive of the bosses, and Screvane's primary campaign had reinforced that charge. Lindsay mobilized thousands of volunteers throughout the city to work in storefront headquarters while Beame relied on the regular Democratic organization clubhouses that had carried him to victory in the primary. Senator Kennedy made a few clumsy attempts to campaign with Beame but in general was conspicuous by his absence. He attempted to take over the campaign in the closing weeks and make Beame a more pugnacious candidate, but this late intervention was of little help. Moynihan endorsed Beame and headed a task force on city issues but did little else for the campaign.

The Beame defeat in November 1965 closed Moynihan out of a role in city government and presented Kennedy with a formidable potential opponent in City Hall. Wagner's prestige had suffered in the defeat of his protégé Screvane and again in the loss in November. In 1965 Lindsay asked Moynihan to serve on a poverty task force, but the group wouldn't listen when he said that the main problem was going to be ever-expanding welfare rolls.

For Moynihan the defeat meant choosing a new job. His relations with Secretary Wirtz were strained to the point that he knew he could not return to the Labor Department. As it happened, on the morning of the primary Paul Horgan, the director of the Center for Advanced Studies at Wesleyan University, called Moynihan to ask if he would be interested in a post at the center if he lost. "If I lose, and I will lose, I'll be delighted to come," Moynihan told Horgan. Two weeks later

Moynihan had installed himself and his family in Middletown, Connect-icut, eager to begin a period of reflection during the 1965–66 academic year.

Wesleyan may have been a retreat for Moynihan, but it was not a retreat from New York politics. The campaign had left him drained emotionally, and he was eager for a respite from the sort of intense working environment he had created for himself at the Department of Labor. Just before leaving the department to begin campaigning, Moyni-han had authored a report on black family stability that was now attract-ing a good deal of attention. The attacks on the report and on Moynihan had not begun until the end of the campaign, yet by primary day Moynihan had become an object of scorn and even hatred in some liberal and civil rights circles. At Wesleyan, where Moynihan hoped to relax and to maintain a low profile, the controversy over the report would bring him national prominence.

6

The Family

The moment came when, as it were, the nation had the resources
and the leadership and the will to make a total, as against a partial
commitment to the cause of Negro equality. It did not do so. The
time when white men whatever their motives could tell Negroes
what was not good for them is now definitely and decidedly over.
—Pat Moynihan, 1967

Late in 1964 Pat Moynihan was having trouble sleeping. His major
recommendations for President Johnson's war on poverty had been
virtually disregarded; worse, the people around the president thought
they were close to solving the problems of race and inequality in American society in the wake of the passage of the Civil Rights Act of 1964
and the Economic Opportunity Act, which created the poverty program. Yet Moynihan knew that these pieces of legislation were not
enough. Something more had to be done to create jobs for impoverished
blacks and to make a positive national commitment to the support of
stable families.

The concerns over employment and family stability went hand in
hand. A man with a full-time job was less likely to leave his family than
was a man without a job. And a man with a family to support was more

inclined to seek employment than was a man living on his own.[1] Moynihan knew from his own painful experience the difficulties of growing up in a broken family. He had seen how children trapped in similar situations had gone on to lead unhappy and unproductive lives.

Moynihan was also familiar with the literature on family stability, and he knew that scholars shared his view of the importance of the family unit. As a Catholic intellectual, Moynihan had always believed that the family was the basic unit of society, an entity far more important than free enterprise, the power of the state, or the fortunes of political parties. He accepted the principal thesis of Pope John's encyclical of 1963, that individual functions should not be given to larger bodies when individuals could best handle their problems through "lesser and subordinate bodies" such as the family.[2] Moynihan believed that it was the job of the government to reinforce these familial institutions.

There appeared to be little thinking along these lines within the administration. A conversation with an optimistic official one day late in November left Moynihan depressed, unable to believe that he could be the only person who realized that civil rights and poverty legislation were merely a first step. The following day he awoke at 4 A.M., knowing that something had to be done, and resolved to write a paper for the administration detailing the harmful effects of black family instability. It would not be a paper for general circulation (he would write a scholarly article on the subject for *Daedalus* at about the same time); its aim would be to stimulate discussion within the administration on the issues of family stability and unemployment.[3]

Late in the afternoon on the last day of 1964 Moynihan called his two closest aides, Ellen Broderick and Paul Barton, into his office and outlined his plans to them. He told them he wanted all the data they could collect on black family stability and its relationship to unemployment, and he warned them that because the subject was so sensitive they should keep their work secret. For the next couple of months Barton and Broderick worked closely with Moynihan, collecting data and then reading the draft of the report that Moynihan prepared. By mid March the report was finished.

Yet for Moynihan the work had only begun. Not wanting the report to be just another Labor Department paper to be considered briefly and then forgotten, he had to make sure that his thesis got the proper attention. In March Moynihan gave the report to Wirtz, who promptly sent it on to the president with a covering memo that said it contained "78 pages of dynamite." Moynihan heard little about the report from the White House until May; in the meantime he tried to interest administration officials in its content. He took the report with him to a Washington hospital when he went to visit Lyndon Johnson's special counsel, Harry McPherson. The two spent four hours discussing it, and Moynihan was hopeful that McPherson would take up his arguments with the president.[4] The first hint of administration interest came in late May when speechwriter Bill Moyers asked Moynihan to draft a civil rights speech based on the report. The administration was prepared to use Moynihan's report as the basis of a new strategy for improving the social and economic position of blacks in America.

The report was a shock to administration officials who had come to believe that with the passage of civil rights legislation the economic position of blacks was bound to improve. At the outset Moynihan emphasized that because of past and present racism the condition of black Americans was becoming worse, not better. In the subsequent controversy over the report's contents, it was often forgotten that Moynihan laid the blame for social disorganization squarely on white Americans. In the report's introduction he noted that "the racist virus in the American bloodstream still afflicts us. Negroes will encounter serious personal prejudice for at least another generation. Three centuries of sometimes unimaginable mistreatment have taken their toll on the Negro people."[5]

The most powerful effect of the mistreatment was to weaken the stability of the black family. True, a small middle class group had managed to extricate itself, "but for vast numbers of the unskilled, poorly educated city working class the fabric of conventional social relationships has all but disintegrated." Poverty and disadvantage would remain serious problems in the black community until the federal government did something to promote black family stability.

The civil rights movement and the resultant poverty and antidiscrimination legislation of the mid 1960s served only to provide equality of opportunity; nothing had been done that offered much prospect of equality of result. Providing civil and voting rights to blacks did nothing to ensure that their economic positions would improve. Nor would the myriad programs incorporated in the poverty legislation do anything beyond making opportunities available.

Before the federal government could do anything substantive for blacks, a stable working class had to exist. For the family plays the central role in shaping the individual's character and his attitudes toward the larger society. Children from families in which education was emphasized more often than not excelled in school. Conversely, children from broken families had few positive role models to emulate and often dropped out of school or engaged in socially disapproved activities.

The emergence of some stable middle class black families allowed white Americans to underestimate the problem or to ignore it entirely. The available data showed that the black family was in dire straits; about 25 percent of urban black marriages ended in divorce or separation, and an almost equal number of births here were illegitimate (which made the black illegitimacy rate about eight times higher than the white illegitimacy rate). Consequently about one-fourth of black families were headed by women. And—perhaps the most startling finding—a *majority* of black children received welfare at some point during their childhood. According to the Department of Health, Education and Welfare, the sharp increase in welfare payments was due largely to the breakdown of stable families. The vastness and seriousness of the problem was underscored by the fact that while Moynihan was writing his report, black male unemployment was *falling* and the number of newly opened welfare cases was *rising.* Prior to 1962 the number of newly opened welfare cases had risen and fallen with the unemployment rate; now, as conditions were improving overall, there was an underclass that was becoming increasingly large. And while black families were becoming more disorganized, white families were becoming more stable.

Moynihan went on to relate present-day black family instability to such historical forces as slavery, reconstruction, and urbanization, each of which had weakened family bonds. He quoted at length from the work of such scholars as Stanley Elkins and E. Franklin Frazier. He described how unemployment served to weaken the family structure, the father becoming a messenger boy between the home and the welfare office, the mother often forced to seek employment, and the children resentful of their change in circumstance. It was obvious that only by providing the male head of the household with a job could family stability be encouraged.

Since 1940 black unemployment had been twice as high as white unemployment, and as the unemployment rate rose and fell the separation rate among black couples moved with it. Low wage levels in the black community further undermined family stability. The minimum wage was not enough for a couple—let alone a large family—to live on. Mothers who worked to compensate for a husband's low income necessarily had to deprive their children of maternal attention during their formative years, and as these children became older, they too had difficulty finding jobs.

Thus the black community had largely adopted a matriarchal structure. But the dominant white society expected male leadership, and a group that did not follow this pattern was at a severe disadvantage. An enormous burden was placed on the black male, and group progress was made more difficult. Children growing up in female-headed households scored below average on standardized tests. Males in particular showed less ambition, and they performed less well than females. These children had higher delinquency and crime rates than children from male-headed households. And military service, which traditionally provided a way out for poor people, was not always an alternative: 56 percent of black draftees were failing the pre-induction qualifying test. The conclusion was inescapable: "the tangle of pathology" in which black Americans lived was tightening.

The report contained no policy recommendations, though it was clear that Moynihan supported employment programs and some form of family allowance to supplement incomes. There were a number of reasons for this. Moynihan's primary concern was to focus attention on the problem itself and to demonstrate that the legislation of 1964 was insufficient to deal with it. A major theme of the report was the interrelatedness of the problems that stemmed from family instability—the growth in welfare, rising unemployment, and low educational achievement. Before considering solutions it was important to determine precisely the nature of the problem.

Although the report contained no explicit policy recommendations,

Moynihan was clearly trying to move the focus of domestic policy from the individual to the family. The New Deal legislative agenda was largely completed in 1965, and he wanted the attention of the federal government to be redirected toward determining whether its policies tended to weaken or to strengthen the family. Policy making needed careful planning; programs designed to aid the black community had to be systematically evaluated to determine their precise effect. In a May 4 memorandum to President Johnson, Moynihan made a series of general policy recommendations that had been at the center of his thinking on domestic policy for more than ten years. The first recommendation called for the establishment of a central policy review body in the White House that would systematically evaluate programs directed at blacks. He also advocated a public employment program in which the federal government would be the employer of last resort. Birth control should be freely available, blacks should have greater access to the military, and the government should provide family allowances to supplement earned income. The task of the Johnson administration was to make it possible for black Americans to raise their families in the same way white Americans raised theirs.

Almost fifteen years after its original publication, Moynihan's report seems a balanced and evenhanded view of the plight of black Americans. It recognized and paid tribute to the strength and fortitude of black people.

> That the Negro American has survived at all is extraordinary—a lesser people might simply have died out, as indeed others have. That the Negro community has not only survived, but in this political generation has entered national affairs as a moderate, humane and constructive national force is the highest testament to the healing powers of the democratic ideal and the creative vitality of Negro people.[6]

Elsewhere he argued that "the plain physical courage Negro leaders and their followers have shown" was a strong reason for white America's having to face up to how bad things had become while its attention was focused elsewhere.[7] Yet when the report became public, it created a storm in civil rights and white liberal circles. The furor was so great that the report and its arguments passed from a central role in framing administration policy to almost no role at all.

In the spring of 1965 the report was taken very seriously in the highest White House circles. It and Moynihan's follow-up communications led to the president's historic address to graduating seniors at Howard University on June 3 (the speech that Moyers had asked Moynihan to draft). Richard Goodwin, a White House speechwriter, reworked the text with Moynihan's assistance, and their efforts produced what Johnson later called his finest civil rights speech.

The Howard speech followed roughly the format of the Moynihan report, emphasizing the need for white America and the administration to take the responsibility for providing equality of outcome for American blacks. Johnson acknowledged, as Moynihan did, that blacks had finally been provided equal opportunity; civil rights legislation guaranteed the rights of blacks to vote, to hold a job, to attend school, and to enter public places. But the legislation did nothing toward placing blacks on the same economic and social plane as whites. Some blacks, among them those graduating from Howard, had made it, but for the majority of black Americans the gap between them and white America had widened rather than narrowed.

The reasons Johnson cited for the ever widening gap were the same ones Moynihan had isolated: slavery and the poverty that had stemmed from it. The major consequence of years of discrimination and oppression was the breakdown of the family structure, the cornerstone of society. Until the family itself was strengthened, social palliatives would never be enough.

The solutions the president offered were largely Moynihan's recommendations—jobs, decent housing and schools, and welfare programs that encouraged family stability. Johnson also acknowledged that he did not have all the answers, and he announced that the White House would sponsor a conference of academics, civil rights leaders, and government officials to explore the problem further in the fall.

Johnson's speech on June 3 marked the end of Moynihan's formal role in the formulation of White House policy. A day later he left the country to attend a conference in Yugoslavia, confident that his major goal had been achieved. The public reaction of civil rights leaders to the Howard University speech was largely positive. The speech had been read in advance to Martin Luther King, Jr., Whitney Young, and Roy Wilkins and had received their endorsement. Accordingly, the White House went ahead with plans for the fall conference, calling in a number of social scientists for informal meetings.

Early planning sessions did not include civil rights leaders, however, and this omission created a problem when the report became public. (Perhaps with a view to demonstrating the depth and intellectual strength of the White House's commitment, portions of the report were leaked during the summer of 1965 until in August the decision was made to release the entire text.) With the report's emphasis on the deterioration of the black family and its discussion of the illegitimacy and desertion rates, it seemed to some civil rights leaders that the report argued that poverty and unemployment resulted directly and solely from immorality in the black community. Press reports that summer gave some civil rights leaders the impression that Moynihan believed that the process he described was a static one—that is, that black families dissolved because of inherent weaknesses within their community rather than from more powerful long-term historical forces such as slavery, urbanization, and the wage structure (which Moynihan had in fact emphasized). The logical policy implication of this static view of the problem was that the black community could get itself back on its feet only through self-help. While some press reports of the speech emphasized Johnson's call for increased federal assistance, others—notably those by columnist Mary McGrory—said that its real meaning was that blacks would have to help themselves. Johnson had said that the black "will have to rely mostly on his own efforts" and had offered no concrete proposals for promoting family stability. The consequent nervousness of civil rights leaders was compounded by the fact that the report was not then available to them or to their contacts within the government.

The report contained another implicit assumption that scared civil rights leaders. By seeming to assume that discrimination had been eradicated through recent legislation, the report appeared to provide a rationale for the administration's turning away from further civil and voting rights legislation. The report certainly did not advocate this course of action, but civil rights leaders feared that this would be the result of government acceptance of the Moynihan report. The concern was voiced by Clarence Mitchell of the NAACP and Floyd McKissick of CORE during a cruise on the presidential yacht in mid September, and they came away with the impression that the administration was using the report as an excuse for not enforcing the civil rights laws vigorously.

The tension and concern over the report were heightened dramatically that summer by the Watts riots and by the changes that were then taking place within the civil rights movement itself. The rioting demonstrated how little legislation had done to improve conditions for black Americans. The moderate civil rights leadership—the group that had given its tentative approval to the Moynihan report—did not have much of a constituency in the northern ghettoes and could not quell the turmoil. In its place a more militant leadership was emerging that, while having an even smaller constituency than the traditional leadership, appeared with its threatening rhetoric to be winning the battle for media attention. In such a situation few black leaders were willing to commend an analysis made by a white middle class official that showed that structural defects in the black family contributed to the problems of unrest and unemployment. Such an approach was seen to be paternalistic at best, racist at worst; it was the government that deserved the blame, totally and without qualification. The debate often grew ugly as black leaders competed with one another to see who could accuse the white establishment of greater discrimination and mistreatment of blacks.

With Moynihan out of government and the civil rights leadership vigorously attacking his report, the White House abandoned the Moynihan approach. The White House wanted no confrontation with the civil rights leadership, even if Moynihan's analysis was valid.[8] Planning for the fall conference was held up, the administration consulted civil rights leaders, and it was decided that a separate civil rights conference would be held in the spring, with a planning session scheduled for November.

The various civil rights organizations invited to the fall conference were not eager to discuss the family, much less make it the central theme of the conference. They preferred to have the discussion limited to three subjects: employment, civil rights, and voting rights. The White House (which controlled the agenda) wanted eight separate panels, one of them focusing on the black family. But the administration had received almost daily expressions of dissatisfaction with the report and threats that the conference would be disrupted if its focus was to be the black family. Thus it was decided that the black family—and the Moynihan approach in particular—would be de-emphasized. The paper on the black family that would be used as the basis of discussion would be written by Hylan Lewis, a Howard University sociologist, who sought to refute Moynihan's arguments.

Prior to the convening of the conference in November there were other, more hostile, and less respectable attacks on the Moynihan report. One came from William Ryan, a psychologist at the Harvard Medical School, who prepared a paper that was widely circulated in intellectual and civil rights circles and subsequently published in the *Nation*. [9] Ryan sought to document his belief that the report was methodologically flawed, and he was the first to charge explicitly that it had "racist" implications. The report, Ryan argued, "encourages (no doubt unintentionally) a new form of subtle racism that might be termed 'Savage Discovery' and seduces the reader into believing that it is not racism and discrimination but the weaknesses and defects of the Negro himself that account for the present status of inequality between Negro and white." [10]

The charge stung Moynihan. He could accept substantive criticism of the report, even if it were hostile, but to be charged with racism was galling. Moynihan had long been active in the civil rights movement; in 1956 he had pushed Governor Harriman to support a strong civil rights plank at the Democratic convention; in the 1960s he had been a foremost advocate of a job program aimed at eliminating unemployment; and in 1964 he had even violated an administration ban and participated in that summer's civil rights march. And what was most galling about Ryan's "poisonous attack" (as he referred to it in a letter to a friend), was that the charges of racism had come from a white rather than a black.

A still more tendentious analysis was prepared in September by Dr. Benjamin Payton, director of the Office of Religion and Race of the Protestant Council of the City of New York. [11] It is not clear that Payton had actually read the report when he wrote his paper, for most of his criticisms were directed at press characterizations of Moynihan's arguments rather than at the report itself. For example, Payton sought to demonstrate that Moynihan's argument failed to explain the recent riots, when Moynihan's report said nothing about them. Payton also attributed to Moynihan the belief that blacks had made gains relative to whites in terms of income levels, when in fact Moynihan had made precisely the opposite point. Payton said that the key problem was not family instability but a lack of comprehensive city planning to break down barriers in segregated schools and housing. Nothing in Moynihan's report indicated that he opposed such plans, and in fact he supported them. And Payton pointed to the Howard University speech as an example of an instance in which the administration had properly used social science data. Moynihan, of course, had inspired that speech and had written the first draft.

When Payton mailed out his critique early in September, he suggested that civil rights groups schedule pre-White House conferences around the country. Under his leadership a New York conference held early in November passed a widely publicized resolution calling for the subject of family stability to be stricken from the agenda of the White House conference. Similar meetings in Detroit and Philadelphia gave grass roots activists further opportunities to criticize the Moynihan report.

The White House did not remove the subject of family stability from the agenda of the November conference in Washington. However, it was now only one of eight topics to be considered. (The majority of the sessions dealt with traditional civil rights issues—voting rights, education, employment, housing, and equal rights.) The family panel was chaired by Hylan Lewis, who sought to refute Moynihan's principal conclusions without mentioning him by name. He noted that two-thirds of black American families had both parents present; that the increase in the proportion of female-headed households had been relatively slight; and that much of the black-white difference in family structure disappeared when people of similar incomes were compared. Moreover, the presence of female-headed households did not necessarily mean that their children would not lead productive lives. In general the paper was a sober and reasoned attempt to refute Moynihan's argument. What was surprising was that the government had retreated so far that the principal paper on the black family was an attack on the document on which the administration had based its thinking only a few months earlier.[12]

Thus the White House and most civil rights leaders hoped to avoid direct debate on the merits of the Moynihan report. (At the opening session of the conference the executive director announced, "I have been reliably informed that no such person as Daniel Patrick Moynihan exists.") Yet while the Lewis paper had a different thrust from the Moynihan report, virtually all of the substantive policy recommendations made by Lewis and other members of the panel were similar to those Moynihan had advocated. Discussion focused on birth control, income maintenance, and job creation—the very kinds of programs for which Moynihan had argued so strenuously. Nevertheless, conference participants were unwilling to level criticisms directly at the black community or to suggest self-improvement programs. The dominant sentiment was that the white power structure was to blame and only it could improve the situation.

Moynihan attended the family panel but did not take a major part in the discussion. On the second day he attempted to rebut Payton's paper by explaining that he too believed that black family instability was directly related to unemployment and low wage structures. Payton replied that there was too much emphasis on the deterioration of the family and not enough on economic factors. They differed again on how the entire subject should be approached; Payton counseled caution because of the delicate nature of the problem, while Moynihan thought it essential to emphasize the seriousness of the problem in order to focus attention on it.

The administration did not regard the conference as a great success. A few high-ranking figures made it clear that they were discouraged that black family instability had not been discussed, and others were angered that the administration had been criticized for not vigorously enforcing civil rights legislation. Civil rights leaders adopted more rigid postures in the aftermath of the conference. There was dissatisfaction with a perceived lack of follow-up on the Howard University speech and with the administration's attitude toward the conference. Once again the Moynihan report was used as a scapegoat. James Farmer wrote in the *Amsterdam News* that the report provided "the fuel for a new racism" and contained data that would "turn the Grand Dragon of the Ku Klux

Klan into a prophet." The report was nothing more than a means for white America to absolve itself of any blame for the plight of black Americans.[13]

As attacks on the report became stronger, the administration sought further to dissociate itself from it. Secretary of Labor Wirtz, no longer on speaking terms with Moynihan, criticized him publicly. In a press release that drew on a public television interview, Wirtz echoed criticism from the Bureau of Labor Statistics that indicated that Moynihan had overemphasized the deterioration of the black family. And Wirtz sought to discuss the problem of poverty and disadvantage not from the perspective of black Americans but from that of all Americans (an approach Moynihan heartily endorsed).

Out of government now, Moynihan refused to retreat from his position that the report offered a basis for formulating national policy. In a series of interviews, one of them on *Meet the Press,* he said again that he had described a dynamic process in which the factors of unemployment, poverty, and family instability were closely related. He pressed his argument for a national family policy and refused to acknowledge that the administration was consciously trying to dissociate itself from the report.

The White House conference on civil rights held in the spring of 1966 virtually ignored the subject of the black family. The Moynihan report was not available at the conference and no consideration was given to it. The purpose of the conference was not to define the problem; the idea was that the assembled representatives of the civil rights movement would reach some sort of consensus about what should be done. The role of social scientists in analyzing race relations was de-emphasized, and greater efforts were made to ensure that all legitimate interests in the civil rights movement would be represented. So eager was the White House to have a consensus that there was no organized debate on the issues and no balloting on the conference resolutions.

Moynihan attended the 1966 conference but remained silent. There was little he could say; the administration had abandoned his report because the civil rights movement had criticized it, and he believed himself betrayed. He waited until 1967, when he was at Harvard and the controversy had died down, to voice his feelings. His article in *Commentary* blamed liberals for the administration's failure to make a full commitment to equality for blacks. In the past, Moynihan wrote, opposition to equality had come from conservatives. But now

> the opposition emanated from the supposed proponents of such a commitment; from Negro leaders unable to comprehend their opportunity; from civil rights militants, Negro and white, caught up in a frenzy of arrogance and nihilism; and from white liberals unwilling to expend a lot of prestige to do a difficult job that had to be done, and could have been done. But was not.[14]

Liberals were unwilling to confront problems such as illegitimacy—or they argued that it was an adaptation to conditions created by a fascist society. This was nonsense. The left, he argued, only wanted to indict society, and in their not wanting to face up to real problems, liberals could be as "destructive" and "rigid" as any force in American society.

Moynihan was more restrained in his criticism of the administration, though he suggested that it had refused to stand behind the report when it was criticized by civil rights leaders. When the planners of the 1966 conference decided not to put the black family on the agenda, he said, the White House refused to take issue with them. Moynihan's article was the first indication that he had at least a measure of sympathy with Republicans and conservatives; he thought it likely that the Republicans would ride a crest of backlash sentiment into control of the national government. True, there was harshness in the nature of their criticism of welfare programs, but at the same time "the number of families receiving assistance is a scandal."[15] The era of white initiatives for blacks was over, as was the time when whites could criticize blacks with impunity.

It was a bitter Pat Moynihan who wrote about the black family controversy early in 1967. His views on two major domestic policy initiatives in the 1960s—the poverty program and the black family—had been overridden, and he had retired from government service to an academe where he would have the freedom to speak out when he wished. As the riots in the cities continued into 1966 and 1967, Moynihan became a national figure for his work on domestic racial problems (he appeared on the cover of *Time* in the summer of 1967), and that work came to the attention of an increasing number of people, among them a corporate lawyer in New York named Richard Nixon.

7

Fulfilling a Dream:
A Harvard Professorship

If you decide to join a University faculty, you must accept the fact
that at any given hour for the rest of your professional life someone,
somewhere, will be saying something unpleasant about you. You
cannot avoid this. Your only option is to choose between having the
successful or the unsuccessful professors take you apart. If you are
successful your less fortunate colleagues will consider the disreputable means by which you have attained your position. If you are not
successful, those who are will remark at length on the shortcomings
which made this outcome inevitable. If you are in between or
otherwise difficult to define, everyone will be nasty about you.
—Pat Moynihan, 1960

In May 1966 Moynihan's eight-month appointment at the Center for
Advanced Studies at Wesleyan University would be up, and he had to
decide what he would do. Arthur Goldberg, now United States ambassador to the United Nations, had asked Moynihan to join his staff, but he
had refused. Early in 1966 another offer came from a friend, Professor
James Q. Wilson, director of the Joint Center for Urban Studies at
Harvard and MIT. Wilson had invited Moynihan to speak at the center

on a number of occasions, and the two had collaborated on an article for the *American Political Science Review.* [1] Now Wilson was planning to leave his post, and he asked Moynihan if he wanted the job.

Moynihan was intrigued. He told Wilson he would take the position if two conditions could be met. First, he wanted to finish the academic year at Wesleyan, where after a hectic period in government and politics he was enjoying a newfound freedom. Second, he wanted to be assured of having a tenured professorship. The directorship of the Joint Center was an administrative post, and for personal and professional reasons he sought an academic post. Liz Moynihan had impressed on him the need for the security of a tenured post, and he felt as well that after having served in the subcabinet anything less than a full professorship would be beneath him.

There were problems involved in finding him a post in Harvard's Faculty of Arts and Sciences. Moynihan had published no substantial scholarly work in his field of international relations and law, and much of his work on domestic affairs had appeared in popular magazines. Whatever Moynihan's abilities as a writer or thinker, the standards of the Harvard department of government required a greater scholastic achievement than Moynihan had yet attained. He had collaborated with Nathan Glazer on *Beyond the Melting Pot,* but Glazer had conceived the work and called on Moynihan only to write the section on the Irish and to draft the book's conclusion. Moynihan's contribution may have made it a better book—Glazer credits him with generally improving the prose style— but Moynihan could not take full credit for the work. And while his historical study of the Irish was first-rate sociology, it was not the sort of work that earns a tenured post in the government department at Harvard.

To resolve the situation, Wilson suggested that Moynihan also be given a post in the School of Education. Theodore Sizer, the dean of the school, was enthusiastic about having Moynihan on the faculty, for he hoped that Moynihan's work on family structure and urban poverty would help diversify the school. Sizer was working to link the school more closely with the rest of the university, and having the director of the Joint Center for Urban Studies on the faculty would help promote that goal. It was agreed that as of July 1, 1966, Moynihan would assume the dual post of professor of education and director of the Joint Center for Urban Studies.

While completing the academic year at Wesleyan, Moynihan's principal project was a book on the black family that was intended as both a serious academic work and a refutation of the criticism that had been leveled at him by blacks late in 1965. The criticism had affected him deeply. When Monsignor George Higgins wrote a column in December 1965 that defended the black family report, Moynihan wrote him that "the column comes at a time when I need help, and am not . . . ashamed to say so."

For the most part Moynihan did little to attract public attention during his eight months at Wesleyan. Soon after his arrival there he began to feel the accumulated strain of five years of intense government service. Late in September 1965 he and a fellow Johnson administration alumnus at Wesleyan, Richard Goodwin, would reach their offices at 9:30 A.M.; in October it became 10:30 A.M., and by November it was 11:30 A.M. "We were both so tired," Moynihan recalls, "I think it took Goodwin and me until February to recover." Most of Moynihan's working hours were spent alone in his study, and Paul Horgan encouraged Moynihan not to do anything that would be too taxing. He was generally quiet, enjoying fully the life in a cloistered academic community. Today Moynihan rates his eight months at Wesleyan in 1965–66, along with his year at Middlebury in 1944–45, as the happiest of his life.

Moynihan's retreat was more than simply a time for healing wounds. He had to redirect his efforts toward influencing government policy; where he had failed in working within the federal government, he would now have to work outside the government.

Over the next four years Moynihan would campaign tirelessly, writing and speaking on behalf of programs that would enhance family stability in America. Again and again Moynihan would say that America was the only Western democracy that did not have a family allowance. Repeatedly he advocated employment programs as a means of giving heads of households stable incomes that would enable them to provide for their families. Anyone who believes Moynihan ideologically inconsistent should read his work from this period; he supported the same programs, often with the same arguments, time and again.

Moynihan set out the basic themes in the course of a long, reflective interview with the *New York Times* a month or so after he arrived at the Center for Advanced Studies. People were mistaken in believing they were "too sophisticated" for a family policy. Slum kids were being "savagely cheated" because society thought itself "too sophisticated" to care whether children had fathers and mothers had husbands. Civil rights and voting rights legislation was not enough; America needed a family policy. And the United States was the only democracy that didn't recognize the welfare and stability of the family as a principal objective of its social policy. Part of the problem was that much of the civil rights leadership, both white and black, came from secure middle class families and had trouble understanding family decay. But Moynihan understood it only too well. "I grew up in Hell's Kitchen. My father was a drunk. I know what life is like."[2] He was angry and hurt at the time of the interview, and his reference to his own family situation marked one of the few times he would ever let his guard down to personalize the issue. Asked about the statement some thirteen years later, Moynihan reddened and said he had made a mistake in speaking as he had.

In May 1966, shortly before assuming his post at the Joint Center for Urban Studies, Moynihan went up to Cambridge one day for a meeting with Johnson administration official Joseph Califano at the Harvard Faculty Club. There Professor Seymour Martin Lipset stopped Moynihan to ask if he had heard about the preliminary findings of the Report on Equality of Educational Opportunity. The study, mandated by the 1964 Civil Rights Act and conducted by Professor James Coleman of Johns Hopkins, was designed to assess, through an elaborate series of surveys, the lack of opportunity available to ethnic and racial minorities. Lipset told Moynihan that the report's initial conclusion was that family background, not schooling, was the single most important variable in predicting a child's development.

Coming on the heels of his long battle with the Johnson administration and civil rights activists over his own report, the news gave Moynihan a great boost. That summer he arranged with Coleman to publish an article on the new report in *The Public Interest,* a magazine he had helped to start, and on returning to Cambridge from his upstate New York farm in September, Moynihan called on Theodore Sizer to ask what the School of Education planned to do about Coleman's report, which had just been released.

"This is the most dangerous report in the history of education," Moynihan said, hurling a copy of the report onto Sizer's desk. It was dangerous for a number of reasons. As an excuse for slashing school budgets conservatives might seize on its finding that variations in expenditures on school facilities had little relation to academic achievement. The report would anger liberals who hoped that integrated schools, which purported to provide each student with equal educational opportunity, would act as a social leveling device, for the report showed that there was, in fact, little discrimination in the provision of school facilities to predominately white and predominately black schools. Moreover, minority children lagged behind whites in educational achievement; the family was a more important factor in predicting academic achievement than was the quality of education; and more could be done to improve poor children's achievement by placing them in classes with middle class and upper middle class children than by spending increased sums on school facilities.

The conclusions were startling—almost counterintuitive—and Moynihan was worried how they would be regarded. He asked Sizer what he was going to do about the report. "The question," Sizer replied, "is what are you going to do about it, Pat?"

Moynihan organized a seminar on the Coleman report that drew on many disciplines, among them government, statistics, sociology, and law. Seminars of this sort are rare at Harvard, and social psychologist Thomas Pettigrew warned Moynihan that Harvard professors preferred to do their research alone and would not attend multidisciplinary seminars. But Moynihan proved Pettigrew wrong. Conceived to include some thirty or thirty-five people, the seminar quickly grew to a total of more than 150 people who participated at one or more sessions. Armed with a $25,000 grant from the Carnegie Corporation, Moynihan held dinners at the Harvard Faculty Club every two weeks; between these sessions researchers would re-analyze the survey data that Coleman and his colleagues had used. Subsequently Moynihan and statistician Frederick Mosteller published a collection of papers that summarized much of the material presented at the seminar.[3]

The seminar, rated a great success, had shown that Moynihan could produce a cooperative spirit in one of the most diverse and diffuse academic communities in America. "Everyone was delighted with the seminar," Pettigrew recalls. "There hasn't been anything like it at Harvard since."

The findings of Moynihan's seminar did not dispute the central finding of the Coleman report, that the variation in achievement among schools was small compared to that among students within schools. The seminar papers did criticize the initial survey's collection of data and the methodology employed to analyze that data. There were specific substantive differences—as on the question of whether racial integration was as important as social class integration—but in general the Moynihan seminar did not constitute an attack on the Coleman report. Rather, Moynihan and Mosteller concluded that more research was necessary, in both the long term and the short term. They suggested that there was cause for optimism over what gains had been made at the same time that they called on the different levels of government to improve the quality of education. And they recommended that employment and income programs be developed.

> Recognizing that what can be done at school is conditioned by the situation in the home, we believe that employment and income strategies designed to strengthen the home environment of the child and his family have over the long run a chance to produce a great additional component to educational achievement of a child.[4]

This section of the introduction to the Moynihan and Mosteller work bears Moynihan's imprint. His summaries of the papers contributed emphasize that some research has demonstrated that family influences are more important than school influences, race being constant. Moynihan even included in his introduction one researcher's advocacy of income maintenance and family allowances when the recommendations did not appear in the researcher's chapter draft.[5] Writing elsewhere at the time the seminar was concluding, Moynihan indicated the direction that he thought should be taken.

> I believe that these and other questions being raised in other fields are all heading us in the same direction, toward concern with the fundamen-

tal issues of social class and family welfare and in particular to a realization
that education is the product of the total environment of the child of
which the school is only one, and probably not the most powerful of
multiple factors.[6]

The demands on Moynihan's time as director of the Joint Center for
Urban Studies were not great. Most of those who were associated with
the center worked independently on a diverse set of problems, and
Moynihan could best provide encouragement. The unifying theme—
one which Moynihan believes applies to much, if not all, social policy
research—was that the crisis was not that the cities were about to be
destroyed by their own problems, but that we know so little about how
to cope with those problems. The center had been generously endowed
by the Ford Foundation, leaving Moynihan free of the burden of fund-
raising. (When Wilson turned over the post to Moynihan, the last thing
he told him was that he had a fund of $100,000 to use as he pleased.)

His administrative duties were comparatively light. One of his major
functions was to bring in speakers for the Tuesday luncheon seminars,
and given his wide range of contacts throughout the government, this
was no problem. John Lindsay and Robert Moses were among the
speakers, and often Moynihan's introductions were more memorable
than the speeches themselves. Urban studies, as Moynihan had predicted two years earlier, was now the "in" subject; he had little trouble
interesting people in the work of the center or broadening the center's
outside contacts. While Moynihan was himself involved in a variety of
projects and did a fair amount of traveling, he tried to spend the greater
part of his mornings writing at home, emerging at about noon for a
luncheon or a class. He taught one large lecture course on the uses of
social science in the development of social policy, which attracted listen-
ers from all over the university. In a community of renowned scholars,
Moynihan quickly made an impact.

Yet Moynihan's impact was not the result of his own academic work;
his associates saw him as a sort of honest broker acting between social
scientists and government policy makers. There was considerable respect
for his broad range of interests and his ability to get to the core of
complex issues. At the same time there was a sense that he had performed little original social science research. "I don't think many of his

colleagues saw him as an academic," one former colleague remembers. "If you look at his books and articles, they aren't what you would call scholarly works." Moynihan had made it to Harvard, but he had not been accepted as a full member of the community.

The Harvard community is not one that really embraces an individual, no matter how powerful or important he or she may once have been. It is an anomic community, and after the first few months Moynihan began to feel somewhat isolated and uncomfortable in Cambridge. While James Q. Wilson, Edward Banfield, and others told Moynihan that what he was doing was important, he could not overcome the feeling that he was not in fact a scholar in the way that people like Fred Mosteller were. Moynihan had never developed sophisticated quantitative skills, and at times during the discussions of the Coleman report he sensed that he was not sufficiently attuned to the methodological subtleties of the research. "It was when I got to Harvard that I realized I wasn't a scholar," Moynihan explains. "I had not been trained as a political scientist or a sociologist. My training in international law really didn't prepare me for what I would be doing." The feelings of uncertainty about the quality of his scholarship, coupled with an unwillingness to rekindle old disputes, led Moynihan to abandon his book on the black family, about 90 percent of which had been finished by the summer of 1968.

Meanwhile a number of liberal intellectuals had decided that Moynihan had betrayed the principles he had worked for during the Kennedy administration by associating himself with a group of largely New York intellectuals who were coming to be described as neoconservatives. This group spanned a diverse community and included such people as Irving Kristol, Nathan Glazer, Norman Podhoretz, and Daniel Bell; in general it had begun to question the extent and degree to which government should attempt to influence social arrangements. By becoming increasingly skeptical about government intervention, Moynihan incurred the wrath of a number of prominent academics in the Cambridge area.

There was further resentment at the way Moynihan handled his job as director of the Joint Center. Some felt that he used the post as a kind of political base for advancing his own ideas. True, Moynihan received a good deal of public attention in 1967, but much of this was because the media and many public officials sought him out when the riots flared that summer. If Moynihan had been declared a nonperson at the planning session for the 1966 civil rights conference, he was now a man much in demand. Mayor Jerome Cavanagh of Detroit begged Moynihan to fly to his city in the aftermath of the riot there. NBC-TV asked him to narrate a documentary on the Detroit riot in the fall. He was on the cover of *Time* late in July, and *Life* ran Fred Powledge's article, "Idea Broker in the Race Crisis: A Troubled Nation Turns to Pat Moynihan" in November.[7] With this confirmation of his position as one of the leading nongovernment authorities on domestic policy making, Moynihan felt more secure about speaking out and did not hesitate to advocate specific policies for alleviating urban problems.

During 1967 Moynihan wrote and spoke on a wide range of subjects: welfare reform, the role of the civil rights movement in diverting attention from his black family report, radicals on college campuses and the proper response to demonstrations and disruptions, and approaches to political action at a time when the stability of the social order was being undermined. His bitterness at the Johnson administration's failure to embrace his point of view on racial problems was obvious, and he did not hesitate to criticize Washington for its lack of a coherent approach to the riots. Moynihan's message was clear: if they had listened to him in 1965, his family policy would have provided a response to those questions that the urban riots raised about the nature of the federal government's approach to urban poverty.

In February 1967 he testified before the Senate Government Operations Committee to reiterate his support for full employment (the government acting as employer of last resort), job training, and income maintenance. Instead of trying to do things for the poor, Moynihan told the senators, the government should give them money and jobs.[8] It is not clear what impression he made; his frustration with administration policies and the Democratic left in general were evident that month in his *Commentary* article on the controversy over his black family report. Taking notice of Republican gains in the 1966 congressional elections, Moynihan speculated that the GOP would soon win control of the national government. He found much to recommend their approach to social problems, even if their reactionary right wing was totally hostile to social reform. A growing backlash against Great Society spending programs would benefit the Republicans enormously, and this boded ill for the poor, the black poor in particular. The government had provided blacks with legal equality but had not given them the economic and political resources that would enable them to win social equality. Liberals and civil rights leaders were largely to blame, for they had failed to stick with his family policy when it had been attacked. "With all of its virtue as a secular conscience, the liberal left can be as rigid and destructive as any force in American life."[9]

Moynihan's bitterness with much of the black community increased as he came to be regarded as something of a pariah because of what people believed was in the black family report. It was as though the report had taken on an identity of its own, quite independent from anything Moynihan had written. Many blacks came to think the report racist and to treat Moynihan as though he were a bigoted Southerner. Amazed and upset that he could be seen in that light, Moynihan became sensitive, even defensive about his attitude toward blacks. And while his resentment stemmed from a very real disappointment with the way in which his ideas had been misinterpreted, his critics regarded his new attitude as proof of his lack of sympathy for the plight of blacks. Defensiveness was interpreted as hostility by black leaders, and in time Moynihan became unwilling to debate the issue and unable to do so without growing angry.

If Moynihan had little success in convincing liberal Democrats and civil rights activists of the importance of a family policy, he had better luck with Republican businessmen. Late in 1967 he addressed a meeting of many of the nation's business leaders, convened by New York Governor Nelson Rockefeller to explore new approaches to public welfare. The conference at Arden House in Harriman, New York, debated the merits of income maintenance as one approach, with Moynihan speaking in favor of a system of family allowances and Professor Milton Friedman speaking for a negative income tax. Moynihan pointed to the growing welfare rolls of the 1950s and 1960s and to the development of an impoverished underclass (of both whites and blacks) that seemed to remain in economic difficulties even when the unemployment rate dropped. Politicians had avoided the problem generally, and now there was need for a full-scale overhaul of the system. To improve the status of this dependent underclass, Moynihan said, the first requirement was to give them enough money to lead what he called a normal life.

In advocating a family allowance, Moynihan called for a policy of income equalization that would elevate those at the very bottom of the wealth distribution scale to a position in the middle. In effect he wanted to create a triangle-like distribution of wealth, in which great accumulation was possible but without permitting anyone to fall below a broad middle level. Such an arrangement would be preferable to the present elongated diamondlike distribution of income, in which the largest group was at the center with substantial numbers of people above and below it.[10]

Moynihan was careful to speak in class terms. While blacks fell disproportionately into the dependent underclass, it was important to recognize that there were whites in this group as well. And while the family allowance approach would have a general redistributive effect, it would provide all families with some benefits—an important consideration in a time of polarized opinion. The strength of the family allowance—as opposed to a guaranteed annual income—was that it would not divide the nation between those who would receive assistance and those who would not. The argument Moynihan made was like the one he would develop in what came to be called the "benign neglect" memorandum for President Nixon early in 1970. Policy makers needed to develop programs that would turn attention away from the divisions in American society and emphasize national unity. "In the present state of race relations, and the mounting radicalism of both the left and the right, it may be argued that what is needed is a program that will benefit everyone, thereby asserting the unities of the nation, rather then emphasizing those qualities which divide it."[11]

The speech was well received by the businessmen, and Moynihan in turn was pleased with their reaction. In a later interview he recalled his surprise at finding that businessmen were interested in the family structure.

I found that the businessmen were very responsive to this subject. The trade union leaders didn't want to talk about this. The social workers

didn't want to talk about this. But the businessmen were perfectly willing
to talk about it. It was a new problem to them. They had no position to
defend, no record to be defensive about. It was absolutely new to them.
They were perfectly willing to talk about it. It made me think that a
Republican Administration would be a lot more willing to deal with this
problem than a Democratic one.[12]

One Republican who showed interest in the idea was Representative
Melvin Laird of Wisconsin, the chairman of the House Republican
Conference. He invited Moynihan to address the conference on the
subject of welfare reform and later induced him to contribute an essay
to a volume he was editing that would be a statement of Republican
policy for the 1968 presidential election. Clearly Laird saw Moynihan
as a potential political ally, and Moynihan was eager to make ad hoc
alliances with anyone who appeared to be interested in programs related
to his family policy.

The spring and summer of 1967 were busy times for Moynihan. In
May an old friend from Middlebury days, Story Zartman, called from
Rochester to ask his help. Zartman was general counsel for Eastman
Kodak, which was then involved in a dispute with a community group,
FIGHT, over jobs for members of Rochester's black community. Eastman Kodak, considered a staunchly antiunion company that over the
years had done little for Rochester's black community, had negotiated
an agreement late in 1966 with FIGHT (then being advised by the
radical organizer Saul Alinsky) that its board of directors had promptly
repudiated. Thereupon communications between the two bodies had
deteriorated, and now there was a search on for a mediator acceptable
to both sides. Zartman hoped that Moynihan would accept the assignment. Alinsky and Moynihan shared similar views on social change—
Moynihan would later write about him in the most flattering terms in
Maximum Feasible Misunderstanding[13]—and Zartman knew that
Moynihan would be trusted by Kodak's executives.

A couple of weeks after Zartman's initial call Moynihan flew to
Rochester and spent an afternoon with Alinsky. Over the next two
months Moynihan acted as mediator between Kodak and FIGHT, helping to negotiate a settlement. It took Moynihan to make Kodak agree
to recognize FIGHT. As a concession to Kodak, FIGHT agreed to drop

its claim for jobs after Kodak promised to make two thousand jobs available to the community through another ad hoc organization. Both sides came away feeling they had won a partial victory, and there was general agreement that Moynihan deserved the credit for producing the settlement. One of the leaders of FIGHT, Dr. Bernard Gifford, was so impressed with Moynihan's performance that he sought him out when he went to Harvard four years later, and in 1976 he was a key organizer of Moynihan's campaign for the Senate.

Moynihan was a man much in demand in the summer of 1967. The nation was torn by urban riots; Newark and Detroit were among more than thirty communities struck. Tensions between blacks and the police and between the black and white communities in general rose to high levels. Black leaders became vehemently militant, thereby alarming further the nation's whites. There was little consensus in the administration or in Congress on what to do. A sort of paralysis had set in; few government officials had any idea of how to respond to the riots, much less a sense of what had caused them. Moynihan had a number of ideas, however, and as the level of violence rose, he became increasingly frustrated. "It was possible to foresee what was coming, but we couldn't get the country to get serious about it. I am angry."[14]

He was angry that liberals had failed to recognize that the riots were a consequence of the development of a black underclass that was made up largely of broken families with at least one member on welfare. Worse, by failing to speak out against black extremism the liberals were legitimizing violence. The rioting demonstrated that "all the things we've tried to help the cities with [haven't] worked out very well," Moynihan said at the time. The president was preoccupied with the war in Vietnam and "dares not and will not scrap the war in order to save the cities."

Just after the Detroit and Newark riots Moynihan went to Washington to offer his help—and came away angry. The administration was paralyzed. "Washington is run by a bunch of old men right now," Moynihan said. "The riots have kind of broken their hearts."[15] The administration could offer no leadership; its attitude was that because it could do nothing, it would take no action.

Moynihan did not claim to have the answers. "Anyone who thinks he knows things that can solve the urban problem is a fool or a fraud," he told a press conference early in August.[16] But he did have ideas. Unlike race relations problems in the South, the problems of northern cities did not come about because the society had willed the development of a poor black underclass. Broken families, larger welfare rolls, high unemployment, and low educational achievement were problems that called for study as well as remedy. The nation had to know why these trends were developing in order to act on them appropriately.

In the wake of the Detroit and Newark riots Moynihan received letters and telegrams from professors and government officials throughout the country that said that the riots had vindicated his black family report.

> People are now saying that I was right and that my report on the disintegration of the Negro family predicted the riots. For the moment I'm a good guy. A year ago my theories of what was going on were powerful enough to explain what was going on. But nothing can explain the dimension of the absolute hatred of the rioters . . . against America. I used to think my proposals would solve the welfare problem. I realize now that they are just the beginning steps. I don't know any more than anyone else what all the answers are.[17]

Moynihan was concerned not only with the problems that led to the riots—chiefly family instability and unemployment—but with their effect on American society. He had begun to feel that American society was coming unglued. A democracy is a fragile thing, and Moynihan feared that the riots would usher in a period of right-wing repression. It was of crucial importance that liberals speak up for the stability of the social order; their failure to do so could lead to the erosion of those democratic freedoms and liberties that most people took for granted.

He spoke on this theme twice, first at Harvard's Phi Beta Kappa oration in June, then to the board of Americans for Democratic Action in September. His focus in June was on student protesters; he told his audience that while much was wrong with American society, there was still great value in preserving the essence of liberalism—due process, the rule of law, an optimistic belief in progress, toleration, and equality. Protest was likely to be successful because its organizers came from what would soon be the dominant social group, the educated middle class, and because protesters had chosen a relatively simple goal, that of disrupting society rather than redirecting it. In the same way that he would one day ask third world countries at the United Nations to come up with a more successful form of government, Moynihan challenged the student protesters. "Things . . . are best in the liberal industrial democracies of the North Atlantic world. I hold these regimes to be the best accommodation to the human condition yet devised, and will demand to know of those who reject it, just what they have in mind as a replacement."[18]

Finally, it was important to recognize that the system could be shaken, even destroyed, if liberals did not defend themselves. Popular confidence in the system was weaker than most people imagined, and only an assertive response to the challenge would demonstrate the value of American society and culture.

> The foundations of popular confidence in the American system are proving to be nothing like so solid and enduring as the confident liberal establishment has supposed. The ability to respond to signs of danger is the essential condition of the ability to survive. It is not too much to declare that our ability is now being tested: it is always being tested. If we respond well to these signs of danger—and if we find a meaningful role in helping to transform the system for those who now attack it—we are likely to evolve a society of considerable nobility.[19]

The June speech only outlined the response that Moynihan sought from liberals; in September, before the ADA, he provided a detailed approach to the problems of social instability. Liberals had to realize that their fundamental interest lay in the stability of the social order, and they must seek alliances with political conservatives (i.e., moderate Republicans such as Melvin Laird) who shared their commitment to peaceful change. Anticipating the later calls for decentralization and neighborhood control, Moynihan urged liberals to "divest themselves of the notion that the nation—and especially the cities of the nation—can be run from agencies in Washington." Innovation has traditionally come from northern cities and states, and liberals should encourage this tendency through such programs as revenue sharing, which effectively allow local choice in policy making. The real business of the government was to deal with international affairs, and in order to keep international crises from paralyzing the domestic policy-making apparatus, it was useful to give localities the impetus for developing social policy. Finally, Moynihan argued that liberals had to avoid the tendency to justify or explain whatever blacks did, however "outrageous" their activity might be. Two groups were agitating in the black community: "One is the vast Negro underclass that has somehow grown up in our Northern cities; a disorganized, angry, hurt group of persons easily given to self-destructive violence." Alongside them stood radical youth, determined to manipulate the poor to produce violent confrontation. "We must prepare for the onset of terrorism. Indeed it may already have begun."[20]

Liberals must not fall into the trap of blaming themselves for the shortcomings of the poor; this only played into the hands of the radical left; moreover, it was faulty analysis. Liberals had to counter the problems of the black underclass with solutions that would make a difference. To do so would deprive white and black radicals of their potential base of support and thus reduce the potential for violent confrontation.

Moynihan's approaches represented something of a change of emphasis on his part. Before the ADA speech he told Ralph Nader that he was beginning to believe more in natural processes. And his recommendations reflected a more pronounced free-enterprise bias. Going beyond family allowances and job training, Moynihan now advocated that the government redistribute income among regions and classes.

> The Federal government is good at collecting revenues, and rather bad at disbursing services. Therefore, we should use the Federal fisc as an instrument for redistributing income between different levels of government, different regions, and different classes. If state and local governments are to assume roles as innovative and creative agents, they simply must begin to receive a share of Federal revenues on a permanent, ongoing basis.[21]

City residents should be given control over their own destinies, which meant that the federal government had to allow municipal governments a greater degree of power. And private business should be brought into policy making. "What aerospace corporations have done for getting us to the moon urban housing corporations can do for the slums. All that is necessary, one fears, is to let enough men make enough money out of doing so."[22]

The ADA speech was a major event. The *New York Times* reported it on page one, Tom Wicker and other columnists wrote favorably of it, and Republicans welcomed it with glee. Melvin Laird began referring to Moynihan as a man who was not necessarily "wedded to old commitments" and who was "sincerely and primarily interested in finding viable and practical solutions no matter where they originate. His solutions may not be our solutions, but his questing search for true causes makes dialogue possible and welcome."[23] Another Republican, Richard Nixon, read the press accounts of the speech and made a mental note to keep his eye on Moynihan. Meanwhile, some liberal Democrats decided that Moynihan had abandoned their cause, becoming in effect a Republican whose background in Democratic politics was the only evidence of his continued association with the liberal wing of the party.

Amid a busy schedule, Moynihan somehow found time in October 1967 for an eight-day trip to Tokyo and New Delhi as a member of the Board of Trustees of the Woodrow Wilson International Center for Scholars (administered by the Smithsonian Institution as a memorial to President Wilson). Accompanied by friend and fellow board member Charles Blitzer, Moynihan shopped in Tokyo (at a restaurant supply store he bought a large wooden bucket to hold fish he would catch on his farm) and had a shoeshine at Minub Qtar, a large tower near New Delhi, where he compared the price structures for shoeshines in Times Square in 1941 and India in 1967.

Moynihan returned from the Asian trip on a Tuesday and took the shuttle to Boston for an afternoon class. On Wednesday he went to Rochester for a meeting on the Kodak dispute; on Thursday he was in Albany to meet with Governor Rockefeller's welfare task force; on Friday he flew to New York for a speech at the Harvard Club on American architecture. After the speech he went to LaGuardia to catch the shuttle back to Boston and found the flight canceled because of the weather. He also found that in his hurry to get to the airport he had lost his wallet. Borrowing a dime from a stranger, Moynihan called his wife in Cambridge to ask her what he should do. She told him to take a taxi back to the Harvard Club and have the doorman pay for it. The exhausted Moynihan spent the next day sleeping.

Another issue on the political horizon that was increasingly drawing attention away from the cities was the war in Vietnam. At the ADA meeting at which Moynihan had spoken, the organization took its first tentative steps toward not supporting the president for re-election. At that time Moynihan fully expected that Johnson would be re-elected, but he had misgivings about the way the war was being handled. However, he had yet to develop a broad conceptual analysis of American foreign policy in the 1960s, and he expressed his doubts with hesitation. Then the increasing controversy in late 1967 and in 1968 drew Moynihan into the debate.

Pat Moynihan was pulled in two directions by the war in Vietnam. On the one hand, he was convinced that the war was a tragic mistake. We could never succeed in bringing democracy to Asia, and we were foolish to try; America would only be seen in an increasingly bad light both at home and in the international community. And given the administration's preoccupation with the war, few domestic policy initiatives would be undertaken—at a time when urban riots were demonstrating the need for a response from the federal government. On the other hand, Moynihan would not join the peace movement in advocating any form of unilateral disengagement. His major concern was for the stability of the social order, and he feared that any appearance of the administration's capitulating to the peace movement would have grave consequences for the nation. Much of the antiwar movement was not only hostile to the struggle in Vietnam but appeared to be hostile to America as well, and liberals like Moynihan could not afford to associate with people who believed the war was "an illegal act of an illegal society." American honor had to be considered in any plan to end the war; any settlement that reflected adversely on the national interest had to be rejected.

Moynihan avoided most antiwar activities and instead joined Negotiations Now, a group of liberal intellectuals who were committed to a negotiated settlement rather than unilateral disengagement. Moynihan became one of six co-chairmen of the organization, along with President Clark Kerr of the University of California and Professor Seymour Martin Lipset of Harvard. Early in 1968 they advocated a bombing halt for a specified period and negotiations involving all parties to the conflict, including the National Liberation Front, with the goal of democratic elections. The organization called on the nations that had partitioned Vietnam in 1954—the United States, Britain, Russia, India, Poland, and Canada—to reconvene the Geneva peace conference as a means of preventing an escalation of the fighting as a result of the battle of Khesanh, which was then beginning. While Negotiations Now was a distinctly moderate peace group—it emphasized that it opposed unilateral disengagement if its own plan failed—the FBI saw fit to add to its files a reference to Moynihan's affiliation with the organization and a statement of the group's platform on the war.[24]

In June 1967 Moynihan's first words on Vietnam were distinctly "dovish." His remarks, coming in his Phi Beta Kappa address at Harvard, must have pleased an audience that may not have been entirely comfortable with his analysis of student radicalism. The war was being carried on by people who were convinced that democracy was an option available to all nations, Moynihan said. They were wrong; American history was unique, and any effort designed to spread the American system worldwide was "doomed to fail." Not only were our efforts inherently impossible, they were—in the words of Michael Oakeshott, onetime professor of politics at the London School of Economics—"a corrupting enterprise." Moynihan elaborated:

> As our efforts repeatedly fall short of their pronounced goals, we begin covering up, taking shortcuts, and in desperation end up doing things we would never conceivably start out to do. Princes of the Church, modest sons of small town grocers, begin proclaiming holy wars in Asia, while the man in the street acquires an appallingly troubled vision of those who protest.
> Liberals have simply got to restrain their enthusiasm for civilizing others. It is their greatest weakness and ultimate arrogance.[25]

In May 1968 Moynihan spelled out what liberals had to do about foreign policy: they had to develop "institutional means of controlling the military-industrial complex which, through no one's fault, so easily leads governments to overestimate the effectiveness of controlled violence—and thereafter the possibility of keeping violence under control."[26] The war was not the fault of generals or munitions makers but of liberal professors who had little understanding of the power of the military-industrial complex and didn't appreciate how important it was that the civilian leadership control that power.

Moynihan's antipathy toward the war grew over time. In 1968 he spoke of our "incredible experience" in Vietnam, "where our Government persists alone and adamant in a course of destruction." While the administration was "outwardly convinced of its rationality," the American people were convinced of its "fundamental immorality" and the rest of the world of its "madness." Administration policy was leading America to the status of "outcast" nation.[27]

Although the war raised questions about a fundamental tenet of post-World War II foreign policy—that the United States would be an interventionist power in situations where totalitarianism threatened the balance of power, and would act generally as a peace-keeping force— Moynihan was not ready to abandon this notion. While it was important that we recognize the limits of our power, it did not necessarily follow that American foreign policy had to be entirely reconceived. True, hard questions should be asked, and Moynihan would come to see a renewed purpose for American interventionism: to assert the primacy of human rights in international politics.[28]

In 1967–68 Moynihan was most concerned about the threats that black violence and the antiwar movement posed to the stability of American democracy. That democracy was very fragile indeed, and the growing domestic violence raised serious questions about whether the system could endure. The left had become violent as a result of the war in Vietnam, black rhetoric was increasingly militant, ghetto riots were almost commonplace, and the right was restive in the face of black and antiwar agitation. "The sheer effort to hold things together has become the central issue of politics in a nation that began the decade intent on building a society touched with moral grandeur."[29] Consequently Moynihan would not place himself in the position of espousing any policy line that might compromise American interests.

So he told the Americans for Democratic Action, at the national board meeting called to discuss the president's handling of the war, that liberals would be wrong to advocate unilateral withdrawal from Vietnam. Organizations such as the ADA had to make it "politically worthwhile and possible for the Administration to disengage." It was a question not just of "summoning the will, but also of finding a way." In taking any decision to withdraw it was important to consider the prestige of the military as well as "the self-regard of the tens of thousands of American youths who perform honorably and well in those jungles because they were asked or told to do so by their superiors." Opponents of the war had to make it clear that their loyalties lay with America, lest the world assume they were sympathetic to the Viet Cong. He could have no sympathy with antiwar activists who saw Vietnam as "the illegal act of an illegal society," whose "indictment of American society escalated as fast, and perhaps even faster than the bombing." Such sentiments led to the belief that the NLF was fighting the same kinds of battles that black rioters were fighting against oppression in America.[30]

These sentiments, Moynihan believed, served to "legitimate—and to some extent [they] did indeed bring on—deliberate disobedience of law and the use of force and violence to promote the cause of peace."[31] It was the "urgent task of liberals and conservatives alike to decry the descent to violence as a way of life, and to decry most especially any legitimation of it in terms that the failure to enforce this right, or to redress that wrong, somehow makes violence inevitable and therefore acceptable."[32] Any efforts by antiwar groups to prevent the president from expressing his views, however noxious, had to be stopped. That the peace movement had justifiable motives did not legitimate their use of force to try to stop the president. "The apparent determination of some peace groups by criminal assault to prevent the President from campaigning is just that—criminal, there must be a stop to it."[33]

The American way to register displeasure with government policy is through the electoral process, Moynihan believed, and as 1968 began Moynihan turned to the candidacies of Eugene McCarthy and Robert Kennedy. Given Moynihan's somewhat unfocused feelings about the war, it is hard to escape the notion that the Johnson administration's failure to adopt his approach to domestic policy led in the first instance to his disaffection with the president. Bitterness over the fate of the black family report ran deep with Moynihan (Harry McPherson remembers that Moynihan often called to alert him to studies that supported his thesis after he had left Washington). If only the administration had adopted a family policy, Moynihan evidently believed, some of the urban violence might have been avoided. Its preoccupation with the war had paralyzed the administration on the domestic side to such an extent that Moynihan came to believe that his approach had been rejected in favor of no policy at all. The Kerner Commission report was evidence of this; there was much in it that was useful, yet Johnson never bothered formally to acknowledge its completion, much less take note of its findings. The war played its role in turning Moynihan against the president—he would describe the president's response to all antiwar activity as "rigid and moralizing"—but it was domestic policy, not foreign policy, that led Moynihan to oppose the president.

When Moynihan spoke to the ADA in September 1967, he assumed that President Johnson would be re-elected the following year. But as 1968 got underway his perception began to change. The McCarthy challenge was more serious than most had supposed, and for the first time the president appeared to be vulnerable. Moynihan felt little residual loyalty to Johnson and was prepared to oppose him, but the man he wanted to support was vacillating about becoming a candidate. (Robert Kennedy did not decide to enter the primaries until just after the New Hampshire primary in mid March.) For Moynihan the only alternative was Eugene McCarthy, whom he respected greatly but did not know well. McCarthy and Kennedy were both part of the same political tradition in which Moynihan had grown up. Like him, they were Irish, Catholic, and from the North. Unlike the student radicals in the street, McCarthy and Kennedy represented "a tradition of common sense and compassion, but also predictability and a measure of caution. It is liberal without being especially ideological; idealistic without being greatly abstract; but most of all it is a tradition."[34] These feelings led Moynihan to vote for McCarthy at the ADA national board meeting in January, when the organization endorsed his candidacy for president.

Moynihan, still waiting for Kennedy to enter the race, did not work actively for McCarthy. When Kennedy announced his candidacy four days after the virtual dead heat in New Hampshire, Moynihan quickly volunteered his services.

Moynihan was pleased with the results in New Hampshire. Until the primary he had felt that the stability of the Democratic system was uncertain, but the results proved that the system still worked: the president withdrew from the race some three weeks after the outcome was known, and administration policy began to shift. Thus the results were a victory for the "center peace movement," which had advocated electoral activity as a means of influencing government policy.

> The retirement of the President is an act without precedent, but the substantive point is that policy changed almost routinely in response to a changed public opinion. This is what is meant by the democratic process. Before New Hampshire, there was plausibility in the idea that the democratic process was breaking down in America. After New Hampshire, we know that it has not broken down, that it works.[35]

Moynihan hoped that Robert Kennedy would be able to restore America to a more moderate posture and bring together diverse groups. Kennedy was the man who could best protect American society as it was without challenging the assumptions on which it was based. After the senator's assassination Moynihan would express surprise that Kennedy had been seen by many as someone who would restructure American society. "Now I find Robert Kennedy turned into some kind of super-contestant of all the arrangements of American society, arrangements he lived very much for and with. And I find myself saying, 'God, that's not the Robert Kennedy who asked me to come to California.' "[36]

The Robert Kennedy he supported offered the best chance of carrying out the reassessment of American domestic and foreign policy that Moynihan thought necessary. The Democratic party, Moynihan believed, had always been the party of stability, and by responding to international and domestic challenges with subtlety and flexibility, the party had helped to enhance that stability. Yet in domestic affairs almost all social initiatives had been abandoned following the 1967 summer riots, and in foreign affairs the administration was rigidly committed to pursuing an effort in Southeast Asia that was doomed to fail. The failure of the administration to alter its policies actually helped undermine that stability. What then had to be done?

Moynihan believed it important that America reassess its commitment to interventionism in foreign affairs as well as in domestic affairs generally. It was important that government not seek out large numbers of new ideas for the sake of innovation alone. Government needed to concern itself more with administering and evaluating the programs it already had rather than propose a panoply of new programs whose effects would be unpredictable. Proposing and implementing new programs was becoming more difficult because of the development of a "conservative majority" that resulted from the growing middle class character of American society. Change was possible only if political issues were approached in class, rather than racial, terms. The conservative majority would certainly try to block any program designed as a reparation to blacks for past white racism. It would also be best that programs intended to improve low educational achievement and to end welfare dependency be framed in nonracial terms because these problems were common to working class people regardless of race.

In general Moynihan thought it time for politicians to lower their voices and their expectations. "The great liberal failing of this time is constantly to over-promise and to overstate, and thereby constantly to appear to under-perform."[37] Messianic rhetoric was harmful to the body politic; it was at least in some part responsible for our disaster in Vietnam. Moynihan even criticized Robert Kennedy for saying that America has a right to the moral leadership of the planet. (Even if there were such a thing as moral leadership of the planet, it was not something Moynihan believed America had a right to.) Domestically, government had to stop using the rhetoric of the civil rights movement to introduce new programs; that kind of language was suitable to inspirational political movements, not to sustained government activity. The government should concentrate on introducing a few programs, such as revenue sharing and some form of negative income tax or family allowance, to demonstrate that the Democratic party has a clear idea of what is needed to keep the country together.

Moynihan believed that Kennedy was more sympathetic to his approach than to that of the more radical social activists who supported him (e.g., Adam Walinsky, Peter Edelman, Allard Lowenstein), yet it is not entirely clear that Kennedy was thinking along the same lines as Moynihan. Before the campaign Senator Fred Harris of Oklahoma had asked Kennedy what he thought of Moynihan, and Kennedy had replied, "He knows all the facts and he's against all the solutions."[38]

There was little time for carefully thought-out planning during the hastily organized Kennedy campaign, and ideological differences had little influence on the flow of events. There was a job to do—winning the nomination—and Kennedy loyalists were preoccupied with doing what practical things they could rather than developing a coherent and conceptually sound campaign platform to impose on their candidate. When Kennedy asked him to go to California early in May, Moynihan joined old Kennedy hands Burke Marshall, Fred Dutton, and Ted Sorensen, flying to Los Angeles to speak for Kennedy at a series of coffee klatches and then repeating the routine in San Francisco. At Berkeley he spoke on the steps of Sproul Hall before a plaza made famous in the early days of the Free Speech Movement. The students were strongly anti-Kennedy, and Moynihan enjoyed bantering with them.

> I came off all right, mostly by the process of being fairly open with the kids, being smart . . . I'm as smart as they are, and I know more, so you can come off moderately well. I mean they would ask me, "Would Kennedy be in this race had McCarthy not won in New Hampshire?" And while your instinct would be to say, "Well, McCarthy didn't win in New Hampshire," my sense at the time said to me to look the man in the eye and say, "No."
>
> Well, they understood that, they accepted that much better than the bullshit.[39]

Moynihan, who had commitments to give four commencement addresses in the East, could not remain in California for the June 5 primary, and on the night of May 31 he left Kennedy asleep in California. The following night he spoke at St. Louis University, where he told the audience that he did not trust the FBI investigation into the assassination of Martin Luther King. If many of those connected with the civil rights movement considered Moynihan to be distinctly hostile to it, the FBI had the opposite impression. They noted the speech in his file the next day and reported that Moynihan had spoken at one of King's Southern Christian Leadership Conference training sessions in February. The SCLC, the FBI report said, was a "pro-integration organization"; the impression was clear—Moynihan's hostility to the Bureau was related to his sympathy for civil rights and liberalism in general.

On the night of Kennedy's assassination Moynihan delivered the commencement address at the New School for Social Research in New York. It was a serious speech; Moynihan came out against ethnic and racial quotas while at the same time he endorsed informal programs that would give disadvantaged minorities special help. The *New York Times* reported the speech on page one of the early edition, but the late editions were dominated by Kennedy's assassination.

Moynihan's reaction to Robert Kennedy's death differed from his earlier reaction to John Kennedy's death. For him the president's funeral had contained in some measure a "sense of triumph"; in contrast, the senator's funeral was a "long, desolate, remorseless demonstration of defeat. We lost." The "we" included people who had once worked with John Kennedy and had reunited to work for Robert. The assassination was a sign that Camelot had come to an end. The supporters of Robert and John Kennedy "hoped much for their country, but those hopes for the moment, at least, seemed to have come to little more than the burial by moonlight of a leader who in the face of setback and disappointment did not lower, but did indeed raise his expectation for that country."[40] On the funeral train Moynihan told author Michael Harrington that the only thing we could do well at that point was to bury our dead. He found himself "suffused with a sense of clarity—and terrible to say—a sense of inevitability" about what had happened.[41] From the funeral he went directly to his farm in upstate New York, where he spent the next seven weeks writing his account of the role of community action in the war on poverty, which was published as *Maximum Feasible Misunderstanding.*

Moynihan had only a minor role for the balance of the campaign. He served on a McCarthy issues task force prior to the convention, and in the fall he gave one speech in New York for Hubert Humphrey. After that he was content to return to teaching, assuming that for the present his political career was over. Then, two months after Richard Nixon's victory, instead of being a former Kennedy aide in the academic wilderness, Moynihan was named to a post that made him perhaps the most powerful domestic policy adviser in the nation.

8

Switching Sides

Let me say with absolute candor that I think he [Nixon] is the most
civil man I ever worked for. He really does have some sense of your
own feelings.

—Pat Moynihan, 1971

Pat Moynihan stayed up late on November 5, 1968, awaiting the final
results of the Nixon-Humphrey contest. When it became clear that
Richard Nixon was likely to be the next president of the United States,
he went to bed angry. The next morning he left his house at 57 Francis
Avenue in Cambridge to walk to the Joint Center. At William James
Hall on Kirkland Street he met Thomas Pettigrew, and soon the two
were commiserating over the election results. Adjourning to a nearby
tavern, they spent the rest of the day in the Penguin Bar discussing the
prospects of a Nixon presidency. Moynihan did most of the talking,
worried about what might happen under a Nixon administration and
unaware that little more than a month later he would be named to one
of the most important domestic policy positions in that administration.

Leonard Garment was probably most responsible for bringing Moynihan into the new administration. A law partner of Nixon in the firm of

Nixon, Mudge, Rose, Guthrie, Alexander & Mitchell in New York, Garment was decidedly more liberal than most members of the new president's inner circle. He knew of Moynihan's work and particularly the 1967 ADA speech, and he wanted to bring him into the government. He had talked with Nixon about Moynihan during the campaign, as had speechwriters Raymond Price and William Safire and a longtime Nixon confidant, Robert Finch, the lieutenant governor of California. In the course of the campaign Nixon had referred to Moynihan as a "thoughtful liberal" because of his commitment to personal freedom and reduced government intervention. Moreover, Moynihan was not merely a liberal Democrat but a Kennedy Democrat who had rejected many of the initiatives of the Great Society. When Nixon expressed misgivings about Moynihan's temperament and worried that it might not be wise to have a friend of the Kennedys in his administration, Garment was insistent. He invited Moynihan to dinner in New York to discuss the subject, and Moynihan made it known that he was interested in serving in the new administration.

Garment relayed the news to Nixon and arranged for Moynihan to see the president-elect. There had been speculation (reported in *Newsweek*) that Moynihan would be offered the post of either secretary of transportation or secretary of housing and urban development, but Moynihan did not take the possibilities seriously. However, the reports did convince Moynihan that he was being actively considered for some post in the administration, so before Garment could set up his meeting with Nixon, Moynihan sent the president-elect a letter outlining his thoughts on welfare reform.

Moynihan was excited when Nixon told him that he wanted him to be in charge of all domestic policy formulation outside the economic sphere. After having been in the political wilderness since 1965, Moynihan was now being given the influence he had unsuccessfully sought in a Democratic administration. Where Johnson had ignored him, Moynihan found that Nixon appeared to be interested in his views on urban affairs, was willing to listen, and even took copious notes on what Moynihan said. He began to sense that service in the Nixon administration might allow him to accomplish at least in part some of the things he had hoped to do in the Kennedy and Johnson administrations. More, he sensed that through his service in the Nixon administration he could get back at all the liberals who had disagreed with him on social policy during the Kennedy and Johnson years; he would try to prove that *more* could be accomplished in a conservative Republican administration than in a Democratic administration.

Yet Moynihan was wary. Presidents invariably promise more than they can deliver, and Moynihan was skeptical that Nixon would give him complete authority over domestic affairs. Having never worked with Republicans before, he was suspicious. His wife opposed the idea and argued vigorously. Nevertheless the opportunity was too good to turn down. After discussing the idea over dinner at the Plaza Hotel with Robert Finch following his meeting with the president-elect, Moynihan decided to accept the post.

There were those in Nixon's inner circle who tried to block the appointment. Bryce Harlow and Arthur Burns vehemently opposed Moynihan's presence in the administration, arguing that his social policy was too liberal and that he was likely to be a disruptive force. They predicted that he would resign over some issue before a year was out, embarrassing the president and his administration. But Nixon wanted some Democratic participation in his administration—he had put out feelers to senators Henry Jackson and Eugene McCarthy, among others —and only Moynihan was interested. Nixon concluded that he was worth the gamble.

Early in December Nixon announced that Moynihan would become assistant to the president for urban affairs and secretary of a newly created body, the Urban Affairs Council, which would consist of the secretaries of Transportation, Agriculture, Commerce, Housing and Urban Development, and Health, Education, and Welfare and the attorney general. The president was chairman of the UAC, the vice president presiding in his absence. Nixon told a press conference that the new council would exactly parallel the National Security Council and that Moynihan's domestic role would be similar to that of Henry Kissinger in foreign policy.[1]

Moynihan sought to minimize the policy differences between himself and the president. Acknowledging that he and Nixon did not agree on all subjects, Moynihan pointed out that "presidents don't need advisers who agree with them on everything." And what he thought about issues did not matter much. "My ideas belong to the president," Moynihan told the assembled press corps. "Only the president has views." Nixon shared in the effort to minimize their differences, telling the press that they both agreed on the need for a good fifty-cent hamburger.[2]

Beyond their ideological differences Nixon and Moynihan developed a warm rapport. Their backgrounds were similar: both had had humble origins, and their early years had informed their thoughts on domestic policy. After he had left the administration in early 1971, Moynihan remembered a conversation with Nixon in which "he always went back to that store in Whittier, California, and he never failed to mention the poor kids coming into the store. Just as poor as he was."[3] Nixon became fond of Moynihan and frequently invited him to the Oval Office for late afternoon chats. In the early months of the administration their relationship reached the point where Moynihan was rarely more than three hours away from a meeting with the president. Moynihan gave the president reading lists and convinced him he could be a social reformer like the nineteenth-century British Tory Disraeli despite the conservative character of his administration. And when appealing to the president's higher instincts didn't work, Moynihan's tone would grow conspiratorial as he told the president how his proposals would hurt the liberals and the social workers, whom they both distrusted. Nixon enjoyed reading Moynihan's memos, which often concluded that to follow the policy option he proposed would be a decision of lasting importance.

At the same time that Nixon wooed Moynihan with the offer of general responsibility for domestic policy, he was seeking economist Arthur Burns to be a special assistant for domestic affairs with Cabinet rank. Nixon had promised Burns the chairmanship of the Federal Reserve Board when William McChesney Martin's term expired on January 31, 1970, and Burns expected to remain outside the government until that time. But Nixon was adamant, and Burns was persuaded to take a post as White House counselor with Cabinet rank. Moynihan, sitting with Nixon's press secretary, Ron Ziegler, when he learned of the appointment, asked why Burns had been appointed. But in a sense Moynihan already knew the answer. He had suspected when Nixon gave him jurisdiction over domestic policy that there would be other officials with similar responsibility who knew Nixon better than he did. It was never clearly determined how Burns's responsibilities would mesh with Moynihan's; as the new administration settled in, it was evident to both that they were headed for conflict.

Moynihan returned to Cambridge in December 1968 to finish the term at Harvard. There many of his liberal colleagues were enraged that he had decided to serve in the Nixon administration. Moynihan's response to his critics was that he felt it his responsibility to serve when the president called. He secured a two-year leave of absence from the School of Education and attended to some final administrative details before leaving for Washington. Moynihan planned to serve only for two years, sensing that if anything were going to be accomplished, it would happen early in the new term. In December 1968 he told an administration planning session at the Hotel Pierre, "If you cannot do what you set out to do in the first couple of years, forget it."[4]

A minor controversy developed a week or so after his appointment was announced, when the first copies of his new book, *Maximum Feasible Misunderstanding,* became available to the press.[5] The book sought to explain why the Johnson administration's poverty program had not lived up to the high expectations its framers had for it in 1964. The main argument was that no one in government then had a clear notion of what community action entailed, and that this led to a disorganized and ultimately disappointing program. Because the government did not really know what "maximum feasible participation" of the poor would mean when it set up the Office of Economic Opportunity, some local community action agencies became focal points for conflict with the established order. The book, seen as a wide-ranging indictment of the development and implementation of the poverty program, led to speculation that Moynihan might bring about the dismantling of the community action and model cities programs. The book appeared just as the *New York Times* was conducting its own investigation of corruption in New York City's poverty program. Former Great Society officials Bill Moyers and Adam Yarmolinsky announced that they backed a continuation of the war on poverty, their fear being that the Nixon administration, fueled by the evidence in Moynihan's book, would eliminate the program.[6] In the end Moynihan was probably the official most responsi-

ble for continuing the poverty program after the new administration
took office.

In the days between his appointment on December 10 and the inauguration on January 20 Moynihan set about recruiting a staff. If he were
to have the authority he wanted, he would need a head start on the other
appointees, and his goal was to be already at work on inauguration day.
At the end of December he set up temporary offices at the Pennsylvania
Avenue Commission in Washington. For his chief deputy Moynihan
chose Stephen Hess, a Republican intellectual who had co-authored a
biography of Richard Nixon. Hess had served on Eisenhower's White
House staff, and Moynihan hoped that he would provide both adminis-
trative assistance and the links to the Republican establishment that
Moynihan lacked. He hired a group of recent Ivy League college gradu-
ates to help with research and work on the domestic council. From the
Nixon transition staff he recruited John Price, a leader of the liberal
Republican Ripon Society, and Chris DeMuth, a Harvard graduate and
aide to Leonard Garment. He added Richard Blumenthal, a recent
Harvard graduate who had just returned from a year in England, and
Chester (Checker) Finn, Jr., a doctoral candidate at Harvard who was
working under Moynihan's supervision. The group was later joined by
a June 1969 Yale graduate, Arthur Klebanoff, a nephew of Nathan
Glazer, who had done considerable research on New York City voting
patterns. Other additions to the staff were Mike Monroe, a public
relations man who stayed only a short while, and Moynihan's longtime
friend Story Zartman, who left Eastman Kodak to go to Washington.

While choosing his staff, Moynihan set out his thoughts on priorities
for the new administration in a memorandum to the president-elect
dated January 3. Taking as his starting point Nixon's campaign slogan,
"Bring Us Together," Moynihan argued—as he had when he was out
of government—that the president's most important job was to restore
the authority of American institutions. To do this, Nixon had to improve
the lot of the black underclass and end the war in Vietnam. This meant
encouraging the continuation of the rate of economic expansion and
eschewing the rhetoric of crisis in which the liberals indulged. Nixon
could not allow himself to be identified personally with a war that was
a "domestic disaster." Elimination of the black underclass would take

the cadres away from the middle class black extremists who routinely threatened white society. Moreover, the alleviation of urban poverty would do much to end crime committed by blacks against other blacks. Finally, Moynihan urged Nixon to stress those aspects of American life that were shared by a large proportion of the population rather than emphasize those things that distinguished one group from another. All in all, Moynihan sought to persuade the president to adopt a moderate, sober approach to progressive social reform.[7] It was an approach for which he would fight throughout the two years he served in the White House.

Instead of taking a large suite of offices in the Executive Office Building, Moynihan opted for more cramped quarters in the White House basement, adjacent to Henry Kissinger's National Security Council staff. Proximity to the president rather than lavish office space was Moynihan's goal; by staying in the White House basement he made himself that much more accessible to the president and his key staff assistants. In Moynihan's words, "It meant I could piss standing next to Haldeman in the same toilet." Efforts to impose order on the staff proved unsuccessful—much of the group's work emerged from the creative chaos that Moynihan cultivated. Checker Finn, for example, served for a time as a sort of confidential assistant to Moynihan, making sure his desk was cleared and taking his shirts to the laundry in a Mercury limousine.

If Moynihan had been angry the day after the election, he was jubilant on inauguration day and at a celebration that night at the Sheraton Park Hotel—so jubilant that J. Edgar Hoover noted in Moynihan's FBI file that he had been drunk. But while Moynihan was pleased with the prospect of spending two years in the administration, Liz Moynihan was not eager to go to Washington. So they arranged that Pat would stay in Washington during the week and fly to Cambridge on weekends. Thus weekends became special times for the Moynihans. Liz organized an informal movie club among a group of close Cambridge friends, and Saturday nights were a time for a dinner with friends followed by a screening of an old film.

On January 23, 1969, Richard Nixon's first formal act as president of the United States was to sign the executive order creating the Urban

Affairs Council. Moynihan and Hess entered the Cabinet room before the president and found that the only fountain pens available were inscribed with Lyndon Johnson's name. This would not do, Moynihan thought, and he searched for a substitute. Hess discovered some felt-tip pens, but these were not suitable either. Finally, Moynihan located some plain White House fountain pens and made certain they were placed where the president would see them. Nixon used the pens to sign the executive order, taking a different pen for each letter of his name. Unfortunately, the pens leaked profusely. Seeing this, Moynihan pulled out his handkerchief and handed it to the president. After the ceremony the president put the handkerchief in his pocket and walked off. Moynihan turned to Hess and said, "Well, I just got an Urban Affairs Council and lost a handkerchief."

The UAC was organized into ten subcommittees, each chaired by a Cabinet member, and each with a Moynihan staff member designated to monitor its proceedings. Subcommittees covered such areas as crime, welfare, and education; their activities generally depended on the degree of interest of the chairman. Attorney General John Mitchell, who quickly developed a strong dislike for Moynihan, refused to convene his crime subcommittee; Secretary of Health, Education and Welfare Robert Finch's welfare subcommittee was very busy during the early months of the administration. At first the president himself attended the council meetings. Nixon presided at six of the first eight sessions, each of them lasting from one and one-half to three hours. Attendance was mandatory for the vice president and those Cabinet members who were on the council. Thus the UAC was clearly a focal point for domestic policy formulation in the early days of the administration.

One of the first areas of attention for Moynihan was District of Columbia affairs, and here he had to contend with the attorney general. Mitchell soon made it clear that he had serious doubts about Moynihan's ability to handle District affairs—or anything else for that matter. Mitchell had had little experience in politics and was accustomed to the life of a Wall Street lawyer; both personally and politically he was very conservative, and he found Moynihan's personality and manner somewhat alien and threatening. Although Nixon came to trust Moynihan in time, Mitchell never forgot that Moynihan was a Kennedy Democrat and never fully accepted him as part of the administration team. As if to emphasize his determination not to take Moynihan seriously, Mitchell refused to call Moynihan by his correct name and insisted on calling him "Monahan."

The two men clashed early in 1969, just as Moynihan was assuming responsibility for District of Columbia affairs. Two major problems faced the government in this area. First, there were strong pressures from Washington, D.C., residents for home rule. Mayor Walter Washington had been appointed by the president, and there would certainly be resentment if the administration appeared to be too heavy-handed in influencing local affairs. Second, the District had been hit hard by the riots that followed Martin Luther King's assassination in 1968, and substantial reconstruction was needed. As a gesture to the black community, Moynihan persuaded the president to go to 7th and T streets and propose that a building lot adjoining a schoolyard be turned into a playground, to be named after a black high school principal who had been killed in a school nearby. Photos of the president touring the area appeared in the next day's paper, enabling Nixon to attain some credibility with the black community in the District and throughout the country.

In announcing his proposed District of Columbia crime control legislation (which embodied the notion of preventive detention), Nixon asked that the District be given home rule and announced that he was authorizing $29.7 million for the restoration of riot-torn areas. (Here there was conflict with Mitchell; Moynihan opposed preventive detention on civil libertarian grounds, while Mitchell strongly supported it.) While Moynihan was instrumental in getting Nixon to provide assistance to the District, he was careful that he himself not be too prominent. His avowed goal was to remain "anonymous" rather than appear to be the white overlord of a largely black city. His critics in the black community had reappeared when his appointment was announced, and if they were to become aware of his responsibilities for Washington's government, a renewed protest might develop. Meanwhile Mitchell moved to diminish Moynihan's influence in the area by blocking two of three proposed appointments to the District of Columbia City Council—Moynihan's first public conflict with entrenched Nixon loyalists.[8]

Although many liberals undoubtedly feared that the publication of Moynihan's *Maximum Feasible Misunderstanding* would provide the rationale for the dismantling of the poverty programs, it proved to be the case that most of those programs survived—if in modified form. Moynihan the government official took a very different view of the poverty program and the Model Cities program than Moynihan the social scientist had taken. Moynihan had said that Nixon's most important task as president was to restore confidence in American institutions, and to end the poverty program would only exacerbate the divisions in American society and create deep mistrust of the administration among the black community. Even though Chris DeMuth reported that vast sums of money were being wasted on the Model Cities program through inefficient programs and high staff salaries, Moynihan could only smile. Such was the price of keeping American society together. In private meetings with the president Moynihan persuaded him to propose legislation to extend the life of the Office of Economic Opportunity and to continue funding for the Model Cities program. The focus of OEO changed from administration to research and development when such programs as Head Start and the Job Corps were assigned to other departments, but OEO continued to exist, if only as a symbol. Moynihan also had a part in getting Nixon to appoint Republican Congressman Donald Rumsfeld to head the Office of Economic Opportunity.[9] Rumsfeld later became a close friend of Moynihan, working with him during the Ford administration when Moynihan was ambassador to the United Nations and Rumsfeld was one of the president's closest advisers.

By far the most important issue to occupy Moynihan during his time in the White House was welfare reform.[10] When Moynihan set up shop in the West Wing, the prospects for significant overhaul of the system were bleak at best. Just before his inauguration Nixon had dictated a memo to Mitchell, Finch, Moynihan, and Harlow, calling for an investigation with an eye toward cutting "costly political programs" that had created a welfare "mess." In the context of such a memo it was surely difficult to imagine that any such meaningful innovation as the development of a negative income tax or a family allowance could be contemplated. Nevertheless Moynihan sought to use his analysis of the breakdown of working class families as an argument for the establishment of national standards for all categories of federal assistance as a presidential task force had just recommended. An investigation Nixon wanted of the situation in New York City would produce few benefits; instead it would give the welfare rights organizations a chance to create martyrs. "The fact is, the more one knows about welfare, the more horrible it becomes: but not because of cheating, rather because the system destroys those who receive it and corrupts those who dispense it."[11]

National standards for welfare payments represented a short-term response to a presidential memorandum that seemed to imply that massive cuts were in order. Advocating national standards "was the most I could do," Moynihan said, and in the following weeks he pressed the proposal in memos to the president. Moynihan's entreaties apparently carried the day. The president directed the UAC welfare subcommittee to take up the proposal for national minimum standards despite the objections of Arthur Burns, who thought the plan too costly.

During the weeks that the welfare subcommittee considered the national standards proposals, Moynihan fed the president a steady stream of memos that provided information about welfare and invariably concluded with a comment such as, "With every day I am more convinced that a national welfare standard is necessary." The memos helped to turn the president's focus away from slashing welfare programs and toward finding the best means for making the system more equitable.

The initial proposal to set national standards for welfare payments was turned over to Worth Bateman, a staff economist in HEW, for analysis. Bateman concluded that although national standards were a step in the right direction, the task force proposal would provide additional incentives for families to break up. If benefits for female-headed households were raised, there would be greater incentive for men to desert their families. What was needed was a proposal that would broaden the scope of assistance to include more of the poor.

Bateman's analysis was of great interest to the council and particularly to HEW undersecretary Jack Veneman. Since the council had been asked by the president to come up with a national standards approach, Veneman was eager to find a way to combine the president's wishes and Bateman's memo, and he asked Bateman to chair a working committee to formulate such a plan. The Bateman task force developed a proposal for a negative income tax with a base payment of $1500, which would provide relief to the working poor and eliminate the costly Aid to Families with Dependent Children program. Ultimately the plan would include a work training program and the food stamps program. The task force took the proposal to Secretary Finch, who expressed concern about the political consequences of giving an additional six million people some government assistance but nevertheless approved the proposal and agreed to have it presented to the UAC welfare subcommittee on March 24, 1969.

Moynihan had little to do with developing the technical features of the welfare reform program, and he was overjoyed when he learned what the Bateman task force was doing. His role was that of advocate rather than policy formulator; he would have to make sure that Richard Nixon bought the final proposal.

When the subcommittee met on March 24, Moynihan took the offensive. "I want to say this is a great, historic plan," he said. "I think we should go to the president with it immediately."

Burns's chief deputy, Martin Anderson, contended that the plan was too expensive and would become a political liability. He saw the program as nothing more than a guaranteed annual income. "I believe in calling a spade a spade," Anderson said.

Moynihan responded, "I agree with Oscar Wilde. Anyone who insists on calling a spade a spade should be forced to use one."[12] The meeting concluded without resolution; the subcommittee adjourned without even proposing that the plan, now called the Family Security System, be forwarded to the full Cabinet for discussion.

Finch himself resolved to take the plan to the president but became ill and left the task to Moynihan. In a memo of March 26, 1969, Moynihan argued that the FSS *"will abolish poverty for dependent children and the working poor."* He stressed that by adopting the plan Nixon could "assert with full validity that it was under your Presidency that poverty was abolished in America."[13] Moynihan was amazed at what appeared to be the very real possibility of the president's approving this plan. Only three months earlier he had been thrilled that the subject of national standards had merely been put on the agenda, and now the president was actually considering a proposal that would radically overhaul the entire system.

Moynihan, Burns, and Finch went to Key Biscayne over the Easter weekend to present the FSS plan to the president. Nixon heard the proposal from Finch and Moynihan, listened to Burns's objection, and reached no decision. This was a victory for Finch and Moynihan to the extent that the president had passed over a chance to kill the program. Following the Key Biscayne meeting, Moynihan acted as though the president had accepted the proposal; thus Moynihan now had to develop a means of presenting it. The presidential message on domestic affairs that was sent to Congress in mid April called for a complete overhaul of the welfare program, thereby giving some support to Moynihan's optimistic interpretation of what had transpired. Meanwhile, John Ehrlichman told Moynihan shortly after the Key Biscayne meeting that the president was sympathetic to his proposal.

Knowing that the president was sympathetic, Moynihan urged him to make the plan public as soon as possible. For the longer it was delayed, the greater the chance was that it would be blocked—and that was precisely what Arthur Burns tried to do. He now came down in favor of the national standards proposal, and his deputy Martin Anderson wrote a paper for the president on the history of England's experience with the Family Security System in the Speenhamland program of the eighteenth century. Relying on advice from his old friend, Professor J. H. Plumb of Cambridge University, whom he hastily telephoned for assistance, Moynihan refuted Anderson's version of the alleged failure of the English income supplement program. But a subsequent Burns memo that attacked the FSS program and advocated national standards along with a work requirement created the deadlock that Moynihan had feared.

To try to resolve the situation, an ad hoc group of Cabinet members who were on the UAC, Secretary of the Treasury David Kennedy, and assorted staff members convened one Saturday late in April to consider the FSS proposal. The meeting failed to achieve consensus and only produced more discussion and further policy papers. One of the papers, by Paul McCracken, chairman of the Council of Economic Advisers, which urged acceptance of the Burns plan and called for an interagency task force to study FSS in greater detail, seemed to be having some impact in the White House.

This angered Moynihan. In May he had arranged for Mayor John Lindsay and other New York City officials to meet with the UAC in Washington. In addition, he and aide John Price had gone to New York to obtain endorsements of the plan from Cardinal Cooke, David Rockefeller, and William Buckley. They had returned to Washington with a letter from the cardinal to Moynihan that endorsed FSS because of its commitment to strengthening family life. Now, with the appearance of the McCracken memo, it was possible that all Moynihan's work would be for naught.

Early in June Moynihan sent Nixon a memo that argued that the technical questions were secondary to whether he could provide the political leadership to "dominate and direct [the] social transformation" that welfare reform would bring. President Johnson's commission on income maintenance would be reporting a plan similar to FSS, and it was important that Nixon realize that the Democratic congress would seek to use that proposal instead of his own as a basis for its discussions of welfare reform. If Nixon released FSS quickly, welfare reform would become "his" issue; FSS would be a "genuinely new, unmistakably Nixon, unmistakably needed program which would attract the attention of the world, far less the United States." Appealing to the president's political instincts, Moynihan pointed out that passage of FSS would give the administration a "solid, unprecedented accomplishment in a vital area of social policy" for the 1972 election. If the proposal were not passed, "in four years time you really won't have a single distinctive Nixon program to show for it all." The memo clearly removed Moynihan from the realm of impartial policy arbiter; he was marshaling every possible argument he could in favor of the proposal—at the risk of being embarrassed politically if the president rejected his proposal.[14]

Why did Moynihan risk his credibility for the negative income proposal? The obvious reason was that he had joined the Nixon administration to obtain passage of just such legislation. The Johnson administration had not listened when he urged the adoption of a family policy, and now he was willing to do almost anything to make sure the Nixon administration adopted the Family Security System—the cornerstone of such a policy. And there was a larger reason. The nation was coming out of a period of turmoil and unrest, and it needed a sign that something could be done to improve social conditions. The best way to respond to the sense of collective inadequacy that was developing in America was to enact a social program that would do much to eliminate poverty. "We have been in a time of deep trouble. The issue has been confidence in ourselves, in our competence, and perhaps most of all in our goodness. We need to show ourselves what we can do. We need a success."[15]

While Moynihan played a critical role in keeping the president's mind on the FSS proposal, a memorandum from Secretary of Labor George Shultz played a decisive role in committing the administration to it. Early in May the president had asked Shultz to try to resolve the impasse between Moynihan and Burns. Shultz's study accepted the FSS proposal for a payment of $1500 but ignored the first $20 of income in the calculation of benefit levels. The $20 added about $1 billion a year to the cost of the proposal, but it would give poor people an incentive to work while receiving assistance. The Shultz proposal allowed Nixon an alternative to choosing between the Finch-Moynihan and Burns proposals. As a palliative to Burns, Nixon adopted his proposal for mandatory work requirements. Then he asked John Ehrlichman to prepare the congressional message in support of the plan—but he did not tell Burns of his decision to adopt the Shultz proposal, and he cautioned Ehrlichman to keep his work secret.

Meanwhile, Burns, along with Paul McCracken, David Kennedy, and Budget Bureau head Robert Mayo, worked furiously to block the proposal and managed to stave off an imminent announcement of the program in mid July. Instead of introducing a proposal, Moynihan announced on July 14 that the president would present "a total change in the welfare system" before the August congressional recess. He referred carefully to the Shultz plan as a compromise between his proposal and that of Arthur Burns, realizing all the while that the Shultz proposal was much closer to his approach than to that of Burns.[16] Ehrlichman pressed the plan while walking with the president in Rumania during the world tour that followed Neil Armstrong's walk on the moon, and ultimately he convinced Nixon to approve it. It was decided that the proposal would be announced August 8 on national television. All that remained was to determine the precise benefit levels. After a good deal of haggling a

$1600 minimum for a family of four was adopted, the first $720 of income to be excluded in computing benefits.

Moynihan would not be convinced that the president would support the program until it had actually been announced.

> For weeks I lived . . . as a person not that certain about his position. I felt like a very young poker player who has the winning hand, but nobody knows it. But he doesn't know enough about poker to know for sure that he has the winning hand. So many persons were acting like I didn't have the winning hand! It could be because I didn't—and it could be because they didn't know that I had it.[17]

His suspicions were well founded. Four days before the scheduled announcement Vice President Spiro Agnew sent the president a memo strongly opposing FSS and endorsing the Burns proposal for national standards. Agnew argued that the plan would not be politically popular and that it would encourage less—rather than more—scrutiny of welfare recipients. Liberals would call it inadequate, and low income groups would not swing to the Republican party over the issue. Worse, the working poor who were just above the assistance level would feel resentment at their exclusion from the plan. Agnew pressed his objections at a Cabinet meeting two days later, and George Romney and Arthur Burns supported his position. But the president stood firm.

Moynihan was relieved. On the helicopter flight to Camp David, Moynihan had seemed distant and aloof to the point where Jerome Rosow, an assistant secretary of labor who had helped to draft the final version of the plan, wondered whether Moynihan really cared about it. But Moynihan's seeming distance only masked his apprehension. "Moynihan was really uptight," Robert Finch recalls. "Three or four times he came to me at Camp David and said, 'You really think he's going to go through with it?' "[18]

On the night of August 8 the president announced to the nation that he had decided to adopt a Family Assistance Program. Knowing that he had to convince the nation and the Congress that this innovative program was in reality conservative, he underestimated the amount of money that would go to each poor family and maintained, somewhat disingenuously that his proposal did not amount to a guaranteed annual income. The figure given as the base payment ($1600) understated the

benefits that each family would receive when food stamps and incre-
ments for more than two children were included. Nixon said the plan
was not a guaranteed income proposal because of the work requirement,
but most Washington commentators believed that this stipulation had
been included only to make the plan more palatable politically. While
it was an expensive program—estimates of the cost ran to $4 billion in
the first year alone—Nixon tried to justify it on the ground that it would
save money in the long run.

Nixon's approach was apparently successful. The Gallup poll showed
that the country favored the plan by a margin of more than three to one.
Major newspapers editorialized in favor of it, and White House mail was
positive, twenty to one. Yet the president needed to be reassured. He
called Moynihan from San Clemente to ask if the American people
approved the proposal. "Like it," Moynihan replied, "why there are
more telegrams coming in than at any time since Johnson announced
he was quitting." Nevertheless Moynihan tried to brace the president
for the criticism he knew would come. "Enjoy it while you can, Mr.
President. The criticism will soon start."[19]

Moynihan knew the president faced criticism from both the left and
the right, for he had just appeared on *Meet the Press,* where reporters
had raised many of the objections that liberals and conservatives would
voice over the next two years.[20] Ron Nessen of NBC-TV had complained that the benefits were too low and argued that the plan dis-
criminated in favor of the South without giving fiscal relief to northern
states with assistance programs that provided more money than FAP
budgeted. Thomas Johnson of the *New York Times* echoed a complaint
that conservatives would raise: Did the administration have the money
to pay for this program and other urban aid programs as well? Don
Oberdorfer of the Washington *Post* raised another conservative objection: it seemed to him that by offering some assistance to 22 million
Americans the government was actually adding people to the welfare
rolls in its effort to end their dependency.

Moynihan answered the objections. He explained that benefits would
in fact amount to more than $1600 a year for the vast majority of families
qualifying for assistance. He pointed out that even the most generous
states, such as New York, would receive at least 10 percent relief of its
welfare burden. And he said that America could afford the program.

"We are not a poor country. Our gross national product increases at a billion dollars a week. We can do what it takes to end poverty."[21] The assistance offered to the working poor was *not* "welfare." It was payments made in recognition of the fact that there were millions of families in America that did not have enough money to make ends meet even though the husband was gainfully employed.

Over the next year and a half Moynihan would answer many of the same questions—and some new ones—time and time again before House and Senate committees and in meetings with various interest group representatives and state legislatures. Moynihan had won a significant battle in getting Nixon to propose the legislation, but the struggle to win congressional approval had only begun.

In the summer of 1969 Pat Moynihan celebrated the twenty-fifth anniversary of his entry into the navy by hosting a reunion of his old Middlebury friends. Story Zartman, Joe Reisler, Angus Deming, and Peter Vogt joined Moynihan at the Army & Navy Club for an evening of drinking and reviewing old photographs. When everyone was thoroughly drunk, Moynihan suggested that they go on a White House tour. He then led his increasingly rowdy friends around the White House grounds, where they had a view of President Nixon at work alone in his study.

Inside the White House the touring visitors heard footsteps and looked around to see Nixon approaching with a notebook and H. G. Wells's *Outline of History* in hand. When Moynihan saw the president, he stood drunkenly at attention. "Mr. President, these are some old navy friends of mine, and we have been drinking."

"Well, Pat, navy men will do that sometimes," Nixon replied.

"Furthermore, Mr. President," Moynihan added, "they are all loyal to you."

"Glad to hear that, Pat," the president said as he walked on, smiling ever so slightly.

Moynihan's personal stature within the White House remained high. After FAP had been announced Nixon left it to Moynihan to reveal that a government study had shown that the ending of the Vietnam War would not free additional revenue for new social programs. (Any additional revenue that was made available by the ending of the war would go to support existing social programs.) This was an unpopular announcement to have to make, and Moynihan made it only after a long meeting of the UAC. The peace dividend, Moynihan said, "tends to become evanescent like the morning clouds around San Clemente."[22] Almost immediately Moynihan's foes in the administration rose to the attack. Arthur Burns, as though drawn to oppose anything Moynihan said, told the National Governors Conference that there would be an $8 billion peace dividend.

The controversy over the peace dividend ultimately drew attention to the policy differences within the White House and strengthened the president's resolve to develop a smoother policy-making apparatus. Yet he continued to give Moynihan important responsibilities. He named him to head a delegation to a NATO Conference on the Challenges of Modern Society that, it was hoped, would develop coordinated strategies for attacking the problems of the environment. By late 1969 it seemed that Nixon distinguished between Moynihan the person—whom he had come to like and trust—and Moynihan the administrator—who was poorly organized.

In October the administration began moving toward a reorganization of the White House. Moynihan had been quoted as saying that "the White House is structured to produce conflict. The President wants it that way."[23] But this was almost certainly not the case. Burns had been named chairman of the Federal Reserve Board effective in late January 1970, and reports began to circulate that Moynihan would get his post. The threat to Moynihan's influence was now John Ehrlichman, who since developing the compromise on welfare reform had been coordinating domestic policy making. Ehrlichman had proved to be an able administrator, and the president found him easier to deal with than the free-floating Moynihan. Moynihan's strong suit was ideas, not organization; Ehrlichman's was precisely the opposite.

To make the domestic policy-making apparatus more effective, the president gave John Ehrlichman control over the entire area, placing the Urban Affairs Council under his jurisdiction. Moynihan was effectively kicked upstairs to the rank of counselor, and the UAC was virtually stripped of its staff. Moynihan aide John Price was named the body's titular head, but it was clear that the UAC would have little or no influence. John Ehrlichman's Domestic Council would now have the influence that Kissinger's National Security Council had in foreign policy. Nixon also made congressional liaison Bryce Harlow a counselor to the president.

There are a number of possible explanations of Nixon's reorganization. First, he had been disturbed by the conflict that had developed over the formulation of the Family Assistance Program, and Ehrlichman could be expected to make policy making more bureaucratic and to perform in a low key. Second, Moynihan's UAC had been effective in the early days of the administration in developing policy innovations such as welfare reform and Burns's revenue-sharing proposal, but now Nixon sought a more broadly based body that would encompass all domestic policy and be responsible for the implementation of policy already formulated.[24] The reorganization indicated that Nixon considered that the bulk of the innovation for his first term was over and that it was time now to put the new programs into effect. Finally, the reorganization was testament to the growing influence of H. R. Haldeman and John Ehrlichman in the White House power structure, for Haldeman had pushed Ehrlichman's appointment.

There was speculation that Moynihan's influence would not diminish because his impact derived from his personality and ideas rather than from the UAC. Yet the reorganization deprived him of important staff support and in effect left him on his own. Even though he now had Cabinet rank, the reorganization was a defeat.

Moynihan accepted the changes calmly. He had not engaged in White House staff infighting to a great degree in the preceding ten months, except as it related to the fight with Arthur Burns over welfare reform (and most of their arguments had concerned policy rather than personality). Moynihan and Ehrlichman, although they were very different individuals, did not have strong personal differences. After all, Ehrlichman had supported FAP at a crucial moment, and he was seen as a person without distinct views on domestic policy. "At that point John Ehrlichman wanted to prove that the Nixon administration had the capacity to do good," Moynihan says now. Ehrlichman was willing, if not eager, to support family assistance. Yet Moynihan had realized early on that "my half life will last only until Ehrlichman discovers the Bureau of the Budget and Haldeman produces a telephone directory."

Doubts about Moynihan's loyalty and some distrust of his staff had lingered. Many administration officials, like Peter Flanagan, did not like the way Moynihan's young, sometimes brash staff operated. (They were thought to be too liberal and brazen for the staid Nixon White House.) As a way of softening the blow, the word went around that Moynihan's staff, not Moynihan, had necessitated the reorganization. And to smooth the transition Ehrlichman offered all the Moynihan people positions on the reconstituted domestic council, even though many of those people were distrusted. Moynihan, who had agreed to serve in the administration for a maximum of two years, resolved to do his best and expressed dissatisfaction to no one. In fact Moynihan was so passive that one longtime antagonist of Haldeman and Ehrlichman, Melvin Laird, was angry that Moynihan had not fought harder against their expansionist tendencies.

In his new post Moynihan came to feel isolated. For research help he had to rely on ad hoc contacts with former UAC staff members who stayed on in the White House. One such staff member, Checker Finn, found himself in the uncomfortable position of drafting educational memos for Ehrlichman as part of his new job and then drafting responses for Moynihan late in the afternoon, on his own time. Moynihan's goal was to remain in the White House until Congress passed the Family Assistance Program; after that his job would be finished. Moynihan had developed a good relationship with the president and a few staff members (e.g., Leonard Garment and Raymond Price), but he was not very close to many other members of the administration.

Early in 1969 Moynihan had persuaded the president to hold a year-end conference on food and nutrition and had induced him to appoint Dr. Jean Mayer of Harvard as a special consultant to run it. Both the conference and Dr. Mayer's appointment backfired against Moynihan. During the summer of 1969 Mayer and Moynihan clashed repeatedly over how the conference would be run. Mayer was eager to recruit as broad a range of representatives as possible, and Moynihan wanted to make sure that those invited were not likely to make partisan attacks on the administration. The Harvard nutritionist wanted the administration, in the president's address to the conference, to make a dramatic rhetorical commitment to feeding the poor. Nixon refused. But Mayer succeeded in inviting a diverse constituency to the conference, and it appeared certain that they would be critical of the administration.

In his keynote address to the conference Nixon reviewed the administration's major proposals in the area—welfare reform, food stamp expansion, a population growth commission. The speech was poorly received. The conferees wanted more money than Nixon was willing to give, and they wanted a commitment to emergency aid. The participants spent as much time criticizing the president as they spent discussing hunger. Nixon subsequently met with six delegates from the conference but refused again to declare a national hunger emergency. In the end Moynihan was enraged. He complained about the "dramatics and theatrics of the conference" and called the conferees "ungrateful wretches" for criticizing the administration. But the damage had been done; the conference, held at Moynihan's instigation, had embarrassed the president.[25]

Moynihan had a substantial role in inspiring a White House report on social conditions in America; he presented his national urban policy to a group of mayors in Indianapolis; he played a major part in drafting a presidential message on educational reform that emphasized the need for determining whether the money being spent actually improved educational achievement. Nevertheless it began to appear early in 1970 that Moynihan's influence within the White House was beginning to wane. He has acknowledged that the administration was never willing to consider seriously a national urban policy.[26] The consensus was that Harlow was now more visible and influential than Moynihan.

Moynihan's position was even more severely undercut late in February when someone leaked to the press a confidential memo he had written to the president. The memo concerned the social and economic progress of blacks in America, and—as had happened with his 1965 report on the black family—Moynihan again became the target of vituperative criticism from within the civil rights movement. The most inflammatory section of the memo called upon the administration to adopt a policy of "benign neglect" toward the issue of race. Here Moynihan's point was hardly new. For three or four years he had been arguing that divisive rhetoric from either the right or the left undermined social stability and made progress more difficult. His article in *Commentary* on the 1968 election had made precisely that point. Nevertheless the use of the phrase "benign neglect" predictably upset the civil rights leadership. They had distrusted him on account of the black family report and because he was working for their avowed enemy, Richard Nixon—and now he was saying that their problems should be neglected! As it was pointed out at the Leadership Conference on Civil Rights a few days after the memo was leaked, black gains had been won by "courageous and aggressive action," not by benign neglect.[27] The benign neglect memo lost Moynihan whatever support he may have had in the black community. Social psychologist Kenneth Clark, one of the few black intellectuals to defend Moynihan's black family report (which had been based on much of Clark's own research), now turned against him, believing Moynihan a racist and regretting ever having defended him.

While the expression "benign neglect" was undoubtedly a poor choice of language, the memo was not meant as a rationale for abandoning all attempts to deal with the problems of the poor. Rather, it was intended to persuade the administration to turn away from the kind of confrontational rhetoric that Vice President Agnew had used during his well-publicized speaking tour in 1969. Only one month before the memo was leaked Moynihan had said, "poverty and social isolation of minority groups is the single most urgent problem of American cities today," and the memo was really an attempt to describe the scope of the problem and to outline a strategy for attacking poverty.

In the memo Moynihan acknowledged that black Americans as a whole had made extraordinary progress. Young black families had almost the same incomes as their white counterparts, and while the black unemployment rate was still twice the overall rate, the situation was improving. Yet black teenagers presented a particular problem. Educational achievement had lagged, and the breakup of the black family that Moynihan had written about five years earlier continued. Moynihan did not address these problems in detail; instead he worried about growing social alienation in the black community. It was their unfocused anger, he believed, that led young blacks to engage in antisocial behavior.

With no real evidence I would nonetheless suggest that a great deal of the crime, the fire-setting, the rampant school violence, and other such phenomena in the black community have become quasi-politicized. Hatred, revenge against whites is now an acceptable excuse for doing what might have been done anyway.

Moynihan also worried about the behavior of middle class black youths who demonstrated "virulent anti-white feeling; it would be difficult to overestimate the degree to which young, well-educated blacks detest white America."

The administration should respond to the social alienation in the black community, he proposed, by trying to remove the political element from the situation. Instead of fanning the flames by attacking black extremists, it should focus its attention on programs that would quietly improve the lot of all blacks. Talking about the problem in the language of the militants only made the situation more tense. This was what Moynihan had meant in that undeservedly infamous paragraph.

> The time may have come when the issue of race could benefit from a period of "benign neglect." The subject has been too much talked about. . . . We may need a period in which Negro progress continues and racial rhetoric fades.
>
> [The administration] should avoid situations in which extremists of either race are given opportunities for martyrdom, heroics, histrionics, or whatever.[28]

Moynihan took exception to the work of Attorney General John Mitchell, who had advocated the controversial no-knock legislation and preventive detention (which had angered much of the liberal and black communities). Lawyers, Moynihan wrote, "are not professionally well equipped to do much to prevent crime." He also called for more carefully made studies on crime.

The memo suggested that the administration give increased attention to the more stable elements in the black working class and middle class, who had received little attention so far. Just as Nixon had tried to focus attention on the silent majority in general, he should now turn his attention away from the militants and toward the black silent majority in particular.

When the memo was reported on page one of the *New York Times,* the calls and protests poured into the White House. Press Secretary Ron Ziegler was besieged with so many questions that he brought Moynihan before the White House press corps to explain himself. Moynihan told the press that he had two purposes in writing the memo: to inform the president of the gains that blacks had made and to offer a strategy for consolidating those gains. He was asked if he thought Vice President Agnew's recent criticism of "kooks and demagogues and social misfits who ought to be brought in with butterfly nets" was an example of the sort of language Moynihan wanted to discourage. Avoiding a direct answer, Moynihan replied, "I think the reference was to Harvard students, and I have ambiguous and complex and evasive views on them, too."[29]

The memo was criticized by civil rights activists, columnists, and editorial writers on several grounds. Some took issue with Moynihan's assertion that there had been extraordinary black progress within the last decade. Others argued that by talking in terms of a strategy of benign neglect, Moynihan might establish the neglect of legitimate black needs as a working principle: conservatives could use the Moynihan memorandum as an excuse for ignoring the problems of the poor. Others argued that the administration had in fact been hostile to the interests of blacks in slowing desegregation, failing to promote voting rights aggressively and doing little to achieve progress in the area of equal employment and fair housing. Regardless of the validity of the criticisms, the phrase "benign neglect" took on a life of its own, quite independent of the arguments Moynihan advanced. It became a symbol of the administration's alleged hostility to the interests of blacks and further stigmatized Moynihan as a racist.

It was never clear who released the benign neglect memo. It may have been Mitchell, Haldeman, or Ehrlichman. There was speculation that liberals within HEW had leaked it out of fear over its policy implications. Soon after the memo was leaked someone in Washington gave the *New York Times* a copy of Moynihan's pre-inaugural memo to the president, thereby causing further embarrassment. (The memo also said in part, "In a sense he [Johnson] was the first American President to be toppled by a mob. No matter that it was a mob of college professors, millionaires, flower children, and Radcliffe girls.")

Moynihan was now distrusted by both the left and the right. Liberals saw him as a veritable traitor to the cause while conservatives considered him an idiosyncratic, free-spending Democrat who supported a guaranteed annual income. His influence in the White House had waned as conservatives scored victories in slowing the progress of desegregation and advancing southern conservative Supreme Court appointees. And with his loss of credibility in the liberal community, his influence with conservatives in the White House was undermined.

Moynihan's doubts about his remaining long in the administration increased that spring when the president announced that American troops would invade Cambodia. Perhaps a military case could be made for the action, Moynihan believed, but there was no political case whatever for it. Moynihan was uncomfortable in the position of having to defend the action and having to put up with the increasingly strident rhetoric that Agnew and others were using to describe college demonstrators. A member of his UAC staff, Arthur Klebanoff, resigned in protest, and Moynihan made no effort to keep him in the White House. Moynihan told Klebanoff, "Maybe there is someone you should talk to here about this, but I don't know who that is." He advised Klebanoff that if he intended to quit, he should do it quickly.

Surely Moynihan was uncomfortable when a group of six urban experts, among them Charles Haar of the Harvard Law School, Bernard Freiden of MIT, and Lee Rainwater of Harvard, called on him to say that as a matter of conscience they could no longer serve the administration. Moynihan was sympathetic to the group's antiwar message and privately dissociated himself from the administration position on Cambodia. But he became angry when some of those who had attended the meeting went to the press. He telephoned Freiden to complain that the same people who had been silent when Johnson was in the White House were suddenly more principled under President Nixon.

Moynihan was also angry with Henry Kissinger, the national security adviser, who had conceived the Cambodia incursion. Moynihan had sat in the Roosevelt Room in May 1970 while Kissinger briefed the White House staff on the action. "[Kissinger] spoke with sexual excitement. He was going to smash the faces of those son of bitching no good bastards."[30] Moynihan realized that while Kissinger enjoyed talking about his military strategy, the Cambodian incursion would doom such domestic initiatives as the Family Assistance Program. Kissinger's reassurance that the incursion would last for only a short period would not undo the damage.

> I had assumed that my small reputation would turn on the fate of these measures and it was clear they were now doomed. And I knew why. Henry Kissinger's damn fool invasion of Cambodia. And Henry Kissinger looking straight at me over lunch, explained that the Cambodian disturbance would soon be over and it was high time the Administration got itself a domestic policy.[31]

Moynihan concluded that he had to leave the administration. He told the president that he would resign and return to Harvard, but Nixon persuaded him to stay to see the welfare reform legislation through Congress.

The administration's legislation had passed the House in mid April under the stewardship of Wilbur Mills, chairman of the House Ways and Means Committee. Moynihan had carefully cultivated Mills, whom he did not know well prior to the committee's consideration of FAP. Before the Ways and Means Committee had reported out the legislation Mills sent a letter to Moynihan at the White House, addressed "Dear Dan," and asking him to speak at Mills's alma mater, Hendrix College in Arkansas, in April. One day after receiving the letter Moynihan responded that he would be happy to speak at any time during the period Mills had specified, except for the one week he had to be in Brussels for a meeting of the NATO committee on the challenges of modern society. Moynihan was careful to send blind carbon copies of the exchange of letters to Robert Finch and Bryce Harlow.

Now the legislation was before the Senate Finance Committee, and the prospects for its passage were gloomy. The committee chairman, Russell Long of Louisiana, was generally suspicious of people who received welfare and had said of family assistance that "for all the defects of the present system, the mind of man is always capable of devising something worse." The ranking Republican on the committee, John Williams of Delaware, thought himself neglected by the White House and had philosophical objections to the program; he was planning to

retire at the end of 1970 and decided that his final major act would be
to block the welfare reform legislation.

To Moynihan the Senate Finance Committee posed greater problems
than the House Ways and Means Committee. Aside from the attitudes
of Long and Williams there were too many southern Democratic senators on the committee who would be hostile to the legislation because
of the profound impact it would have on their states. The committee's
Republicans were largely from western states that had few major welfare
problems, and they were not likely to become forceful advocates of the
legislation. Worst of all, Long viewed the legislation as welfare reform
rather than a provision for a guaranteed annual income. Taking the
administration at its word, Long focused attention on abuses in the
present welfare system and viewed FAP in terms of how it would change
that system—instead of seeing it simply as a new program that would
put a floor under the income of every American. It could be shown that
under FAP there were disincentives to work, and findings such as this
doomed the bill. The legislation would not eliminate the abuses in the
present system, and for this the legislation would not pass the Senate
Finance Committee.

Moynihan acted as a sort of public and private lobbyist, speaking in
favor of FAP before organized groups such as the American Newspaper
Publishers Association and lunching with key Democratic senators like
Connecticut's Abraham Ribicoff, who had proposed a number of
amendments to the bill. Moynihan tried to work out an agreement with
Ribicoff, but this proved to be impossible.

Early in May 1970 the administration suffered a defeat when the
committee sent the bill back to the administration for major reconstruction, to include a determination of how existing family programs would
be integrated with FAP. The legislation was revised, but to no avail.
Conservatives now complained that under the revised plan work incentives were inadequate, and liberals protested that coverage was not broad
enough. On July 1 the committee still had taken no action on the
legislation, and Moynihan publicly called on it to report the legislation
out. In a speech before a group of businessmen Moynihan said that if
Congress did not pass the Family Assistance Program, "I do not see how
we will get it in this decade." "A dance of death has commenced,"

Moynihan continued, "our chance is slipping away." The success or failure of the legislation will do much to determine "the fate of the United States in the decade ahead, and probably even beyond that."[32]

Administration sources were saying privately that there was less than a 50 percent chance that the bill would pass by the end of the year. During the summer Nixon met with Republican members of the committee in an effort to obtain favorable action. In late August he agreed to accept an amendment by Ribicoff that called for a year's test of FAP before it went into effect. Time was running out, and many who were involved in the FAP effort believed that the president's commitment had begun to falter.

Moynihan tried to remain optimistic. He predicted in mid October that the legislation had enough support to pass the Senate, but he was almost certainly overstating the case.[33] The congressional election campaign, replete with Agnew's harsh attacks on radical liberals, dampened the political climate and made cooperation with the liberal Democrats more difficult. The administration's conservative posture made it appear that it opposed welfare reform. As the 1970 election returns came in, it could be seen that Republicans who had supported FAP had suffered. The administration tried again to win passage of the bill following the election, but the Senate Finance Committee failed to report out the legislation. A last-ditch effort to attach the measure to social security amendments failed to win Senate support; Senator Long had pilot FAP projects stricken from the legislation. For the 91st Congress, welfare reform had failed.

By the time FAP died in the Senate Finance Committee, Moynihan had decided to leave Washington. His influence had fallen to the point where his choice of former UAC staffer Richard Blumenthal as head of VISTA (the choice of presidential counsel Donald Rumsfeld as well), was blocked by conservative elements in the administration led by Bryce Harlow. Yet Moynihan's personal relationship with the president remained strong. In fact Nixon had asked him to replace Charles Yost as ambassador to the United Nations. While some of his training had been in international relations, Moynihan had done little in the area until his service in 1969–70 as American representative to the NATO Conference on the Challenges of Modern Society. But the idea appealed to him. He had spent enough time in Cambridge over the past two years to know that many Harvard liberals were not especially pleased with his having served Richard Nixon, and he was not eager to have to defend himself and the administration's record at every turn. He would have to surrender his tenure to take the post, but he was willing to make the sacrifice. The decision was reached in the fall, and the president decided to withhold the announcement until the end of the year.

In Cambridge Moynihan let it slip out that he had been offered the post. On November 20, in a copyrighted article in the Boston *Globe,* Charles Whipple reported that Moynihan had been offered the position. The news was a shock to Yost, who had not been told. The appointment disturbed the foreign service, where there was a sense that Moynihan did not have the requisite experience in foreign affairs. On November 25 the *New York Times* suggested that while Moynihan "has outstanding qualities in public life . . . he is simply not qualified for this job."[34]

Moynihan was upset that he had been the unwitting source of the *Globe* report, his wife was unhappy at the prospect of returning to New York, and both were annoyed at the criticism that had been directed at him. Moynihan decided that he would not go to the United Nations. He wrote Nixon that he would return to Harvard, and he cited family pressure and Yost's embarrassment as reasons for his decision.

Now Moynihan had only to make his valedictory speech to the president and Cabinet. Addressing the Cabinet just before Christmas, Moynihan offered an evaluation of the president's performance to date, the performance of his administration, and the response that that performance had won. Moynihan gave Nixon credit for having done much to heal the wounds of the 1960s—winding down the war in Asia and ending racial polarization and social unrest. All in all, it was "a record of some good fortune and much genuine achievement." Moynihan also had high praise for Nixon personally.

> To have seen him late into the night and through the night and into the morning, struggling with the most awful complexities, the most demanding and irresolvable conflicts, doing so because he cared, trying to comprehend what is right, and trying to make other men see it, above all, caring, working, hoping for this country that he has made greater already and which he will make greater still.[35]

Yet "depressing, even frightening things are being said about this Administration." In part this was due to the fact that mistrust of the Johnson administration had weakened the credibility of government in general. Disapproval of government actions became distrust of government. With their habit of reducing complex problems to simple moral issues, Americans had made it more difficult for policy makers to think honestly and seriously about their problems. The result was that "a set of myths and counter myths about ourselves and the world . . . create expectations which cannot be satisfied, and which lead to a rhetoric of crisis and conflict that constantly, in effect, declares the government in power disqualified for the serious tasks at hand."[36]

The president had tried to change policy and restructure the government. In foreign affairs he had asserted the limits of American power and attempted to defuse outdated Cold War patterns. Domestically he had sought to reorganize the government and fulfill commitments to the poor through new policy innovations. His achievements had been "considerable, even remarkable."

Yet it was difficult for the president to discuss such problems in complex terms because of the moralistic propensities of the populace. "Moralism drives out thought," Moynihan said. It was hard for the administration to avoid the tendency to act as though it were "lurching from crisis to crisis"—thereby undermining the policy initiatives the president advocated. Unfortunately, the moralistic style is effective in election campaigns, and the president could only respond in kind. There was little time in which he could speak for a broad national constituency.

Moynihan's advice to the Cabinet and staff was to avoid the tendency to engage in demagogic rhetoric. That could only damage the goals President Nixon sought. It was important "to resist the temptation to respond in kind to the untruths and half truths that begin to fill the air." The "essence of tyranny was the denial of complexity. . . . What we need are great complexifiers, men who will not only seek to understand what it is they are about, but who will also dare to share that understanding with those for whom they act."[37]

Moynihan obviously had in mind the tough-talking Spiro Agnew and those in the administration who counseled the president to take a hard line in general. Not only was their rhetoric destructive, their motives were suspect. Moynihan accused members of the administration of not following through effectively enough in implementing the president's proposals. Members of the administration must "be far more attentive to what it is the President has said and proposed. Time and again, the President has said things of startling insight, taken positions of great political courage and intellectual daring, only to be greeted with the silence of incomprehension."[38] The president's initial advocacy of policy was often ignored by much of his staff. "Deliberately or not, the impression was allowed to arise with respect to the widest range of Presidential initiatives that the President wasn't really behind them. It was a devastating critique."[39]

The reference to the Family Assistance Program was clear. Commentators had doubted the president's commitment to the legislation because many staff members had publicly and privately expressed skepticism toward it. Senators who began to believe that the administration was not fully committed to the program would feel no compulsion to support it. The implication was obvious: had the administration supported the legislation more strongly, it might have cleared the Senate Finance Committee.

The speech contained a broader message, one that may not have been recognized at the time. This was that Nixon had addressed himself forthrightly to the issues and problems that Moynihan had isolated between 1966 and 1968. Nixon had recognized the inherent limits of American power, had sought to restructure government through such measures as revenue sharing, and had tried to fulfill the nation's commitment to the poor through programs—like FAP—that Moynihan had recommended in one form or another. In a sense Moynihan was trying to demonstrate programmatically that his service had been of value to Richard Nixon.

President Nixon was similarly gracious to Moynihan. Introducing him to the Cabinet, Nixon had said, "Every time we get a little down, every time we need a little inspiration, we're going to want to call him back to give it to us."[40] After Moynihan had left the White House Nixon gave an interview to four White House correspondents, and in the course of it he defended Moynihan's "benign neglect" memorandum.

He got a bad rap on that, Mr. [Howard K.] Smith . . . Dr. Moynihan is
one of the most dedicated men to racial justice and to justice for all people
that I've ever known . . . When he talked about benign neglect, he was
not referring to neglecting black Americans or any Americans. What he
was referring to was not to react to violence, not to react to attacks that
might be made—verbal or other—by minority groups, black Americans
and extremist groups.

But I want to say I'm proud that he was a member of our staff for two
years, and his legacy—and I promised him the day that he left, the day
before Christmas—his legacy was, will be, that we are going to have
welfare reform, and that every family in America with children will have
a minimum income.[41]

If Moynihan was pleased with the way the president treated him on
leaving Washington, he was disappointed with his reception on returning to Cambridge. In keeping with its informal policy of giving no one
special treatment, the faculty made no special effort to welcome Moynihan back. He was annoyed at being assigned cramped office space at 24
Garden Street after having enjoyed more spacious quarters in the White
House, and he complained when he was given only part-time secretarial
service. "Moynihan felt he was being persecuted because he had worked
for Nixon," one faculty colleague said. "This just was not true. He got
the same treatment any returning faculty member would get." Within
a couple of months of his return Moynihan came to feel that the
Kennedy Institute of Politics, set up by the Kennedy family in 1966 as
a bridge between the academic and political worlds, was excluding him
from its major policy decisions. As one who had served in the last three
presidential administrations, and as a tenured professor, Moynihan believed he had a special competence for running the institute programs
—and he was not being consulted. His close friend Professor James Q.
Wilson told him not to worry about the institute; it was primarily for
undergraduates, and senior faculty did not give it much of their time.
Moynihan nevertheless felt neglected.

Moynihan's major concern now was to escape the School of Education, which ranks near the bottom in prestige among the various Harvard
faculties. Moynihan was eager to transfer to the government department, where he could settle in to work in his own field. But changing
faculties is not an easy matter to negotiate, and many in the government

had of the Nixon administration in its first term, which may have explained in part why the press saw itself in an adversary relationship with President Nixon and his administration.

Now that his relations with the administration were limited to an occasional telephone conversation, Moynihan was eager to continue in public service. His opportunity came in the fall of 1971 when he accepted President Nixon's invitation to serve as United States representative to the United Nations Committee on Social, Humanitarian and Cultural Affairs (known as the Third Committee). In this capacity Moynihan began to see how the third world majority and the Soviet Union exercised their influence in what he considered to be a hypocritical fashion. Since 1963 the United Nations had issued a periodic Report on the World Social Situation, and by 1971 its drafters had concluded, according to Moynihan, that "social justice means social stability and that social stability means the absence of social protest." Under this standard the Soviet Union appeared to be doing quite well while America, with its tradition of encouraging the free expression of opinion, came off badly. Moynihan concluded that the third world concurred in this analysis because many of their regimes were totalitarian and did not allow dissent. And since their economies were nominally socialist, they had an interest in criticizing a capitalist society such as the United States. It was a terrible report, Moynihan decided, and he vowed to speak out against it.

Moynihan was further disturbed that he had been the first American to take issue with the report, which had been in the works for three years without American criticism. The American foreign policy establishment had "actively participated in preparing this sustained assault on American institutions." America failed to realize that behind the report lay a distinctive third world ideology that had to be challenged.[46]

Moynihan's speech on the report to the Third Committee at the UN in late October 1971 was an attempt to respond both to the specific inaccuracies in the report and to the critics of American society. After detailing the technical errors of the report and concluding that it contained scarcely a sentence that social scientists could approve, Moynihan pointed out what he considered its larger errors. The authors of the report failed to recognize that there were two types of societies in the world: those that allowed no criticism and those that encouraged criticism. Liberty lives in protest, Moynihan said, and the United States would fear its absence. He was glad that the Soviet Union had pointed to the discord and division in American society; these were signs of the nation's political health. It was fatuous for the Soviets to say they live in political harmony simply because there is no evidence of sustained dissent, for the U.S.S.R. is a totalitarian nation that allows no criticism of the state. Addressing himself to the United Nations, Moynihan recommended that future world situation reports stick to presenting useful statistical information rather than attempt to develop an international definition of social harmony or to agree on what processes impede social change. As it was, the United Nations was "settling into a swamp of untruth and half-truth and vagary."[47]

The speech was Moynihan's first step in developing his "opposition" strategy, which he outlined in March 1975 in an article in *Commentary*. The 1971 speech recognized the need to respond to third world and Soviet attacks, but the speech offered only a bare outline of the critique he would eventually develop. The speech gave the first hint that Moynihan believed the administration had to take a different posture in foreign affairs than it took in domestic affairs. In his communications with the president in 1969 and 1970 Moynihan had stressed the need for issues to be discussed in complex terms. Absolutes were to be avoided, voices were to be lowered, and moral appeals were to be shunned as being counterproductive. But he believed now that the same approach could not be taken in international relations. The nonideological, technocratic approach was perhaps most appropriate for the efficient management of domestic policy, but it was not at this point appropriate in multinational diplomacy. Americans had to be able to abstract from their domestic experience to describe the essence of democracy to the rest of the world, and they were not doing this well. What was more, very few American diplomats or politicians were equipped to engage in the type of sustained ideological debate that became necessary when the fundamental principles on which the American system is based were questioned. "We have a lot of experience about how you run a decent country, surprisingly little experience at describing the process. This is a weakness of our foreign policy and the strength of our democracy."[48]

Moynihan was not really confident that America was prepared to express the spirt of its democracy in an international forum. "I don't think we're very good at ideological argument, " he concluded. The leadership strata had not learned, at their universities or in public service, how to debate the fundamentals of government organization. A facility for such debate would be crucial to America's success internationally, Moynihan had become convinced, even though he deeply hoped that the United Nations would renounce polemics and adopt the more re-strained mode of discourse he thought appropriate in the theatre of American domestic politics. The approach that he recommended to the Nixon administration was the one he wanted the United Nations to adopt.

> What we would like to hope is that we'd have a little less of the symbolic politics of the divided, post-colonial world and a more mature concern with specifics, with agreements, with undertakings. The U.N. should do business, but it should not be in the world business.[49]

In the course of events Moynihan concluded that when the United States was under attack and serious discussion was impossible, it should respond in kind. A hostile defensive posture—with all the impediments that it created to the smooth development of multinational cooperation —was necessary when the nation faced a sustained concerted attack by the forces of totalitarianism.

It was not entirely clear that the United States mission to the United Nations was pleased with all that Moynihan said. He had objected to one section of the report that claimed American youths were becoming hippies and addicts in reaction to their sense of powerlessness to change American society after the General Assembly had unanimously approved a resolution that the United Nations deal with the problems that world youth face. At a news conference following the vote a mission spokesman pointedly refused to comment on Moynihan's criticism of the report.[50] This was perhaps the first time the State Department and the mission staff tried to moderate a Moynihan statement. It would not be the last.

Moynihan continued to teach while serving at the United Nations, traveling to New York a day or so each week. He still did not find Cambridge hospitable. His home was on Francis Avenue, a quiet, winding street populated mostly by upper middle class professionals and Harvard professors, but the relative tranquility there did not assure Moynihan that he and his family would be left alone. There was still an active chapter of Students for a Democratic Society at Harvard, and Moynihan feared that he or his family might be harmed in reprisal for his work in the Nixon administration. The antiwar movement was winding down in the spring of 1972, but there were still antiwar demonstrations in the Cambridge-Boston area. Bad enough, Moynihan thought, that the old ROTC building near his house had been turned into a rather desultory day care center, but he could not abide the radical students and "outside agitators" who wanted to "trash" Harvard buildings to protest the university's supposed complicity in the war effort.

One evening in the spring a group of demonstrators left a march that was returning from a rally in Boston and broke into the Center for International Affairs, some two blocks from Moynihan's house. The demonstrators did considerable damage to the center and destroyed the research materials of a number of professors. The action took place while Moynihan was teaching his seminar; afterward he was drawn to the building by the noise of fire engines and police cars. Recognizing a colleague standing before the center, Moynihan rushed up and embraced him emotionally. "They're fascists," he cried turning to survey the damage. Not only radicals were hostile to Moynihan; other members of the Harvard community criticized his service in the Nixon administration, and it became possible to detect a defensive tone in Moynihan's voice as he spoke approvingly of the administration's record on domestic affairs. When challenged, Moynihan would cite the number of schools in the South that had been desegregated and the potential benefits of FAP as evidence of the positive work the administration was doing. Students found it difficult to argue with him in seminars, for he was charming as a discussion leader and often offered them sherry during late afternoon meetings. When someone attempted to criticize the president, Moynihan's face would redden with the forcefulness of his rebuttal. He enjoyed ridiculing liberal and black opponents of FAP, and he seemed almost to take pleasure in telling the story of a black Mississippi state representative who went to Washington to lobby on behalf of legislation for a higher level of benefits but instead gave southern conservatives who opposed Nixon's bill further ammunition to use against the legislation.

Moynihan was eager to know what his students in 1972 thought about the coming presidential election. Early on he had decided to be officially neutral on the ground that as a Democrat who had served in the Nixon administration it would be improper for him to take sides in the campaign. He publicly expressed a preference in the presidential race only when he appeared on *Meet the Press* late in December 1971 and said he would like to see Eugene McCarthy win the Democratic nomination. Otherwise he refused to take sides, though he indicated that he had little sympathy for George McGovern (whom the majority of his students supported).

In interviews given after he left Washington Moynihan maintained that he still considered himself a Kennedy Democrat, yet it is hard to avoid the conclusion that Moynihan wanted Richard Nixon to win in 1972. He steadfastly refused to join Democrats for Nixon, despite the entreaties of his close friend Leonard Garment, but this was entirely a practical political decision. Moynihan did not want to destroy his ties to the Democratic party (he had firmly refused to engage in partisan political activity on behalf of the administration during his two years in Washington). Yet he had powerful reasons for wanting Nixon to be re-elected. Family assistance had not passed, and he hoped that it and other progressive legislation would be introduced during Nixon's second term, thereby justifying the time he had spent in the administration. On the personal level Moynihan genuinely liked Nixon and felt a strong measure of loyalty toward him. Thus Moynihan maintained a deliberately low profile during the campaign, and in the end he voted for Nixon.

Despite the very evident differences between George McGovern and Richard Nixon, Moynihan was struck by the similarities between the positions of the two candidates on domestic policy. According to Moynihan, both parties were emphasizing income redistribution and offering proposals for welfare reform, tax reform, and revenue sharing. The substantial differences between Nixon and McGovern in the levels of redistribution were less important than the fact that their recommendations were headed in the same direction. The thinking on American social policy had changed, Moynihan argued, from the emphasis on the "services strategy" that had predominated in the 1960s to the "income strategy" that he had been advocating for some time. Yet it appeared that both Nixon's and McGovern's proposals were about to be shelved. McGovern's "$1000 plan" had proved to be a major political liability in the California primary, and the FAP legislation was still mired in the Senate Finance Committee, the administration either unwilling or unable to reach a working compromise. Thus Moynihan was trying to keep alive a rapidly fading idea.

For progress to continue, Moynihan believed, Americans would have to realize that things had improved; to despair over what had not been achieved would be destructive. Americans would have to recognize what government could do and what it could not do. The issue was not one of spending more money but of spending it more wisely—on programs such as family assistance. Finally, Americans had to understand that the private sector played a strong positive role in American society through helping to reinforce its stability. Private enterprise had to be allowed to grow without being overwhelmed by the public sector. Moynihan outlined his view of the presidential election and the issues involved in a special Fourth of July column in *Newsweek*. A fair reading of the article suggests that his views placed him much closer to the positions taken by Republicans in 1972 than to those taken by the Democrats.[51]

If Moynihan showed any partiality in 1972, it appeared in his article for *Life* early in September, a sympathetic view of how Nixon viewed his second term through Moynihan's eyes. Such an article could only be seen as an implicit endorsement of Nixon's candidacy, and an examination of Moynihan's language reveals his obviously warm feelings for Nixon and his goals.

Moynihan began by noting that a central feature of the administration had been the president's "steadfastness of purpose," which led him to develop a "well conceived order of priorities" that would probably continue throughout the next four years. He proceeded to outline Nixon's vision of world peace: an end to the war in Vietnam, continued progress in arms limitation, and a further relaxation of tensions with the Soviet Union and China. To accomplish this America had to remain strong, retaining both its military might and its self-respect. In the domestic sphere Moynihan indicated that Nixon believed he had only begun to institute fundamental changes such as welfare reform and revenue sharing. Such efforts would continue, as would efforts to break down prejudice against disadvantaged minorities—while racial quota systems would be resisted.

Nixon's domestic and foreign policy plans were part of a larger goal: to build a new coalition "around the grand mosaic of concerns which he feels a majority of Americans share with regard to the future of the nation and the world." His new coalition would be based not on fear but on hope. Its unifying principle would be "the need for civility in working out ways to approach the great goals of the society. To his thinking, the question of how we are to conduct a rational debate about the issues that divide us has become at least as important as the issues themselves." With purposeful action, Nixon believed, a "Stevensonian" concept of civility was achievable as an alternative to apathy or aimless destruction.[52]

The article was well written, and it touched on most of the major themes of the election campaign: America's role in the world, Nixon's hopes for a new majority, and topical domestic issues. A number of liberals, including a Harvard colleague, Martin Kilson, complained in subsequent letters that Moynihan's article was nothing more than campaign propaganda; for undecided voters the article no doubt provided a sympathetic and appealing picture of the president's views. In response Moynihan said that he merely acted as a reporter, conveying what the president had told him. Yet Moynihan had skillfully used Nixon's comments as a means of focusing his *own* view of the second term, and in that way the article did more than present the president in a favorable light. It gave administration officials a coherent statement of strategy for the new term that was closely based on what the president had said and done. The article, if an apology for a candidate, was also a blueprint for use after election day.

Another Moynihan pre-election article in praise of the administration's achievements appeared in the *New York Times*. President Nixon had worked to develop coherent policy so as to make things better, and the result was proof that the "political system [could] respond to new and sudden demands. Revenue sharing was a major event and the Administration's proposals for income redistribution went to the heart of the matter." Just as the term was ending its efforts had "brought forth a spurt of energy and cooperation that was beginning to show some pay-off." Again the article reflected well on the president. Appearing less than two months before the election, it must have had a positive effect on the president's standing with predominantly liberal *Times* readers.[53]

Such was the extent of Moynihan's role in the 1972 presidential election. For the first time since 1956, Moynihan had not been actively involved in a national campaign. While he sensed that the "benign neglect" memorandum had reduced his usefulness in government to a low point, his work at the United Nations had rekindled his interest in foreign affairs—an interest that had largely lain dormant since his time at the London School of Economics in the early 1950s. As the election approached, Moynihan sensed that his opportunity to return to government service was in that avenue.

9

A Retreat to India

I left India in silence. But I was on to something and I knew it. I
was sure [Mrs. Gandhi] would do what she indeed did do, and had
come to think it was possibly necessary to speak about the threat
to democracy and freedom in the world in newer and bolder terms.
—Pat Moynihan, 1978

Moynihan's *Life* article, a sympathetic view of Nixon's plans for his
second term that reached a wide audience, can best be seen as Moynihan's "tilt" to Nixon. It could only have reinforced the president's warm
feelings for his former urban policy adviser, and in the wake of his
overwhelming victory Nixon sought to bring Moynihan back into the
government, hoping to use his talents in the area of foreign affairs.

In December 1971 Moynihan had argued with Nixon about his decision to support Pakistan in its war with India. It was one of the few times
that Moynihan had called Nixon to discuss a foreign policy decision, and
he had told the president that he believed the United States was on the
wrong side. The Bengalis were going to win, Moynihan said; it was
wrong for us to be siding with Pakistan in its effort to block the creation
of what would later become Bangladesh. The United States, he com-

plained, always appeared to be in the position of crushing national liberation movements. Apparently the conversation had had an impact on Nixon. Moynihan believes it was this advocacy of the Indian position that led Nixon to appoint him ambassador to India after the 1972 election. In fact during the summer Moynihan had predicted to his wife that Nixon would offer him the assignment if he were re-elected.

The post of ambassador to India had often been filled by a leading American intellectual (John Kenneth Galbraith, Chester Bowles), and Moynihan fit that mold well. Moreover, he was willing—perhaps eager —to leave America for a short time. The Nixon administration was unpopular in Cambridge, and Moynihan often drew indifference and even scorn from many Harvard faculty members and outright hostility from a small but vocal segment of the undergraduate and graduate communities. The controversy surrounding the "benign neglect" memorandum still haunted him and undermined his credibility on issues concerning the black community. In Washington the consolidation of power by John Ehrlichman and H. R. Haldeman left little room in the White House for a man of Moynihan's temperament, had he been inclined to return there. Liz Moynihan had come to like Cambridge and was not at first eager to disrupt their family life by moving to India, but when she had been persuaded to go, Moynihan told Nixon that he would accept the appointment.

The idea of going to India excited Moynihan. "If I were a physicist, this would be like being sent to Los Alamos," he told a reporter from *Newsweek* when the appointment was announced.[1] It was by no means an easy assignment. Despite the fact that the two countries are the largest democracies in the world, relations between the United States and India had never been entirely harmonious. Indian distrust of America began shortly after independence, when the United States allied itself with Pakistan as a means of countering Soviet influence in South Asia and India interpreted the alliance as a threat to its well-being. India's anxiety increased in the face of the Nixon administration's "tilt" toward Pakistan in the war between the two nations in 1971. American assistance to India during the 1960s had provided needed technological and economic assistance but had also produced something of a backlash, for India was sensitive to the fact that it was becoming increasingly dependent on America. By February 1973, for example, India still owed America 3.3 billion rupees (over $3 billion) for wheat and grain shipments in the 1950s and 1960s. (In fact Moynihan's major task would be to find a means of settling India's enormous debt to the United States in a manner acceptable to both nations.) There was strong sentiment in India for casting off excessive links to foreign nations. And some Indians believed that America of late had been too preoccupied with normalizing relations with China and not concerned enough with building firmer ties with India. India wanted to be treated as an equal by the superpowers and to have supremacy on the subcontinent.

For its part, America had always been suspicious of India's studied neutrality in world politics and its nonaggression and friendship treaties with the Soviet Union. India had traditionally not sought to emphasize the similarity between it and America and had articulated more of a socialist line. Although Moynihan was sympathetic to Indian concern over American military aid to Pakistan (unlike Kissinger, Moynihan shared India's fear that Pakistan could use such aid not only against the Soviet Union but also against India), he was distrustful of Indira Gandhi, the Indian prime minister. Moynihan and State Department officials (Joseph Sisco, for one) sensed that Mrs. Gandhi had a particular hostility to America, that she viewed it as an essentially expansionist and imperialist nation. These feelings made the normalization of relations still more difficult to achieve. It was against this backdrop of mutual tensions, then, that Moynihan prepared to go to India.

India received the appointment favorably. Its ambassador to the United States, L. K. Jha, gave a party for the Moynihans at his Washington home in January 1973. A festive occasion, it was attended by three former ambassadors, John Kenneth Galbraith, Kenneth Keating, and John Sherman Cooper. Nevertheless the Indian ambassador found the opportunity to take a jab at Moynihan and the United States. Alluding to America's covert intervention on behalf of Pakistan in 1971, Jha told Moynihan that it would help if the Americans followed a policy of benign neglect toward the subcontinent. Diplomatically, Moynihan only smiled. Galbraith similarly put Moynihan on the spot by advising him after a toast that ambassadors were at their best when they ignored their instructions from Washington, and he urged the newly appointed

Moynihan to follow this precedent. Keating was surprised by the remark; Cooper smiled knowingly.[2]

At his Senate confirmation hearings Moynihan made it clear that he was not likely to take Galbraith's advice. He was an instructed ambassador who reported to the secretary of state. Recent exchanges of correspondence between Indira Gandhi and President Nixon boded well for relations between the two countries, and Moynihan told the Senate Foreign Relations Committee that those relations were much improved. He expressed concern that India had limited the number of American students who would be allowed into India at one time while the United States maintained a virtual open door policy—yet he did not consider this a major problem. In general Moynihan was optimistic about the prospects for future American-Indian cooperation.[3]

Mrs. Gandhi, however, was not at all satisfied that it was time for improved relations. American involvement in Vietnam had left her angry about United States policy toward South Asia. The day after Moynihan testified before the Senate Foreign Relations Committee Mrs. Gandhi told a gathering in New Delhi that she doubted that the "savage bombing" of Vietnam would have been tolerated had it been Europeans that were being killed. Nor did the Nixon administration's gradual efforts to wind down the war do much to restore confidence in America. In her view the Vietnam ceasefire agreement might lead to continued conflict: "I cannot help feeling that the very manner of ending the Vietnam War may create new tensions." State Department officials were unprepared for the harshness of Mrs. Gandhi's remarks and asked for a clarification. They also released a letter Mrs. Gandhi had sent President Nixon in November 1972 that praised him for de-escalating the war. The State Department then delayed indefinitely Moynihan's departure for New Delhi.[4]

The press in New Delhi reported that Americans had overreacted to Mrs. Gandhi's speech, and Mrs. Gandhi indicated that she had only been trying to assess the situation in Vietnam and had not intended to offend any nation. Yet there was some suspicion in New Delhi that the United States had deliberately overreacted to the speech as a means of undermining relations between the two countries.

The State Department reacted cautiously to events in India. At

Moynihan's swearing in on February 10 the department would not say when Moynihan would leave. Secretary of State William Rogers had struck back at India in his testimony before the House Foreign Affairs Committee by saying that comments such as Mrs. Gandhi's only prolonged the Vietnam War. But efforts were made to minimize the controversy. When Moynihan and Nixon met for the final time before Moynihan took up his assignment, the president denied that the delay in Moynihan's departure had anything to do with Mrs. Gandhi's speech. Moynihan's departure had been held up only for Senate confirmation; he would now take up his post promptly.[5]

India gave the Moynihan appointment great prominence. While the *New York Times* had a small article about his swearing in, the *Times* of India displayed a large photograph of Moynihan on page one.[6] When Moynihan arrived in New Delhi on February 20, his speech emphasizing "the community of interest" between India and the United States also received front-page attention. Moynihan indicated that the two nations' common interests did not necessarily lead to uniform judgments about world affairs; but, he said, frank expressions of different views were the hallmark of free societies.[7]

His arrival occasioned more than page-one coverage in the Indian press. Air India hung a poster above New Delhi's central shopping center that showed its symbol, a cartoon maharajah, kissing a photograph of Moynihan. The inscription said:

> Oh Danny Boy
> You're Irish, Puckish, Controversial, Unorthodox,
> Oh Danny Boy, we're going to love you so.[8]

By far the most impressive event was the formal presentation of Moynihan's credentials to India's President V. V. Giri in Ashoka Hall at the Presidential Palace on February 28, 1973. The event was meticulously planned; the president's secretariat had issued a five-page list of detailed staff instructions on how the ceremony should be conducted, complete with a drawing of the arrangement for the platform where the installation would take place.[9] The ceremonies began at 8:50 A.M. when the chief of protocol, Shri Mahboob Ahmad, in a Mercedes Benz convertible followed by fourteen house cars, a spare car, an escort car, and a police pilot picked up Moynihan at his residence and took him to Ashoka Hall. On his arrival a guard of honor gave the Indian national salute and played the national anthems of both nations. The Indian and American parties then proceeded to the hall, where Moynihan gave a short speech and was received by the president.

In his speech Moynihan tried to draw attention away from the differences between the two nations. "It is a moment of global rapprochement, a time of healing, a time for understanding, a time for sharing," he said, being careful to avoid controversy on what was a purely ceremonial occasion. Nevertheless one remark caused some concern in Indian diplomatic circles. Moynihan referred to the reduced presence of the United States in India, emphasizing that he hoped the quality of the relationship would compensate for the small size of the American community there. To Moynihan the statement seemed innocuous enough, yet some Indian diplomats interpreted it as a response to recent Indian charges that the CIA was taking an active role in Indian affairs. These diplomats understood Moynihan to say that the United States wondered how four hundred people could be a threat to India's security. But for the most part Moynihan's speech was received in the spirit it was intended, and President Giri responded with a standard speech emphasizing that his government also hoped to strengthen ties between the two nations. Following the speeches the diplomats gathered with Moynihan and the Indian president for a group photograph before proceeding to a reception in the palace's Yellow Drawing Room.[10]

The ambassador's residence in New Delhi matched the formality of the installation ceremony. Pat and Liz Moynihan settled in Roosevelt House, the official United States residence, where they were surrounded by a horde of servants that included three bearers, two inside sweepers, two cooks, two laundrymen, assorted drivers, outside sweepers, gardeners, and guards. The house was elegantly decorated (Moynihan would later call it Van Nest Polglase House, after the set designer of the 1930s Fred Astaire-Ginger Rogers movies) and perfectly suited to entertaining, but it was not really adaptable to raising the Moynihan's two teenage children, Maura and John. A relaxed and unassuming Liz Moynihan found it difficult to be comfortable in a "ghastly" house she found inhibiting for normal family life. To make the house as livable as possible, she put a Ping-Pong table in the main reception room and scheduled informal family get-togethers in place of the more rigid morning coffees and afternoon teas. In her own time she pursued research on mogul gardening.

The adjustment to India was difficult for Moynihan for a more compelling reason: the food and water did not agree with him, and he spent much time trying to weather a bad case of Delhi Belly. He had hoped to enjoy well-prepared Indian food, but his cooks persisted in preparing tasteless and unappetizing English food. Like his wife, Moynihan tried to encourage a more relaxed atmosphere at the embassy and in Roosevelt House. He frequently showed movies at home or in the basement of the consulate. A devotee of Gene Kelly and Fred Astaire movies, Moynihan often prefaced the films with five-minute lectures on the various styles of dancing the audience was about to see. His favorite film, *Singin' in the Rain,* was shown on a number of occasions. The guest lists for the movies were never formally organized; on a given evening twenty or twenty-five people would gather in the lobby of his house, and the crowd was usually composed of Indians, Americans, the children's friends, and diplomats. When movies were shown at the consulate, the Moynihans would traipse across the street to the American Club for hamburgers, hot dogs, and beer after the showing.

Moynihan ran a fairly informal embassy; staff members were free to wander in and out of his office almost as they pleased. At the same time he tried to reinvigorate a rather demoralized staff that had suffered a lack of attention from the State Department. (When Moynihan arrived the embassy's principal reputation was for having the best pansy display in town.)

Yet Moynihan was a stickler for dress, and he insisted that his staff wear ties and jackets on virtually all occasions. Moynihan himself would occasionally take out his red-cuffed London School of Economics blazer and wear it with white trousers and white shoes, thereby affecting a traditional British upper class look. On seeing people dressed in open-collar bush suits, Moynihan suggested that they looked as though they were dressed for a "bloody barbecue."

The embassy staff found it difficult at first to adjust to Moynihan's work schedule and his way of doing things. In the morning Moynihan often arrived at about 10 or 10:30, worked for an hour, then received visitors such as local journalists. After a late lunch (and occasionally a swim) Moynihan would nap, then return to the office at around 5 P.M. and work until 8 P.M. In the evening Moynihan sometimes held small discussions with his staff on subjects unrelated to embassy business. The subject might be a public affairs topic or something he had just read in a newspaper.

Initially Moynihan's style confused the foreign service officers and diplomats stationed in New Delhi, and his personal assistant, Chester Finn, who had worked for Moynihan in the White House, came to act as a sort of interpreter between the ambassador and his staff. This, too, created problems. The staff did not like having to learn what the ambassador thought from a young Ph.D. candidate in his late twenties, and they could not always be sure whether Finn was speaking for himself or for Moynihan. In time, as the staff came to know Moynihan's habits better, their relations became more harmonious.

John Yates, the staff director at the embassy, and his administrative assistant, David Schneider, soon realized that Moynihan was careless of security to the extent that he idly took classified documents home and treated any wastebasket as though it were the burn basket. Yates and Schneider quickly decided that if they were to maintain proper security, they would have to clean up after him. But these were minor irritants; Moynihan quickly proved to be a stimulating—if slightly eccentric— ambassador who got to know the staff (most of whom he had to lunch at one time or another) and won people over.

Perhaps the most difficult person for Moynihan to win over was Indira Gandhi, whose hostility to the United States was well known. The Nixon administration's first contact with Mrs. Gandhi had come when she met Secretary of State William Rogers at the United Nations and subjected him to a long tirade about CIA activities in her country. It was with knowledge of this lingering hostility that Moynihan approached her for their initial meeting in mid March 1973. The meeting lasted a relatively brief twenty-five minutes and accomplished little. Moynihan assured Mrs. Gandhi that the United States had decided not to supply India or Pakistan with weapons and confirmed that Pakistan would be getting more armored personnel carriers, parachutes, and some ammunition. He gave her a personal note from President Nixon and chatted briefly about United States policy toward Southeast Asia. For her part, Mrs. Gandhi was pleasant, but she expressed concern about the resumption of military assistance to Pakistan. After the meeting her external affairs minister, Swaran Singh, said the resumption of arms shipments could produce a break in the normalization of U.S.-Indian relations. Moynihan's statement following the meeting glossed over the differences between the two nations. "We hope to begin a relationship of realistic and pragmatic involvement with our governments, based on mutual respect and based on the fact that we are natural friends with no conflicting interests," he said, failing to explain why Pakistan was not a "conflicting interest."[11]

There were those in India who did not share Moynihan's optimism. A week after the meeting with Mrs. Gandhi a group of five hundred Indians demonstrated outside the United States embassy in New Delhi to protest the resumption of arms shipments to Pakistan. The crowd was unruly and the police had to be called in to control the demonstration. Some twenty-five people were injured when the police resorted to using tear gas. A number of the demonstrators carried placards attacking the United States and Moynihan. One read, "Go back to Harvard Moynihan [sic]. Teach Well and Save America."[12]

Moynihan did what he could to allay Indian suspicions about American intentions toward the subcontinent. He met with Swaran Singh and other Indian government officials and assured them that America had no military designs on the subcontinent and would do nothing to disturb the balance of power there. Throughout these meetings Moynihan stressed that he was only acting as a vehicle for the communication of presidential policy. He was deliberately circumspect, made few public comments, and generally adopted what one official called "an aggressively low profile." Moynihan specifically eschewed personal diplomacy, maintaining that his job was to represent only official United States policy.

As much as possible Moynihan tried to turn public discussion of U.S.-Indian relations from military issues to economic questions. In April he told a meeting of the Indo-American Chamber of Commerce that trade was the most important exchange relationship between the United States and India, and he spoke of his hope that there would be continued expansion, with the two nations dealing as equals.[13]

Following his initial round of talks with Indian officials in New Delhi, Moynihan went to Calcutta, where he met with urban planners and the West Bengal Chief Minister Sidhartha Sanker Ray. On this trip he was questioned at an airport about rumors that America planned to give Pakistan a submarine to replace one that India had sunk off its east coast during the 1971 war. Moynihan called the rumors groundless; he said that the United States had not given and would not be giving a submarine to Pakistan. The denial was page-one news in the Indian press, another indication of the seriousness with which India viewed any potential United States involvement in Indo-Pakistani relations.[14]

In his first months in India Moynihan began work on a problem that was a major obstacle to the normalization of relations between the two countries: the settlement of India's debt to the United States for rice and wheat purchased during the 1950s and 1960s. India was slowly paying off the debt, and in the process the United States was acquiring a huge surplus of rupees. Yet the sizable debt had the effect of creating a sense of dependency in the Indians that often turned into resentment against the United States. It was an irritant to bilateral relations, and Moynihan wanted it eliminated as soon as possible.

Other American officials failed to share Moynihan's sense of priority with regard to the settlement of the debt. Many career diplomats did not care to settle the debt because they believed India was ungrateful for the aid it had received; others simply thought it unimportant to even discuss the issue because a resolution satisfactory to both nations was impossible to achieve. Still others, who considered the debt worthy of Moynihan's attention, saw it as an insoluble problem and predicted he would have little success. Nevertheless Moynihan prevailed, and he actively encouraged negotiations with Indian officials to find an agreeable compromise. The United States government was supportive; in fact the State Department had commissioned a study of the rupee debt some years earlier, and the study had concluded that a portion of the debt should be written off. A number of Indian officials went even further, insisting that the entire debt be forgotten because America had tremendous grain surpluses and because they believed food aid should have come in the form of direct grants rather than through sales. There was also some feeling in India that the Watergate affair had drawn attention away from attempts to resolve the rupee debt and that State Department officials Kenneth Rush and Joseph Sisco had not been straightforward in their meetings with Indian officials in April 1973.

If Watergate had distracted Washington from settling the rupee debt, Moynihan was determined to refocus the government's attention. He flew to Washington in June 1973 for consultations with the State and Treasury departments and the Office of Management and Budget and managed to greet Mrs. Gandhi during her stop in upstate New York en route to a state visit to Canada. More important, Moynihan met with Nixon at San Clemente to discuss the rupee debt.

Nixon was then preoccupied with Soviet Premier Leonid Brezhnev's visit and John Dean's testimony before the Senate Watergate Committee. But Moynihan had Kissinger's permission to discuss the issue with the president, and he flew to San Clemente in the hope of getting a few minutes with Nixon. When he spotted Nixon riding across the grounds in a golf cart, he rushed after him, followed him into his office, and secured an appointment. Moynihan, Kissinger, and Nixon agreed that the debt should be resolved quickly—but Moynihan came away concerned about the president, for Nixon's dress was somewhat disheveled, and Moynihan took this as a sign of "internal disorder." Then, with the president's approval for a prompt resolution of the rupee debt, he went to Washington to meet with State Department officials and India's ambassador to the United States, T. N. Kaul, who would supervise his nation's part in the negotiations.[15]

Moynihan returned to New Delhi to begin the talks, and the State Department announced that the ambassador had been instructed to negotiate a compromise. In mid July he met with Mrs. Gandhi and told her that the State Department had agreed to turn over a $3 million complex of buildings and to end the twenty-one-year-old technical assistance program. Moynihan initiated the first formal negotiations in search of a rupee debt settlement by offering to cancel the debt in fifteen years, with some of the money being used to pay United States embassy expenses and to support a series of schools and technical institutions in India and Nepal that American funds had helped to create. Moynihan emphasized that, given his ties in Washington with Kissinger, Rogers,

Secretary of the Treasury George Shultz, and Roy Ash (the head of the Office of Management and Budget), the time was right to reach a settlement. Yet he insisted that America would never consent to the unconditional write-off of the debt that the Indian left sought. At a follow-up meeting with Y. B. Chavan, the Indian finance minister, Moynihan repeated these points and both sides termed the discussions productive.[16]

A snag occurred when the State Department asked Moynihan to try to retain a number of the buildings that he had promised to turn over to India. The cable requested a priority reply, prompting Moynihan to respond that he had expected that the first such concern would be over office space or staff housing and now he was being proven right. Moynihan made it clear he had promised the prime minister he would turn over to her the South Building. "I quite understand that it might appear that we are off our rocker out here, but it comes down to a simple matter of good faith. . . . We might have tried to weasel out but you will need another Ambassador for such work. The United States of America keeps its word."[17]

Moynihan never intended to resign over the issue, but he believed it important that America keep its promises. Thus it was also important for America to relinquish the South Building, which contained Las Vegas slot machines, a Paul Revere cocktail lounge, and a Williamsburg dining room that served authentic American Chinese food. The building was used by a dwindling number of AID people and the Moynihan family, and much of the time the Moynihan family were the only people in the building. "I don't need it," Moynihan cabled, "and so I have gotten rid of it like we agreed to do. Let this sad ending be a lesson to the next U.S. administration tempted by an edifice complex."[18]

Moynihan's cable caused him some embarrassment, but it probably won him considerable goodwill. The Indian press was pleased that he had stood up to the State Department, and the incident gave Moynihan greater credibility in the eyes of some Indian officials with whom he was negotiating the debt settlement. The talks with Indian officials continued throughout the summer of 1973 as Moynihan met periodically with T. N. Kaul. One by-product of the talks was a tentative plan to restructure Indian and American economic ties that would involve small amounts of selective assistance rather than large doses of aid.

Moynihan returned to Washington again at the end of August for consultations with Kissinger. In September William Rogers resigned and Kissinger became secretary of state. Kissinger, who had a high regard for Moynihan, wanted to bring him into the State Department as an assistant secretary for Latin American affairs. When Moynihan declined the post, Kissinger offered him a freewheeling position as counselor in the State Department. Kissinger was so eager to have Moynihan in Washington that he prevailed on Robert McNamara, the head of the World Bank and a former secretary of defense, to talk to him. But Moynihan was eager to return to New Delhi to conclude the rupee debt negotiations and improve Indian-American relations, and he turned down Kissinger's offer.

One of Moynihan's efforts to improve relations between India and the United States involved inviting Edward J. Epstein, Nathan Glazer, and other American friends to address Indian intellectuals on issues in American politics. The exchange of ideas was intended to show India that "we're more than a country that knows how to grow good wheat, a country with a high standard of living, a country that bombs Vietnam. I want them to see that we come from an extremely vigorous and argumentative political world." Moynihan thought the lectures were more worthwhile than concerts and development seminars. "I don't think piano recitals and free economic advice are worth a damn. The success of Indian democracy matters to us. That is a fact of our foreign policy." And the best way to demonstrate that concern was to have a wide-ranging exchange of ideas on the contemporary problems that faced democracies.[19]

Given these feelings, it was no surprise that Moynihan reacted angrily when the Indian government announced in September 1973 that only twenty American scholars would be permitted to study each year in India. Such a move certainly did not encourage a free exchange of ideas. Moynihan was all the more upset because he had urged Nixon to support higher education grants for American students who wanted to attend universities in European and Asian nations that were usually ignored as places for study. India contended that entry was being restricted for all foreign students, not only Americans. The Indian government was particularly sensitive about research on local politics and religion; it contended that foreign scholars were practicing a form of intellectual colonialism.[20]

The Indian decision may have been a temporary setback for U.S.-Indian relations, but it did not impede the rupee debt negotiations, which were drawing to a conclusion. A consensus was reached in September 1973, with the anticipation that the agreement would become effective in February 1974 if ratified by Congress. Final agreement was reached early in December, and the document was signed on December 13, 1973, by Moynihan and India Foreign Minister Chavan. The settlement resulted in the outright cancellation of 2.2 billion rupees in debt and the cancellation of the interest on the remaining 1.1 billion, which was placed in the Reserve Bank of India for use on projects in India and Nepal in which America had an interest. Another 50 million rupees annually were to be made available for the support of the American embassy and related facilities in New Delhi over a ten-year period. India agreed to pay the United States $64 million in hard currency instead of $51 million, as had been provided in the initial purchase agreement for the food. America agreed to buy $100 million in nontraditional goods from India over the next ten years—a move intended to help the Indian export trade—with the stipulation that $25 million would be applied to the Indian debt. Thus, as Moynihan pointed out at a press conference following the signing of the trade agreement, India would get an additional $75 million in hard currency.[21]

The Indian press and Indian Foreign Secretary Kewal Singh gave Moynihan the principal credit for the agreement, recognizing that he had pushed a sometimes reluctant bureaucracy in Washington. American officials in India also gave Moynihan credit for engineering the agreement and applauded his familiarity with the technical economic questions involved.

The agreement still needed approval in Washington, however, and there were fears that congressmen eager to find an issue for the coming election year would attack the agreement as a massive American giveaway plan. So Moynihan went to Washington to sell the proposal on Capitol Hill. Late in January he testified before a House Foreign Affairs subcommittee and defended the agreement to relinquish 2.2 billion rupees in debt. Five of the seven members of the subcommittee were sympathetic, but a liberal Democrat from New York and a conservative Republican from Iowa attacked the settlement. Lester Wolff of New York called it one of the "greatest giveaways America has ever had" and walked out of the hearing. H. R. Gross of Iowa concurred, claiming that all America was getting was "hot air." But the subcommittee chairman, Peter Frelinghuysen of New Jersey, congratulated Moynihan, and his comments probably reflected the opinion of most congressmen. Moynihan had talked with about fifty members of Congress the previous summer, while the agreement was being negotiated, to prepare them for the final settlement. Now he spent another two weeks briefing congressmen and encountering little objection. It was a moving time for Moynihan; the process made a strong impact on him.

> Finally I came before the Senate Foreign Relations Committee and talked to these very serious men. Then Senator Fulbright said to me, "Do you think what you propose is in the best interests of the United States?" and I said, "Yes, sir, I do." I think it was the most solemn moment in my life since I made the same reply at my wedding.[22]

In mid February Moynihan returned to New Delhi triumphant. The agreement was formally signed by Moynihan and Kaul, and the ceremony concluded with the United States ambassador giving his Indian counterpart a check for the two-thirds of the rupee debt that was being written off. It was Moynihan's idea that a check be drawn up for the absurdly large amount of 2.2 billion rupees ($2,046,700,000), and he got a kick out of presenting it to the Indian officials. It may have been the largest single check ever drafted in India.

Scarcely two weeks after the agreement had been signed an anonymous article in the *National Herald,* the newspaper of Mrs. Gandhi's ruling Congress party, sharply attacked Moynihan. Moynihan, the article said, spoke only in platitudes, and in spite of all the American talk about equality the United States still wanted to dominate India. Moynihan was criticized for emphasizing the links between India and America because of their democratic tradition. This was "an old cliché," the article said, and the Indian people should not "be taken in by such platitudes."[23] There was speculation that the article was the result of pressure from the Congress party's left wing, which feared closer U.S.-Indian ties in the wake of the rupee debt agreement.

A second controversy developed one day later, when comments Moynihan had made to a group of Indian journalists "on deep background" (not for publication) were published. He had said that the small island of Diego Garcia in the Indian Ocean was of more importance to the United States for use as a naval base than it was to India. India, Moynihan said, had no fundamental interest in the Indian Ocean. "Why call it the Indian Ocean?" he joked. "One may call it the Madagascar Sea."[24] Publication of the remarks brought furious calls to the American embassy in New Delhi, and the Indian newspapers were filled with criticism of Moynihan. In Parliament Foreign Minister Singh asked, "Who is he to change the name based on the geographical situation? It is no gift of the United States or the ambassador." In response a State Department spokesman, George Vest, refused to comment directly on Moynihan's statement but said that the department had full confidence in him. Another State Department official, Seymour Weiss, told a House Foreign Affairs subcommittee that the Middle East situation made it imperative that the United States maintain a naval presence in the Persian Gulf and the Indian Ocean. Thus the State Department supported what Moynihan said but left him pretty much on his own to fend off his critics.[25]

When it seemed that U.S.-Indian relations were about to take a turn for the worse, Indian officials, worried about food shortages and a weak economy, asked the United States to resume aid to India. In April 1974 Moynihan went to Washington to begin negotiations on an aid package, with both sides wary about the resumption of assistance. Moynihan and the State Department agreed that America could only adopt a policy of "zero net aid" for India, which required full payment for each aid package before additional assistance could be offered. The idea was to end the dependence on foreign assistance that was regarded as a handout by both donor and recipient. India did not want to become dependent on America, and Americans disliked the customary Indian reaction to foreign aid—resentment and anger rather than gratitude. The $75 million aid package that was assembled was tied up in Congress during much of 1974 as a result of skepticism that America would get anything but ill will for its trouble. Ultimately a $300 million food program was put together, and Moynihan announced it just as he was to depart India.[26]

Despite occasional outbursts from left-wing critics, differences over the need for an American military presence in the Indian Ocean, and general suspicions of American intentions, there was some sense in Mrs. Gandhi's government that Moynihan had done a good deal to improve relations. An official government review of foreign policy issued early in 1974 gave Moynihan credit for negotiating the rupee debt accord and called him "a distinguished American and an eminent scholar." Yet the same report noted that while relations with the United States had improved, there were much stronger ties to the Soviet Union which had now "stood the test of time."[27]

India's deep-seated suspicions of American intentions seemed to surface whenever concrete progress was made toward improving relations. Despite Moynihan's efforts to put the nations on a more equal footing there was still a sense in the Indian government that the United States would try to undercut Mrs. Gandhi when it could. In September 1974, for example, Moynihan cabled Kissinger that the recent controversy over CIA activities in Chile had confirmed Mrs. Gandhi's "worst suspicions and genuine fears about American policy toward India." The cable criticized the CIA's secret activities and noted that Moynihan had told Mrs. Gandhi that the United States had not intervened in Chilean affairs. Mrs. Gandhi, Moynihan said, did not believe that America accepted her government, and she was genuinely concerned that the CIA might engineer a coup. Accordingly, Moynihan predicted with prescience, Mrs. Gandhi would develop nuclear weapons and a missile delivery system while advocating nonviolence.[28] Shortly after the cable was released Kissinger told the Senate Foreign Relations Committee that Mrs. Gandhi had been given assurances that no American was authorized to become involved in Indian domestic politics. Kissinger also reaffirmed his personal respect for Moynihan.[29]

Moynihan returned to the United States in September for consultations in preparation for Kissinger's visit to India in late October. He said then that he planned to return to Harvard at the end of the year in order to protect his tenure. Moynihan had grown tired of India; he had

accomplished his major objective—the settlement of the rupee debt—
but diplomatic relations had not improved noticeably. Moynihan and his
wife had been subjected to a number of attacks in the press which he
resented deeply. There was little he could do; America would not pay
enough attention to India, and relations had "regressed" to a suspicious
equilibrium. Although the volatile diplomacy of the past had largely
disappeared, Moynihan was bothered by the pervasive anti-American
attitudes in India, his isolation from Indian scholars and government
officials, the thinness of the economic links with the United States, and
the Indian government's socialist rhetoric, which failed to distinguish
between regimes that supported individual liberties and those that did
not.[30]

Moynihan believed America had made a mistake in the early 1950s
in arming Pakistan in order to create a military ally against Soviet
expansionism; naturally the action had produced fears in India that the
weapons given to Pakistan would be used against it. Now Americans
were preoccupied with China to the exclusion of India and, as Moynihan
put it, "We've gone from the stage where we were overinvolved in India
to where we now pretend it doesn't exist." India was not an underdeveloped country but a poor nation. A country with the third largest
working force of trained scientists and technicians, the tenth largest
GNP, and a nuclear capacity was not underdeveloped. The Indian government had decided to emphasize internal stability over economic
growth, and consequently the economy had suffered. Planned economies
do not work very well, Moynihan suggested, and the introduction of
more free enterprise in India would benefit the nation.[31]

At his final press conference in India he considered voicing his
thoughts about the drift he had seen in Indian politics. Moynihan had
come to believe that Indian democracy was in danger and that Mrs.
Gandhi was turning the country into a more rigid state socialist economy. He was also disturbed at the degree to which India had fallen into
the orbit of the Soviet Union—at a time when Mrs. Gandhi was still
cooperating covertly with the CIA, even while publicly assailing it for
interfering in Indian affairs. In the end Moynihan decided not to speak
out. His comments would inevitably have provoked a response from the
Indian press, and by then Moynihan would have departed. He left India

worried about the changes he had seen—changes trust stirred in him the concerns that he had just described in an article, "The United States in Opposition," prepared for the March 1975 issue of *Commentary*.

On leaving India Moynihan received high praise from all quarters, including those on the Communist left (who admired his cable criticizing CIA activities in Chile). Even Mrs. Gandhi, who had maintained a purely professional relationship with Moynihan, had Pat and Liz to dinner for the first time early in December. Mrs. Gandhi said Moynihan had "made a very genuine effort and did achieve a certain breakthrough." But despite these warm personal feelings Mrs. Gandhi clearly had not been persuaded to accept Moynihan's view of the links between the two countries. "Well, it is obvious that in your admiration there has not been much understanding of India. I don't think democracy comes into it. When you see American friendship with other countries, democracy has not really come into the picture at all."[32]

On a personal level Moynihan had made a good impression. Otherwise he had effected few lasting changes other than the rupee debt settlement. His departure probably raised the greatest hopes in Pakistan, where President Zulfikar Ali Bhutto looked forward to renewed arms shipments to Pakistan.

It was a somewhat gloomy, introspective Moynihan who prepared to return to Harvard—following a short trip to China at Ambassador George Bush's behest—in February 1975. Late in 1973 he had said, "Before I came here I was a professor of government at Harvard. And I would rather be a professor of government at Harvard than anything else. That doesn't mean I don't like India. But when I leave here I'm going back where I came from."[33]

Moynihan was ready for a period of serious research. His desire to return to Harvard was so strong that he turned down a chance to become Librarian of Congress—a post that he feared would consign him to political and intellectual obscurity. In some sense his desire to return to Harvard was motivated by a feeling that his service in the Nixon administration had effectively destroyed his credibility as a public servant—even through he had continued in the president's service as ambassador partly because his association with the administration made life in Cambridge unpleasant at times. He had gone out on a limb in serving in the Nixon administration to begin with, and this had made him suspect in orthodox liberal circles. Now that Nixon had resigned in disgrace, and it was as though all that the liberals had said had been proved true.

Rather than join critics of the Nixon administration, however, Moynihan felt compelled to defend it even when virtually no one else would. He praised the administration's achievements during its first two years (when he was in the White House), telling anyone who would listen that "there was some damn good government then." He continued to refuse to criticize the administration when the Watergate disclosures were being made public between 1972 and 1974, even when it became clear that Nixon's presidency had been destroyed.

Moynihan felt a strong loyalty to Nixon, who had resurrected him after he had been largely discredited in liberal Democratic circles. Nixon had reached out to Moynihan when Moynihan was in the wilderness, and Moynihan believed he had an obligation to Nixon. Moynihan also sensed that to some extent his own reputation would rise and fall with that of Richard Nixon. If Nixon's presidency were totally discredited, this would reflect badly on Moynihan. Moynihan emphasized that while Nixon's personality may have had a dark side that led him to engage in behavior which shocked the American people, he had also done many things that were still worthy of praise. "Nixon had two personae. If you knew one, you didn't know the other." And Moynihan knew the Richard Nixon who pretended to be shocked when someone used profane language in his presence.

Moynihan believed that "the Watergate break-in itself was a small event. A crime but not a massive one. Nobody was hurt. Unimportant." In April 1973, newly arrived in India, he had hosted a dinner for visiting New York *Times* columnist C. L. Sulzberger and had predicted that the Watergate scandal would blow over.[34] Moynihan believed that Nixon could have defused the whole controversy had he said, "Look here. I didn't know anything about it at the time, and later I thought it better not to rock the presidency; but in point of fact, there was a break-in at Watergate, and I did use bad judgment, and that certainly isn't going to happen again." But Nixon could never do that. "Nixon did not see it develop into a question of character. But it did. And, in the end, it was not the crime of Watergate but the crime of concealment that destroyed him."

Moynihan believed that Nixon had a tragic flaw, and therefore Moynihan was able to maintain his respect for him after the disclosures of what had happened following the break-in.

> You can't understand Nixon if you don't understand that he could not destroy the tapes. It was a combination of, one, being—at that level—an honest man and, two, being a self-destructive one. He did not destroy the tapes and he did not blow up the world. He went peacefully from office. And I thought he left well. . . .
> If you accept the idea of tragic flaws in people, if you accept the idea of sin, if you accept a tragic view of life [it is still possible to have respect for Nixon]. He chose not to tell just one truth, in a dramatic context. It was a struggle of character and morality. Read William Shakespeare. That's what it's all about.[35]

It was just as well that Moynihan was ready to return to Harvard, for his political prospects appeared to be weak. He had lost many liberal allies when he joined the Nixon administration, and the Republican right had remained suspicious of him throughout the period of his service in the White House. Now the president who had appointed him had been deposed. And because of the manner in which Moynihan expressed his views—particularly those on race—there was little that he said or did that failed to arouse passion in some quarter.

His resignation did eliminate a number of troublesome personal constraints. Moynihan would no longer have to adopt a low profile and speak only in platitudes to the press. He would no longer be in a position of having to give away things (buildings, rupees) to a frequently ungrateful constituency and having to listen sympathetically to their often unreasonable complaints.

Though he did not know it then, Moynihan was headed for a job that would require precisely the opposite from him. Within six months Moynihan would become one of the most outspoken individuals on the American political scene and develop a reputation for being among Western diplomats one of the most intolerant of hypocritical third world nations. In India Moynihan had learned a lesson about how developing nations behave, and he put it into practice at the United Nations.

10

Turtle Bay

There's very little success in politics. I'm not a failure, but I would bring liabilities of the past—just or unjust—with which a wise president would be advised not to encumber himself.

—Pat Moynihan, 1974

Before leaving India Moynihan told a reporter that he wanted no more government service. "Thirteen of my last 20 years have been in the Government and that's enough," he said with an air of finality.[1] The 1960s and early 1970s had been painful for Moynihan; he had been shaken by two assassinations, continuing charges of racism by blacks, and a close association with the only president in American history who had been forced to resign. Now Moynihan wanted to get out of the limelight. "I think I've been too trendy. I'm interested in some long-term serious work—the problems of legitimacy in government, the problems of maintaining legitimacy in a culture that is questioning and is in some ways an adversary culture."[2]

Moynihan could not forget all the criticism he had taken on domestic policy. He was tormented to the point that he doubted he would ever again be able to serve effectively in government. In some sense his

turning toward foreign policy may have been motivated by a feeling that
he could no longer be taken seriously in domestic policy. During his last
year in India he indicated the degree of his despair in a comment on the
impact of the "benign neglect" memo. "It killed me. I can never be
usefully involved in those matters that I had been involved in. It won't
ever be forgiven; that's all there is to it."[3]

Moynihan returned to public attention with the appearance in *Commentary* of his article "The United States in Opposition," which urged
the United States to present an alternative to the view of the third world
nations that capitalism and Western exploitation were exclusively responsible for poverty.[4] International liberalism as practiced by the
United States had accomplished good for world society, through both
private corporate investment and quasi-public bodies such as the World
Health Organization. America must recognize that capitalist policies
made economic conditions better, not worse. Third world socialist policies often produced low levels of growth, and poverty was often the result
of poor development strategies, not capitalist imperialism. It was important that the United States speak out on behalf of liberty and freedom
in the world; America should stop being complacent when attacked and
should apply to the third world nations the same standards they used to
judge the United States. America should stop apologizing for an imper-
fect democracy and instead proclaim that the values on which it was
founded have universal application.

The third world was to be confronted not for the sake of confrontation
alone. That third world nations had an anti-American bias did not mean
they were unalterably hostile to the United States or totally committed
to the Soviet point of view. The United States would be most successful
in international forums by vigorously pressing fundamental American
principles and values that could serve as an alternative to the third world
analysis.

Moynihan's advocacy of an aggressive posture in international affairs
represented something of a change of emphasis for him. While he had
taken a firm anti-Communist position from the late 1940s and was
always quick to defend American values, he had been less sanguine about
the feasibility of trying to export those values. He had not believed that
America could extend democratic government to Asia in the Korean

War and the Vietnam War; at the height of the Vietnam War in 1967 Moynihan had attacked the notion that democracy was an option available to all nations. The American experience was unique and could not be replicated; any effort to do so would be a corrupting enterprise—and America had in effect become a corrupting force overseas. Liberals had to restrain their enthusiasm for trying to civilize the world.[5]

Then, when Moynihan went to the General Assembly as a member of the United States delegation in 1971, he saw what happened when America was complacent: the honor of American democracy was freely impugned. Our allies did not defend us assertively, and nations that depended on us for support felt free to attack us. These thoughts had germinated within Moynihan during his two years in India, and, at the end of that time, "I was on to something and only I knew it. [I] had come to think it was possible and necessary to speak about the threat to democracy and personal freedom in the world in new and more urgent terms."[6]

Before leaving India Moynihan wrote a paper that argued that Indian democracy was in jeopardy as a consequence of Mrs. Gandhi's autocratic rule. Because he was about to leave the country he was persuaded to remain silent. Now, returned to America, he would remain silent no longer and would speak frequently and without reservation of the importance of freedom and liberty in the world and of the threat to these values that the third world nations posed. President Gerald Ford and the United States ambassador to the United Nations, John Scali, were advancing similar arguments in December 1974. Scali even believed (incorrectly) that Moynihan had stolen his views without acknowledgment.

Secretary of State Henry Kissinger had never gotten along well with Scali, and when Moynihan's *Commentary* article appeared, he was looking for a new ambassador. Despite the article, Moynihan was not his first choice; he had hoped to persuade a former governor of Pennsylvania, William Scranton, to take the job, but Scranton had repeatedly refused. When Kissinger read the *Commentary* article, he told Moynihan he was absolutely right and asked him to head a State Department committee that would prepare strategy for the next General Assembly. Kissinger then showed the article to President Ford, told him that he was giving Moynihan the chair of the planning committee, and suggested that he could do an even better job for the United States at the United Nations.

Six-month-old Patrick gets a "riding lesson" from Granddad Harry Phipps on the family farm in Kentucky (1928).

Summertime in Jeffersonville, Indiana. From left: Michael, Ellen and Patrick Moynihan (1936).

Middlebury graduate, Ensign Moynihan aboard U.S.S. repair ship *Quirinus* (1946).

Moynihan was twenty-nine
when he was appointed Assistant
Secretary of Reports in the
Harriman administration (1957).
(Wide World)

Moynihan joins the Screvane ticket. From left: Jane and Orin Lehman, Paul Screvane,
Pat and Elizabeth Moynihan and their children, Maura, Timothy and John (1965). (UPI)

Moynihan, adviser on urban affairs, meets with President-elect Nixon and black leaders (1969). *(UPI)*

The Rev. Ralph Abernathy of the Southern Christian Leadership Conference and Moynihan at the White House to discuss the 1969 Poor People's Campaign. *(UPI)*

Moynihan merges his professorial
and political personas while briefing
newsmen on an education proposal
(1970). *(UPI)*

In 1969 Nixon reshuffled the White House staff and Moynihan became a counselor to
the president with cabinet rank. Here at a press conference are Bryce Harlow,
Ehrlichman, Haldeman, and a skeptical looking Moynihan. *(UPI)*

New U.S. ambassador to India, a splendidly turned out Moynihan reviews an honor guard of Indian Gurkha soldiers as he presents his credentials at the presidential palace in New Delhi (1973). *(Wide World)*

Participating in an archery contest at Thimphu Sports Stadium, Ambassador Moynihan is dressed in a native Buhtanese costume (1974). *(Wide World)*

U.S. Ambassador to the United Nations Moynihan holds the United States aloft in an attempt to introduce a point of order during a meeting of the General Assembly. Seated next to him is Pearl Bailey (1975). *(UPI)*

The candidates for the New York Democratic Senate primary race, City Council President Paul O'Dwyer, Moynihan, businessman Abraham Hirschfeld, former U.S. Attorney General Ramsey Clark, and Representative Bella Abzug meet prior to a TV debate (1976). *(UPI)*

Confident that Moynihan's bid for the nomination to the Senate will be successful, the Moynihans go to vote in the New York State primary election (1976). *(UPI)*

Moynihan campaigns in New York City at a noontime rally in the last days before the 1976 senatorial election. *(UPI)*

Moynihan did little to quell the intense public discussion of his article. While he was probably not lobbying for the ambassadorship, neither did he retreat into the world of scholarship. Interviewed at the offices of Nelson Rockefeller's Commission on Critical Choices, Moynihan amplified his remarks with rhetoric that brought him headlines in the *New York Times*. It was time for the United States to go into such international forums as the United Nations and "raise hell," Moynihan told a reporter. On the question of political prisoners Moynihan was blunt. "We should rip the hides off everybody who presumes to talk about prisoners—shame then, hurt them, yell at them." A Cuban resolution before the Colonialism Committee that attacked the United States for its repression of Puerto Rican rights was "an obscene lie." Moynihan demonstrated his broad grasp of international politics by discussing the Middle East and the revolutionary government in Algeria and by reiterating his belief that the United States had to take the offensive against the third world nations.[7] This was a different Daniel Patrick Moynihan, one unconstrained by a government post and eager to speak freely on a wide range of subjects, one whose manner suggested that he expected to have a voice in the formulation of American foreign policy.

A month after the interview Moynihan spoke before Freedom House, an anti-fascist, anti-Communist human rights organization, and attacked the liberal foreign policy establishment. Moynihan told the crowd at City College that the liberal elites were to be criticized for their "failure of nerve," which had resulted in an accommodation to totalitarianism that was "without precedent in our history." The defeat in Vietnam had led many foreign policy makers to abandon their concern for freedom abroad; now many of them cared only about freedom from involvement in the international sphere.[8]

Late in March Kissinger invited Moynihan to his office for a drink and asked him to take the post of ambassador to the United Nations. Moynihan was pleased that Kissinger had liked the *Commentary* article, but he was wary of Kissinger, who he believed first helped destroy Richard Nixon and William Rogers and then "left their bleached bones behind him." If Lyndon Johnson had diminished those with whom he had associated, one ran the greater chance with Kissinger that one would "end up destroyed. He could not help this." Moynihan hoped Kissinger would not lie to him—or would at least warn him when he could not be entirely candid. In time he came to believe that he could not expect it. Moynihan recalls what the counselor to the State Department, Helmut Sonnenfeldt, told him when he was considering taking the post: "You do not understand. Henry does not lie because it is in his interest. He lies because it is in his nature."[9]

Moynihan believed he had advantages that others lacked. He was as close to being Kissinger's intellectual equal as anyone he knew; he believed he knew Kissinger better than Kissinger knew him; he thought he understood the United States better than Kissinger did. Thus Moynihan concluded that while Kissinger had "considerably greater ability" than he, he was not Kissinger's inferior and he could hold his own with the secretary of state. Later he would recruit Leonard Garment as his chief adviser, a man who Moynihan believed "knew every mood and every device, and most of the secrets" of Henry Kissinger.[10] Together, Moynihan thought, the two would be the equal of Henry Kissinger. Personality differences aside, Moynihan also sensed that Kissinger needed him to help restore America's sagging prestige. Cambodia had fallen, the Middle East peace shuttle had collapsed, and Vietnam was about to fall. Moynihan could stand up for America and turn its attention away from its defeats.

For his part Kissinger felt that he was taking a risk in appointing Moynihan, who was erratic and unpredictable and who might resign at an inopportune moment, thereby embarrassing him and the administration. Yet Moynihan would be an asset to the government, and Kissinger was willing to take a chance.

Moynihan accepted Kissinger's offer, but it was not entirely certain that he would actually take the job. Liz Moynihan did not like the life of an ambassador's wife, least of all the endless round of cocktail and dinner parties. (Her resistance had in part been responsible for Moynihan's not taking the job in 1970.) This time Moynihan agreed to accept the position but refused to play the diplomatic game in the usual manner. Having no desire to disrupt the normal routine of family life by bringing in large numbers of servants, Moynihan stationed a papier-mâché butler (made by Pat's son Tim Moynihan) at the door of his suite at the Waldorf Towers.

Again the *New York Times* published the news of the appointment before the present ambassador had been officially notified, and Moynihan avoided comment. In May the *New York Times* editorialized that while Moynihan was better qualified than he had been before he went to India, there was still doubt that he had tact enough for the job. Third world nations should not be allowed to level unfounded attacks on the United States, but neither should the United States engage in verbal fisticuffs with those nations. The editorial praised Moynihan's intellectual ability but expressed concern about the possible effect of his rhetoric at Turtle Bay.[11]

The ready criticism jolted Moynihan, and he called Kissinger to tell him he was considering withdrawing because of it. Kissinger reassured Moynihan of his support and urged him again to take the post. Yet the editorial gave Kissinger himself moments of unease. It did not surprise him; he remembered Moynihan's White House resignation before taking the foreign post in 1970, and his threat to resign while serving in India. Kissinger's misgivings about Moynihan grew stronger.

Nevertheless his enthusiasm remained high. Much of his enthusiasm sprang from Kissinger's belief that the two men shared similar views of the world and international politics. Certainly both believed that America had to speak out for democracy in the face of third world hypocrisy at the United Nations. But there were substantial ideological differences between the two men that neither appreciated at the time and that in large part explain the bitterness which eventually developed between them. These fundamental differences were at least as important as the personality differences that were often cited in attempts to explain the pronounced conflicts between the two during Moynihan's tenure at the United Nations.

For Moynihan, America's prestige was at its zenith in 1919 when Woodrow Wilson helped to found the League of Nations.[12] Wilson had shaped the century as had no other human being by trying to provide "a world dynamic of political independence accompanied by a rhetoric of personal freedom."[13] Wilson had instilled in America a duty to define and advance democratic principles in the world. While not ignoring peace and security, the Wilsonian outlook gave priority to morality in policy making—a morality with an almost religious conviction at its core. America during Wilson's presidency was no more influential than

France or England, but the rest of the world came to be jealous of its economic, military, and political success.

The United States had few imitators; developing nations after 1948 chose Britain or the Soviet Union as models. American liberalism attracted few followers, the principal chosen paths instead being totalitarianism and democratic socialism. The Soviet system was explicitly anti-American and anti-capitalist, and in British socialist doctrine similar biases were latent, if not apparent. Third world leaders—many of whom had studied at the London School of Economics—by and large adopted some variant of British socialist ideology as their model and incorporated hostility toward the United States into their world view.

America had not been equal to the onslaught it received from Communist and emerging socialist states of the third world. As America's pre-eminent military and economic position declined, so had its influence in general. And the decline in American influence had occasioned a decline in the regard for the ideals that Wilson championed—the primacy of individual freedom and liberty as against the demands of the state. Most nations favored equality over liberty, and economic growth was no longer associated with freedom. In the same way that communists believed that the capitalist class exploited the working class, developing nations believed that capitalist America exploited the third world. Consequently their concern lay with the redistribution of wealth rather than with building self-sufficient economies.

On the ideological level the American case had been poorly presented. American spokesmen were inexplicably ashamed to state the American position, and thus the United States was put on the defensive. The situation had to be changed. "We must play the hand dealt us: we stand for liberty. For the expansion of liberty. Anything less risks the contraction of liberty, our own included," Moynihan wrote.[14] The United States must bring its influence to bear on behalf of those nations that offer the promise of personal and national liberty. In the aftermath of the defeat in Vietnam it is especially important that America speak out for freedom. That defeat must not encourage a retreat from America's worldwide commitment; it is strong reason for America's case to be presented more emphatically. And hypocrisy can no longer be tolerated. Nations that systematically deny individual freedoms should not be allowed to criticize aberrational abuses in America.

Moynihan had long believed that the Soviet Union was an expansionist and imperialist power whose quest for world hegemony could be checked only by an assertive American power. Soviet power had grown steadily, to such an extent that the Soviets held the leading, if not the dominant position in world politics, and they showed no sign of cutting back their military buildup as America reduced its own presence around the world.

Détente is not a condition but a process that can lead to peace or to war, depending on how it is managed—this was Moynihan's view. A relaxation of tension on the technological and military side may mean only a redistribution of tension to the ideological side. If the Communists cooperated with the West on arms control and scientific experimentation, there would inevitably be increased ideological conflict between the two nations. Americans must be aware of this fact and must increase their rhetorical support for the United States position in the world—especially when détente with the Soviet Union seems most secure.

Kissinger, on the other hand, had been far more concerned with maintaining a balance of forces in the world. To him the threat of nuclear war was the reality that informed all foreign policy making in the present era. Any effort to promote freedom in tyrannical regimes would necessarily be limited by the threat that such a campaign might pose to world peace.

> Where the age-old antagonism between freedom and tyranny is concerned, we are not neutral. But other imperatives impose limits on our ability to produce internal changes in foreign countries. Consciousness of our limits is recognition of the necessity of peace—not moral callousness. The preservation of human life and human society are moral values, too.[15]

Kissinger held that all American foreign policy making must begin with security—a posture that inevitably led America into cooperation with nations whose internal practices it could not condone. Only in situations where America had latitude could it "seize the moral opportunity for humanitarian purposes."[16] Kissinger was suspicious of political leaders and nations that claimed that their own systems have universal applicability. With leaders of this sort the domestic structure becomes a major issue in international politics and consequently an impediment to understanding, he thought. Symbolic politics overshadows substantive elements of foreign affairs, and issues are framed in terms of ultimates. Disputes cannot be considered in terms of the issues presented for resolution but invariably return to the basic values that underlie each system in question.

> When policy becomes excessively moralistic, it may turn quixotic or dangerous. A presumed monopoly on truth obstructs negotiation and accommodation. Good results may be given up in the quest for ever-elusive ideal solutions. Policy may fall prey to ineffectual posturing or adventuristic crusades.[17]

The unabashed advocacy of American principles that Moynihan advocated could be tolerated only in a world where American influence was unchallenged. In that situation (which both agree existed in the period immediately following World War II) America's disproportionate influence gave it a broad margin of error in its attempts to mold the world according to its own design. But as American nuclear and strategic influence was challenged and American dependence on the world economy grew, the margin of safety was drastically reduced. Diplomacy must now be conducted with subtlety and flexibility, Kissinger believed. Absolute moral judgments will not win broad support—though the United States has a special responsibility to go beyond narrow conceptions of self-interest. Kissinger's was a pragmatic foreign policy that allowed for moral concerns where they do not interfere with the construction of a peaceful world order.

Kissinger's view of United States policy toward the third world and the Soviet Union also differed from that of Moynihan. America's interest in the third world stems from its concern with international order, Kissinger asserted. To achieve order it is necessary to have stable domestic systems in the third world nations, and the United States should do what it can to promote political legitimacy. Yet it is not our mission to try to transfer American institutions to the new nations or even to prevent the spread of Communism where it is firmly entrenched. For the overriding goal is to build a stable world order.

Kissinger believed that the nuclear imperative imposed restraint on the Soviet Union just as it did on the United States. Kissinger had concluded that there was no real consensus in the Soviet Union on whether it should adopt a conciliatory posture toward the West or whether it should be intransigent. The dynamics of the Soviet system produce changes in policy that explain more about Soviet actions than do changes in rhetorical posture, he believed. Soviet policy making is never entirely free from the exigencies of the balance of power and is never divorced from tactical pressures or adjustments. The Soviet Union's acceptance of détente in the 1960s indicated a desire to lessen tensions with the West. The Russians had not been as expansionist militarily as they might have been expected to be, and competition with the United States had made the Soviets willing to stabilize conditions somewhat through negotiation. Their expansionist urges had not disappeared, but they had joined with the United States in a mutual relaxation of tensions. It would undo past progress to tie concern over abuses of freedom within the Soviet Union to the continued process of détente. Ultimately American policy toward Russia should be one of resisting expansionist impulses while working to build a more constructive relationship.

Kissinger specifically opposed what he called "a rhetoric of confrontationalism" that portrays the Russians as "masterful, purposeful, and overwhelming while America is bumbling, uncertain, and weak."[18] Tough rhetoric and contrived confrontations would not build confidence in America; rather, they would serve to undermine America's position. Threatening the Soviets would only serve to weaken our bargaining position in negotiations.

Thus the differences between Moynihan and Kissinger on the conduct of American foreign policy were considerable. An equally powerful basis for conflict between the two men was that both had large egos; their mutual friends found it hard to imagine that the two could get along peacefully in a situation in which Moynihan was working directly for Kissinger. So all the ingredients were present for a clash between the two. With the benefit of hindsight, the most interesting question is not why did the two men clash but why did they not clash sooner?

In the beginning Moynihan did all he could to avoid conflict with Kissinger. He told one interviewer that "I've not the slightest illusion that I work for anyone but Henry Kissinger. I'm an instructed Ambassador, and I will go with the Secretary of State."[19] At his confirmation hearings in June Moynihan emphasized that he served the president and the secretary of state and hesitated to express his personal views on most issues. When asked about the new economic order, Moynihan said that his views were similar to those of Kissinger and that after his confirmation his views would be "precisely" those of the secretary of state. On sanctions against South Africa, Moynihan twice told the Senate Foreign Relations Committee that he would have to wait to be instructed before making specific policy recommendations. When asked whether the United States should vote to seat North and South Vietnam, Moynihan said that as of that moment he would seat their delegations but that he would find out following his confirmation whether he would continue to take that posture.

One difference between Moynihan and the administration did reveal itself at the hearings, however. Moynihan told the senators that he agreed with former Supreme Court Justice Arthur Goldberg's suggestion that the United States withdraw from the General Assembly and cut off financial support for the United Nations if Israel were expelled. At the time Kissinger would not comment on what the United States should do in that event, but he informed the nonaligned block that the United States would strongly oppose any move to curtail Israel's participation in the General Assembly.[20]

But the most interesting aspect of Moynihan's testimony was not that he opened up a small difference in policy with Kissinger, but that he explained in some detail the posture he thought the United States should take in the face of the hostile actions of third world countries at the United Nations. What happens at the United Nations, Moynihan said, is planned long before the various ambassadors reach New York. For example, the nonaligned nations, meeting at Havana in March, had produced a document calling for strong measures against Israel, including the possibility of expulsion. The document had then been discussed and the nonaligned nations had worked out a joint position before going to New York. The task of the American government was to consider seriously these early indications of potential General Assembly action and to impress on those nations that the United States would tolerate no action against Israel. "We are beginning to learn if you want to influence opinion in October in New York you first of all notice what they do in Havana in March and get out to the capitals and try to turn them around."[21]

Following Moynihan's unanimous confirmation by the Senate, he was sworn in by President Ford at a Rose Garden ceremony. The president associated himself with Moynihan's views on handling the third world by saying that the United States would resist all efforts "to exploit the machinery of the United Nations for narrow political interests." The president's praise for Moynihan was unreserved; at the close of the ceremony Moynihan smiled and told him, "I would like to associate myself wholly with your remarks."[22]

After appearing at an AFL-CIO dinner for Aleksandr Solzhenitsyn (where Henry Kissinger was conspicuous by his absence) Moynihan went to New York. He breezed into the United States Mission to the United Nations, greeted a few old friends, and began to get acquainted with the mission staff. Asked how he felt about taking the job, he replied, "I don't know. But they have a paper upstairs that tells me." His first meetings with the mission staff did not go well; on the whole they were not sympathetic to his "opposition" strategy, and he would have little to do with most of them during his time at Turtle Bay.

Following his brief visit to New York Moynihan made a quick trip to Geneva for an Economic and Social Council meeting and met members of his staff there, then returned to New York to present his credentials to Secretary-General Kurt Waldheim. In mid July he began his new job, his first task being to help negotiate a three-month extension of the Sinai peace-keeping force, an agreement that was scheduled to expire at midnight the day the new accord was to be signed.

Moynihan was forced by Kissinger and the State Department to alter his posture with regard to United Nations membership for North and South Vietnam. At his confirmation hearings Moynihan had said he believed that all nation-states had a right to join the body. However, Kissinger instructed Moynihan to veto the applications because the totalitarian nations had blocked consideration the week before of membership for South Korea. The United States opposed selective universality (as Moynihan called it) and therefore had to oppose the applications of North and South Vietnam.

Thus their first difference came over an issue on which Kissinger appeared to be taking a harder line than Moynihan. The secretary of state believed that Moynihan was willing to be more conciliatory than he. Moynihan's view was that by allowing the Vietnams to join the United Nations even though South Korea was blocked, the United States would seize the ideological initiative. By not vetoing North and South Vietnam's entry, Moynihan thought the United States could make a firm statement on behalf of the principle of universal representation—a principle that Communist nations reject. Most Communist nations did not have representative governments, and Moynihan wanted to use America's acceptance of the principle both domestically and internationally to criticize those nations. To veto the admission would be "a calamity. We would be seen to act out of bitterness, blindness, weakness, and fear."[23] Nevertheless he complied with his instructions to veto the resolution, writing a speech that stressed the link between the refusal to tolerate democracy at home and the democracy of the United Nations. The State Department held up the speech and required that he speak only of universality.

This was one early sign of the impending clash with Kissinger. Another was Kissinger's rage at Moynihan's attending the dinner for Solzhenitsyn. The Soviets regarded Solzhenitsyn as their most prominent public enemy, and Kissinger believed that Moynihan's attendance at the dinner would jeopardize détente. Kissinger also advised that the Russian dissident be shunned by the White House for the same reason. A third instance in which the two differed was on how the State Department could best respond to third world imprecations against an American official at the World Food Council. These differences were small, but they were harbingers.

Moynihan had an early victory in the committee of twenty-four when he succeeded in winning narrow passage (11-9 with 3 abstentions) of a proposal to shelve the Cuban resolution criticizing American involvement in Puerto Rico. Moynihan took some pride in this victory, for he believed he had persuaded Kissinger to send a cable to each of the nations involved, pointing out that a vote against the United States in the matter would be regarded as an unfriendly act. This was a threat, and the world would see it as such; nevertheless the situation was one in which a threat was appropriate.

Moynihan's first major test at the General Assembly came after Labor Day 1975, when the Seventh Special Session met to discuss international economic cooperation. For two years prior to the session the West and developing nations had engaged in bitter debate concerning their mutual obligations and responsibilities. And given Moynihan's seemingly hostile posture toward the third world, most observers expected that the United States would have little more success in 1975 than in the previous two years. But Moynihan surprised everyone; when an agreement was reached, both his enemies and his friends agreed that he had done a remarkable job in producing a consensus.

Moynihan opened the session reading Secretary of State Kissinger's speech to the General Assembly pledging increased aid to developing countries through the International Monetary Fund and the establishment of institutes to assist technological and industrial development. Although a few states criticized the speech, in general it was well received. But the real work of the special session was to hammer out an accord that would satisy both the West and the Group of 77 (the organization of more than one hundred developing nations). It was in negotiating this accord that Moynihan made his mark.

The Group of 77 had advanced a number of proposals for a new economic order, including a plan in which Western nations would give 0.7 percent of their GNP in aid to poor nations each year. Another troublesome proposal would tie the price of the natural resources of the poor nations to the price of the manufactured goods of the rich nations. The third world also advanced a plan that would give it special drawing rights (SDRs) from the International Monetary Fund to finance development.

Much of the responsibility for fashioning a response to these proposals was left to Moynihan, his staff, and Thomas Enders, an assistant secretary of state who did technical work. After the first week of talks Moynihan, Leonard Garment, and another ambassador in the United States mission, Jacob Myerson, responded. Their document was never accepted

formally by the State Department because it did not have the approval
of the Treasury and Commerce departments, both of which were involved in the negotiations, but it was used as a statement of America's
unofficial position and thus served as the basis for bargaining in the final
week.

The group worked through the second week in September and
reached agreement (after a number of all-night sessions) on a resolution
that consisted of 87 long, technical passages that would serve as guide-
lines for international economic cooperation. Basically the document
provided for a new American willingness to consider the problems of
developing nations in return for the Group of 77's abandoning the
notion that there should be a planned world economy independent of
supply and demand. It was a document of moderation: both sides had
agreed to negotiate rather than threaten one another.

Just before agreement was reached the entire proposal was jeopardized
when third world nations attempted to add new language condemning
the West's role in international economic exploitation. Moynihan would
not accept such a change. "They want a symbolic surrender from the
U.S., an admission of guilt. But we are not guilty. Sorry. That's not going
to happen."[24] The United States filed a set of reservations about the
agreement, specifically dissociating itself from any idea of a new economic order and any commitment to pay a fixed share of GNP in aid
to third world nations.

In the end Moynihan's firmness with the third world produced consensus as moderates rejected the demands of the more radical states. The
exercise proved that "we can negotiate in good faith and, in doing so,
reach genuine accord," Moynihan said. "Not least we have shown that
this can be done in the unique and indispensable setting of the United
Nations. This system works."[25]

Many people were surprised that the author of "The United States
in Opposition" had achieved such an accord between America and its
erstwhile opponents. Such surprise betrays a misunderstanding of
Moynihan's point. Ever since the publication of the *Commentary* article
Moynihan had maintained that he favored confrontation with the third
world only if the United States were hectored; otherwise the United
States would be willing to engage in constructive dialogue. The United

States would listen to the third world if it would talk sense, Moynihan had said; America would hit back if it were attacked unfairly. In this instance there was dialogue: for the majority of third world nations preferred negotiation to confrontation.

Within two weeks the situation had changed dramatically—and so had Moynihan's posture. Two related events had occurred: the tabling in the Third Committee of a series of amendments equating Zionism with racism, and Uganda President Idi Amin's address to the United Nations General Assembly. These events set off a series of actions and reactions whose effects are still being felt in international politics.[26]

On October 1 President Amin received an ovation in the General Assembly when he called for the extinction of the State of Israel and told the American people to rid themselves of Zionists. At the same time five diplomats from Somalia, Southern Yemen, Libya, Syria, and Cuba were meeting in the United Nations basement to prepare a series of seven amendments to a resolution before the Third Committee on dedicating a decade to combat racism. The amendments would have added Zionism to the forms of racial discrimination scheduled for attack.

Moynihan was not present when Amin spoke, and Clarence Mitchell, the senior American representative in attendance, issued the American response. Then, without consulting Washington, Moynihan boycotted a dinner that was given in honor of Amin by Waldheim.

Moynihan received some criticism from Jewish organizations for not responding immediately to Amin and the Zionism resolution. The day after Amin's speech the Conference of Presidents of Major American Jewish Organizations called on Moynihan to reply publicly to the Amin speech. A phone call from the president of the Conference of Major American Jewish Organizations prompted Moynihan on October 2 to call Chaim Herzog, the Israeli ambassador, to urge him to exert pressure in other areas—such as the American Jewish community, which had not yet spoken out against the resolution. "I don't need the pressure," Moynihan told Herzog. "Tell them to use their influence where it's needed." Herzog complained that western European nations had not grasped the importance of what had happened in the Third Committee, and Moynihan assured Herzog that even if the United States had to stand alone, it would make an impassioned defense of Israel.

Moynihan more than lived up to his commitment. The following day, October 3, he delivered a strong rebuke to Amin at the AFL-CIO convention in San Francisco. "Every day, on every side, we are assailed," Moynihan told the delegates. It was no accident that Amin had called for the extinction of Israel and that Amin was head of the Organization of African Unity. Moynihan repeated the *New York Times'* characterization of Amin as a "racist murderer" and said that despots seek to destroy that which threatens them most—democracies like Israel. He predicted that the resolution equating Zionism with racism would be passed by the General Assembly, and he ended his discussion of Amin and Zionism with an expression of hope that the African nations would disavow Amin and oppose linking Zionism with racism. Moynihan also credited the African nations for having headed off an attempt to suspend Israel from the General Assembly.[27]

In diplomatic circles Moynihan became a target of vituperative criticism for having joined in the characterization of Amin as a racist murderer and for having said it was no accident that Amin was head of the Organization of African Unity. Moynihan was angry that the African nations did not repudiate Amin; that they continued to accept him in a leadership role in the OAU was even worse. In light of the events of early December 1977, when the African nations forced other nations to withdraw a resolution criticizing human rights abuse in Uganda, Moynihan's argument appears even more persuasive. It should be considered, however, that the leadership of the OAU rotates among the heads of member states; the fact is that Amin's chairmanship was an accident of timing rather than premeditation.

Kissinger and other State Department officials were disturbed that Moynihan had identified Amin too closely with the OAU—many of whose member nations were privately outraged and embarrassed by Amin. Moynihan and Kissinger had spoken in general terms about the content of Moynihan's speech before it was delivered, and Kissinger had approved a strong speech. But he had not seen the text in advance, and he believed that Moynihan had far exceeded his authority in the language he used and had damaged the American position with the African nations by linking them to Amin. Kissinger feared that they would react to the speech (as in fact they did) by closing ranks with Amin and attacking the United States. He sensed that the hostility generated by Moynihan's remarks would jeopardize much of the progress that had been made at the Seventh Special Session.

When reports of the speech were made public, the State Department wanted Moynihan to issue an immediate retraction. Returning from San Francisco, Moynihan was met at the airport by Courtney Sheldon, the mission press officer, who had been instructed to suggest that a substitute text be released with the reference to the OAU excised. The mission had also prepared a press release that said some of General Amin's statements had "earned wide approval" while others "were morally offensive." Moynihan refused to consider any modification of his position; two alternative drafts of the substitute text had been prepared, but Moynihan was interested in them only to the extent of learning who had written them. The suggestion that it had been no accident that Amin was head of the OAU remained in the final text and in the various reprints.

Aside from the policy considerations involved, Kissinger was perhaps most disturbed that President Ford himself endorsed the statements of Moynihan and Mitchell. Press secretary Ron Nessen told reporters the week after the San Francisco speech that "the President believes Ambassador Moynihan and Clarence Mitchell said what needed to be said."[28] Kissinger believed that the president did not approve of the language Moynihan had used but felt compelled for political reasons to indicate his support. Thus Moynihan ended up with the full support of the president (even if it came a week after the speech) while Kissinger, it appeared, had been left out on a limb.

There remained the Zionism resolution. The Zionism amendments were tied to the resolution proclaiming a Decade for Action to Combat Racism and Racial Discrimination pending before the Third Committee, and the African nations worried that if they supported the Zionism amendments, the Western nations would oppose the Decade resolution. Accordingly, the United States mission staff assistant assigned to the Third Committee, Cameron Hume, sent the State Department a memo urging that the United States call on Western European nations to tell the Africans that their Decade Against Racism would be in trouble if the amendments were passed. The Western Europeans responded, though not as forcefully or unequivocally as some in the United States mission would have liked. Ultimately the Zionism amendments were withdrawn and a separate resolution introduced that said simply that Zionism was a form of racism and racial discrimination. Some Africans wanted to add a provision deploring anti-Semitism, but this even-handed move was rejected.

There was little lobbying in capitals the two and a half weeks between the presentation of the Zionism amendments and the vote in the Third Committee. One Western European diplomat, looking back on the event, said that if the resolution were to have been blocked, it would have to have been blocked during that period. Yet the Western Europeans and the State Department did not use the leverage they had. Hume believed that the only way to defeat the resolution was for the Western nations to continue to tell the Africans point-blank that the Decade would not pass if the Zionism resolution were approved. Washington was wary of this approach, however, and public attention had been diverted from the Zionism resolution to the Moynihan-Amin controversy, so there was not the continual discussion of the resolution that its opponents wanted.

The Zionism resolution came to a vote for the first time in the Third Committee on October 17, 1975. Worried that the Decade would be imperiled if the Zionism resolution were passed, Sierra Leone introduced and Zambia seconded a proposal to postpone consideration of the issue for one year. The motion to postpone failed, 45-68, with 16 abstentions. Given the numerical majority that third world and Communist states enjoyed, the opponents of the Zionism resolution did about as well as could have been expected. Twelve African nations supported the Sierra Leone proposal and four abstained. Seven Latin American nations voted to defer consideration and five abstained.

The Zionism resolution carried, 70-29, with 27 absentions. Only two of the twelve African nations that had supported the Sierra Leone proposal voted to oppose the resolution. Despite strong pressure from the Arab states, the other ten African nations abstained in hopes of mitigating the potential damage to the Decade for Action to Combat Racism and Racial Discrimination. Fiji, Japan, Nepal, and Colombia had supported the Sierra Leone proposal and then abstained on the

Zionism vote. Bolivia, which had supported the Sierra Leone proposal, was absent on the Zionism vote. Other nations that had supported the postponement voted against the Zionism resolution. On the other side, virtually all the nations that had called for an immediate vote on the resolution voted in favor of it. Only Peru and Rumania abstained on the Zionism resolution after having pressed for an immediate vote. But their places were taken by Spain and Mexico, which had abstained and been absent on the postponement vote, respectively.

The United States' reaction to the resolution was unequivocal. When the result was announced, Moynihan walked over to Chaim Herzog and embraced him. Leonard Garment, the American representative on the Third Committee, had told the body prior to the vote that "this committee is preparing itself, with deliberation and foreknowledge, to perform a supreme act of deceit, to make a massive attack on the moral realities of the world."[29] At a press conference following the vote Moynihan associated himself with the language Garment had used, labeling the vote a "reckless" and "obscene" act. The United States, he said, would oppose the Decade for Action to Combat Racism and Racial Discrimination if the Zionism resolution passed in the General Assembly, and he indicated that other nations would do the same.[30] While he refused to concede that the resolution would ultimately pass, it was clear from his tone that he did not expect it to be defeated. Moynihan would not be drawn into a discussion of who he believed was behind the resolution; he said he read the newspapers for that kind of information.

The following week, at the annual award dinner of the Appeal of Conscience Foundation, he argued that in fact it was not Zionism that was under attack but the State of Israel. Israel had been singled out because it was one of the few places outside the West where democratic principles survived and because it was most vulnerable to attack. The totalitarian nations were perverting the truth in equating racism with Zionism in formulating their targets for their Decade. Racism was, in fact, allied with anti-Semitism, and thus the antithesis of Zionism. Yet there was hope; for the first time in a long while the democracies of the world had gotten together. The resolution had received the support of less than a majority of the United Nations membership. Only the United States and Israel had opposed the inclusion of Zionism with racial discrimination in the program of the International Women's Year Conference in Mexico City in the summer of 1975, but in the Third Committee the democracies of the West had by and large voted together. Conceding that it was likely that the resolution would pass the General Assembly, Moynihan said the United States was nevertheless determined that it should not pass.[31]

If the State Department had been lax in the weeks before the Third Committee vote on the Zionism resolution, it tried to make up for its inattention in the period leading up to the final vote by sending packets of information on Zionism to ambassadors from nations which were undecided, aimed at persuading them to oppose the resolution. Kissinger himself made a few phone calls, but by this time there was little that could be done.

Moynihan and Ivor Richard, the British ambassador, tried to get Edward Blyden, the Sierra Leone ambassador, to propose deferral once more. But the issue had become too hot for Blyden, and he told them he could no longer be involved. Francis Boaten, the Ghanaian ambassador, made overtures to the Arabs, but they would not accept a postponement. Boaten relayed their message to Richard and seemed to indicate that there was little he could do. On the day of the General Assembly vote Boaten decided to propose a ten-day deferral in the hope that the resolution could be eliminated. He was never recognized during the session.

Two weeks before the vote in the General Assembly Moynihan expressed his views on the Zionism resolution on *Face the Nation*. The votes against Zionism, he said, were votes against democracy as it existed in Israel and in America. The coalition that supported the Zionism resolution was an alliance of regimes of the left and the right, united only in that they were despotic regimes; the opposition by and large were democracies. The radical Arab states and the Communist nations had pressured the third world nations (many of which were predominantly Moslem) to support the resolution as a show of solidarity. The American response to the almost certain defeat was to act as though the United Nations did not matter much. Moynihan also advanced an idea that he had proposed to Kissinger that fall: when countries oppose the United States in a multilateral context, the United States should make some response in terms of bilateral relations. Countries that depend on the United States for food and yet vote against America in such organizations as the United Nations and the International Labor Organization should not be tolerated.

Perhaps the most memorable part of the interview came at the end, when CBS correspondent George Herman asked Moynihan if he were using his position at the United Nations to build a constituency in New York State for a race for the Senate in 1976 against Conservative-Republican James Buckley. The question had been asked of Moynihan repeatedly in the weeks following his AFL-CIO speech and the charge had been leveled at him by third world diplomats who wanted to discredit him. Moynihan had anticipated the question; on the morning of the interview he had told Leonard Garment that he would put an end to all such speculation. Thus, when Herman raised the question, Moynihan almost jumped on him to reply.

> Can I speak right quickly to that. It is not so. It might please some of the people who see us as enemies to think that this is so, to explain positions we are taking on matters of principle as in fact having some squalid personal ambition. I am not. I would consider it a dishonorable thing, this charge having been made, I would consider it dishonorable to leave this post and run for any office, and I would hope that it would be understood that if I do, the people, the voters to whom I would present myself in such circumstances, would consider me as having said in advance I am a man of no personal honor to have done so.[32]

Moynihan could not have been more sincere. When he appeared on *Face the Nation* he really had no intention of running for the Senate, and he hoped that his statement would improve his credibility at the United Nations. His concern then was to do all he could to defeat the Zionism resolution and defend democracy, and he was even willing to engage in a little hyperbole if it would help that cause.

The cause, however, was pretty much lost. The African nations were no longer willing to lead the fight for a delay, and that task fell to Belgium, which proposed that the issue be held off for a year. Opponents of the resolution mustered a large vote for postponement, but the motion failed, 55-67, with 15 abstentions, while many argued that Moynihan's rhetoric was responsible for inducing third world nations to support the resolution. The vote indicated that the American position had improved since the postponement vote in the Third Committee (45-68, with 16 abstentions). By and large the new support came from Latin American and African nations that either had not participated in the Third Committee postponement vote or had abstained. In spite of the offense Moynihan had allegedly caused third world nations with his rhetoric, their opposition to the Zionism resolution had become stronger.

Fourteen African nations voted for the postponement, two more than had supported the postponement motion in the Third Committee. Nine nations (six of them Latin American) that had either abstained or not participated in the postponement vote in committee supported the Belgian resolution. Four nations that in committee had supported an immediate vote now abstained. On the other side, the countries that continued to support an immediate vote on the resolution were the Communist nations and the radical (heavily Moslem) third world nations that comprise an almost automatic majority in the United Nations. Their only gains came from two nations that had been absent in committee: one nation that had opposed an immediate vote in committee, and one nation that had abstained in committee.

The Zionism resolution itself passed the General Assembly by a vote of 72-35, with 32 abstentions and 3 nations absent. The movement to the Western position came from third world nations—the group presumably most likely to have been offended by Moynihan's rhetoric. Seven nations that had not taken a position on the resolution in the Third Committee voted against it, and four countries that had supported it in committee now abstained. Only one nation that had opposed the resolution in committee now abstained. In contrast, only two nations that had abstained in committee now supported the resolution, and another four that had not participated in the Third Committee vote now endorsed it. Thus the proponents of the resolution were basically the same nations that had supported it earlier; their lobbying effort had clearly been less effective than that of the Western nations.

Moynihan's speech to the General Assembly after the vote followed the lines of his earlier statements on the question; he made an extended argument for racism's being the antithesis of Zionism, and his rhetoric suggested the importance he attached to the issue. The United States, he declared, "does not acknowledge, it will not abide by, it will never acquiesce in this infamous act." The resolution was obscene to begin with because it was introduced in secrecy; worse, it was now being voted on with a "shameless openness." Passage of the resolution would mean that "the abomination of anti-Semitism has been given the appearance of international sanction." In taking such a step the General Assembly would be granting symbolic amnesty to the murderers of six million Jews in Europe. Finally, passage of the resolution would do irreparable damage to the concept of human rights: to equate Zionism and racism would inevitably be to pervert the meaning of racism, and soon such notions as national self-determination and national honor would inevitably be similarly perverted.[33]

Analysis of the voting on the resolution makes it difficult to accept the conclusion that Moynihan's rhetorical "overkill" caused the resolution to pass. The twelve-vote margin on the resolution to postpone was about as close as America could have expected to come to the third world–Communist majority in the General Assembly. Moreover, what movement there was between October 17 and November 10 was toward the Western position, and most of the changes occurred in the positions of African and Latin American nations, nations that presumably would have been most offended by Moynihan's remarks. The actions of the individual countries reflect a self-interested approach to international politics, their votes representing realistic appraisals of their own benefit.

Japan, for example, abstained on the final vote in order to avoid offending the oil-producing Arabs, but it was willing to vote to postpone for a year. Guatemala abstained in large part in order to win Arab support for their fight with Britain over the territory of Belize. Mexico, under heavy pressure from the United States, voted to postpone but supported the final resolution in an effort to maintain a leadership role in the third world. The twenty Arab nations voted for the resolution out of a desire to maintain solidarity, yet moderates such as Egypt did so with little enthusiasm, fearing United States retribution. Pakistan, Cyprus, and Brazil were other nations influenced by their dependence on Arab oil and economic support.

Moynihan thought it important that the United States show it had muscle. On *Today* two days after the vote he told Barbara Walters that

the countries that had supported the Zionism resolution should suffer
for it. He said he would introduce that day a resolution calling for a
worldwide amnesty for political prisoners in order to make things more
difficult for those nations that had been making life uncomfortable for
the democracies.

Moynihan introduced his resolution on November 12 without final
approval from the State Department and without notifying the nine
members of the European Economic Community that it would be
introduced. Moynihan had become increasingly displeased with the
manner in which Secretary Kissinger and the International Organizations Bureau of the State Department scrutinized everything he wanted
to say or do. Just three days before the vote on the Zionism resolution
the State Department had forced Moynihan to delay a speech on Palestine so that his text could be reworked, and he was chafing under this
kind of treatment. Now Moynihan thought it essential to respond
quickly to the Zionism resolution. When State Department clearance
was not immediately forthcoming—Kissinger could not be located and
Moynihan could not wait—he took it upon himself to introduce the
political prisoners resolution. Kissinger had not expected this; he had
given general approval to the idea in September, but he did not want
the resolution introduced without his specific approval.

In his speech introducing the resolution to the Third Committee
Moynihan called it probably the most important social, cultural, and
humanitarian proposal the United States had made in many years. The
United States believed that resolutions that attacked abuses of freedom
only in some countries were too narrow. While South Africa and Chile
should be condemned for human rights violations, they were not the
only countries that abridged individual liberties. Indeed, many of the
sponsors of the resolutions against Chile and South Africa were themselves nations in which significant abuses took place regularly. Moreover,
one reason why the world was aware of abuses in Chile and South Africa
was that these countries were more open than some totalitarian regimes.
South Africa had the freest press in Africa according to neutral observers, Moynihan believed, and Chile had provisionally allowed investiga-
tors from Amnesty International and the Red Cross to visit the country
after the military coup. The language of human rights was being used

increasingly against regimes that at least acknowledged some validity in the charges leveled at them—while the abuses of the more repressive and unrepentant regimes went unquestioned. If language of this sort could be used against some democracies, it was likely to be used against all democracies. Now the free nations of the world must fight back. The totalitarian nations appeared to have a plan to attack only nations that were partially free (Chile) or totally free (Israel); to demonstrate to the world that no such plan existed, the member nations should support a resolution calling for amnesty for all political prisoners.[34]

The political prisoners resolution was apparently the last straw for Kissinger, who was tired of fighting with his ambassador over the language of every speech and angry with Moynihan's show of independence. Worse, Kissinger believed that Moynihan exaggerated every disagreement into a fight over principle. The arguments they had been having were the usual ones between ambassadors and secretaries of state, Kissinger conceded, but Moynihan made every disagreement take on a monumental quality.

On the afternoon of the day Moynihan introduced his resolution Kissinger struck back. At a press conference in Pittsburgh he said he did not believe it was possible to punish all the countries that had voted for the Zionism resolution, though he shared Moynihan's belief that the resolution was anti-Semitic and harmful to mideast diplomacy. He said that while he was displeased with Amin's comments, he probably would have expressed himself in a more restrained manner than Moynihan had. The secretary dissociated himself from Moynihan's remark about its having been no accident that Amin was head of the Organization of African Unity. Amin was not a typical representative of the organization; he was chairman only because of rotation, and this was no indication that the organization was abandoning its responsible posture in world affairs. Kissinger played down the possibility of America's punishing nations that had voted for the Zionism resolution: the emotions of the day would not lead the United States to abandon its long-term program of aid to third world nations.[35] Whereas Moynihan had endorsed a punitive strategy, Kissinger preferred the carrot to the stick.

Because the amnesty proposal had obviously been introduced in response to the Zionism resolution and because it had been presented in such a hasty way, it stood little chance of serious consideration. The African nations were annoyed that Moynihan had indirectly praised South Africa for its supposedly free press, and the Western European nations were offended because they had not been consulted. This state of affairs led Moynihan to abandon the resolution, and later Leonard Garment withdrew it after it had been saddled with fifteen hostile and tendentious amendments.

On November 12 Moynihan dined at the White House with Ford and Kissinger at a State Dinner for Prime Minister Gaston Thorn of Luxembourg. Kissinger and Moynihan spoke privately after the dinner, but Kissinger neither criticized Moynihan nor urged him to change his ways. Yet *Newsweek* the following Monday, November 17, reported that Kissinger had taken Moynihan to the proverbial woodshed—and Moynihan suspected that Kissinger was the source of the story.[36] Kissinger of course denied it and later said that State Department aides had released the story based on their interpretation of what had occurred at the meeting. But Moynihan concluded that in the future Kissinger would discuss Moynihan's work with him in a balanced manner and then tell reporters he had dressed him down.

So when British Ambassador Ivor Richard told a meeting of the United Nations Association (a private support group for the United Nations in New York) on November 17 (the day the *Newsweek* story appeared) that the United States would best be served by lowering its voice and shunning confrontational rhetoric, Moynihan sensed that Kissinger had inspired the speech. To be sure, Richard used particularly graphic language to describe Moynihan; without mentioning Moynihan's name, Richard compared him to Wyatt Earp looking for outlaws in the Old West. Nothing could be gained by ideological dispute of the kind Moynihan provoked—it served only to encourage the West's enemies, alienate its friends, and isolate the country. Moynihan's posture was that of a Savonarola preaching retribution and revenge. Moynihan's flailing away was a bit like Lear "raging amidst the storm on the blasted heath."[37]

Richard had not discussed his speech with Kissinger—or for that matter with anyone in London. He had had one dinner with Moynihan, Leonard Garment, and Norman Podhoretz (a close friend of Moynihan), and he had come away with the impression that Moynihan was unwilling to listen and lacked an understanding of third world politics. Moreover, like Moynihan, Richard was not a career diplomat and thus similarly felt free to speak his own mind. Having taken on a difficult constitituency in the February 1974 general election, he had been defeated, but he hoped to stand again for office in the the near future. Publicity of the sort he got for his attack on Moynihan was likely to improve his chances of winning a seat in the next general election and improve his stock in the Labour party. He was so primed to return to electoral politics that he maintained he would board the first plane to London when the P.M. called a general election.

Moynihan was certain that Richard had been put up to the speech by Kissinger. He believed then that Kissinger had met British Prime Minister James Callaghan at an economic summit conference in Rambouillet, France, and instructed him to have Richard attack Moynihan. Never before had a British ambassador attacked an American ambassador in such a manner, and to Moynihan it was inconceivable that Washington had not inspired the attack. In fact Richard had made similar comments before a group of congressmen a day before Kissinger met Callaghan, and he had drafted his speech on index cards only while shaving at 6:30 A.M. on the day of the speech. It took the British embassy two days to reproduce the text, and it got into the press four days after Richard delivered the speech—and only then because Richard took special care to have it released.

Richard's speech served as catalyst to the boiling over of Moynihan's resentments at Kissinger and the State Department. Kissinger had not given him sufficient support in his attack on Idi Amin; he had made overtures to Cuba while Moynihan was fighting a Cuban initiative for United Nations recognition of a Puerto Rican liberation movement; the State Department had not lobbied hard enough against the Zionism resolution; it had delayed and hamstrung his amnesty resolution. If Kissinger had not inspired the Richard speech, he should at least have defended Moynihan from its charges—it was the least the secretary of state could do for his ambassador. Whatever his attitude, Kissinger "was not on top of events any longer, at times not even abreast of them. He was worn out. His power, as [New York Times columnist William] Safire put it, truly was ebbing and he was in some ways losing his skills."[38]

Moynihan believed that his position had been undermined and it was time for him to resign. He told Leonard Garment of his decision and scheduled a press conference for the early afternoon of November 21. But Garment wanted Moynihan to stay at the United Nations, and he called President Ford's chief of staff, Richard Cheney, to tell him what was happening. Cheney called Moynihan before the press conference could take place and persuaded him to withhold his resignation until he and the president had a chance to meet in Washington on Monday.

Word leaked out that Moynihan would announce his resignation on November 21, while Kissinger was testifying before a congressional committee. Told the news, he thought the story was a joke. When he realized that it was not, he had the State Department issue a statement in support of Moynihan. He also called Moynihan to reiterate his support, and he spoke with Richard Cheney.

Kissinger wanted Moynihan to remain at the United Nations, and had little sympathy with the reasons that Moynihan was giving privately for resigning. The Richard notion was insane; Kissinger had never met him, and he and Callaghan had not discussed the United Nations at Rambouillet. He had done all he could on the Zionism resolution. Nor had the State Department needlessly delayed Moynihan's political prisoners resolution; Kissinger had expected that the final text would be cleared with him before it was issued. Kissinger was angry. Moynihan was upstaging him, and with the ambassador's growing popularity and his own sagging support he could see no way to bring Moynihan into line. Moreover, members of Ford's inner circle, like Donald Rumsfeld, were so worried about Ronald Reagan's threat in the Republican primaries that they were willing to do anything to keep the administration's most visibly hard-line foreign policy spokesman on their team.

Kissinger was not present for the greater part of the discussion between Ford and Moynihan. The two spoke together for thirty minutes, and the president offered his full support. Ford needed Moynihan; the president's popularity in the polls was sagging, and he faced an aggressive challenge from Ronald Reagan on the right. He had just relieved Kissinger of his National Security Council duties and had fired Secretary of Defense James Schlesinger; another change at this time might give an impression of instability. Moynihan had wide popularity, and insofar as he was popular he helped the administration. Beyond the purely tactical considerations Ford personally liked Moynihan's bluntness; Kissinger may have privately opposed the language Moynihan used, but Ford generally approved of it.

Kissinger joined the two for ten minutes and also offered his support. But he could not avoid a trace of sarcasm when he commented later on his meeting with Moynihan. In announcing that Moynihan had his full confidence and support, Kissinger said jokingly that Moynihan would continue in his "calm, measured, and quiet way to do his job." For his part, Moynihan told reporters on returning to New York that Ford and Kissinger had expressed complete support. When asked if he would leave at the end of the current session of the General Assembly, Moynihan would say only, "everyone leaves eventually."[39]

Moynihan's relations with the State Department improved slightly when Samuel Lewis, a career foreign service officer, was appointed head of the International Organizations Bureau. Moynihan had not worked well with the former head of the bureau, William Buffum, whom he had used as his sounding board when he was frustrated with what he saw as the sluglike responsiveness of the State Department. Often Moynihan yelled not at Kissinger but at Buffum, who consequently developed an intense distaste for the ambassador.

Lewis assumed his job with admiration for Moynihan. Earlier in the fall he had been given a memorandum Moynihan had written on the reorganization of the State Department, which argued that the United States should condition its bilateral relations with certain nations (those with which it had few important interests) on their behavior in multilateral settings. Lewis, who was asked to evaluate the memorandum for the policy planning staff, found that he agreed with Moynihan's proposals and also got along well with him personally.

Nevertheless Lewis had no illusions about the difficulty of mediating between Moynihan and Kissinger. His ultimate loyalty was to Kissinger, and he knew that he must do what he could to prevent Moynihan's resignation. Kissinger feared that Moynihan might want to quit over a Middle East issue, siding with the Israelis and thereby making the administration appear to be equivocal in its support.

While Moynihan never reached the point of resignation over Middle East differences with Kissinger, the two did differ on the issue in the next few months. The Security Council again had to vote an extension to the mandate of the peace-keeping force in the Golan Heights, and the Syrians offered a number of troublesome amendments. The Syrians would agree to an extension only if the resolution stated that the Palestine Liberation Organization were allowed to participate in any Middle East talks. Moynihan lobbied to have the reference to the PLO removed from the resolution itself, but was only partially successful. A compromise was put forward in which the Security Council president would state that a majority of members interpreted the resolution to mean that the PLO would be permitted to participate in a future debate. The United States and Israel opposed this set of conditions, yet Kissinger decided to support the compromise package and to have Moynihan state that the United States did not accept the determination by the Security Council president. The United States said it could not support any resolution that called for council-sponsored talks with a PLO presence. Moynihan, uncomfortable with having to accept the Syrian conditions in any form, had to negotiate with the Syrians even though he personally opposed any interpretation that included the PLO. Moynihan's colleagues credit him with having conducted exceedingly delicate negotiations in support of a position with which he had little sympathy. Yet Moynihan came away with the sense that he had not received enough direction from Kissinger and that Washington was perhaps conceding too much. Kissinger believed that there were no significant differences between him and Moynihan on the issue.

While Moynihan was careful to follow the administration line in the Security Council, he continued to speak freely in other forums. At a time when the administration and Congress were formulating the United States response to the civil war in Angola, Moynihan charged in a speech in Washington that the Soviet Union—through its own activities and those of its putative surrogates, the Cubans, in Angola—was trying to colonize Africa. Moynihan was concerned that the Communists' success in Angola would give them control of shipping lanes from the Persian Gulf to Europe, making Brazil their next target and transforming the balance of power. While Kissinger was concerned about the African balance of power, he did not see the Angolan conflict in quite such broad terms.[40]

Moynihan's criticism of Soviet activities in Africa continued. A week after the Washington speech he addressed the General Assembly to oppose a resolution criticizing South Africa for its alleged intervention in Angola. If evidence of South African involvement were presented, Moynihan said, the United States would of course consider supporting such a resolution. But it was a "big lie" to say that South Africa alone had intervened in Angola, for there was massive evidence that Cuba and the Soviet Union had furnished troops and arms to aid the struggle of the Marxist Popular Movement for the Liberation of Angola (MPLA). Moynihan's speech apparently had some effect; seven African nations withdrew an amendment that condemned South Africa without mentioning Cuba or Russia. And the Soviet Union and Cuba replied with strong personal attacks on Moynihan: the Russians accused him of "slandering the Russians with the big lie," and the Cubans labeled him a "pseudo-professor."[41]

Moynihan's assault on the United Nations continued unabated. He criticized a report of the Special Committee on Colonialism that called the United States' bases in the Caribbean a threat to the sovereignty of the nations in that region and that condemned NATO for allegedly providing military assistance to South Africa and Rhodesia. "Now, these are lies—lies," Moynihan told the General Assembly. The United Nations was "becoming a theater of the absurd." The United States would not be bullied into endorsing this report by the threat of even stronger language being used against it; America was a nation of free people who would not be frightened by "thuggery." Any nation that voted for this resolution should not tell the United States afterward that it had not read the report or was not fully aware of what it was voting for—"that game is over," Moynihan concluded.[42]

It is important to realize that while Moynihan spent considerable time attacking third world hyprocrisy during the General Assembly session, he had to ensure that the United States was itself carrying out an even-handed policy. Thus South Africa was subjected to intense scrutiny when Prime Minister John Vorster indicated that Clarence Mitchell had been lying when he said that South Africans were being detained only because they criticized apartheid. At the time of the attack Moynihan said that Vorster's statement was "completely unwarranted" and that Mitchell's facts were right and South Africa's policy wrong. He promised that Mitchell would reply with specifics, and one month later Mitchell did just that, presenting one of the most comprehensive American critiques of South African policies ever delivered.[43] But in the furor created by the events of that autumn Mitchell's speech went largely unnoticed.

The session ended less than a week after the vote on the colonialism report, and in the closing days Moynihan described in the General Assembly how the session had been viewed by the United States. The picture he drew was a gloomy one. The Thirtieth General Assembly was "a profound, even alarming disappointment." Numerous actions were taken that America regarded as "abominations." Because the General Assembly did not have the legitimacy of a parliamentary body it was not capable of enforcing resolutions which condemned or accused nations of misconduct. The majority of the member nations were not democracies and therefore were not representative of the peoples they purported to represent.

Moynihan advocated the creation of a quasi-parliamentary caucus within the United Nations to enforce standards of basic human rights throughout the world. Such a caucus would presumably follow the example of American behavior in the Thirtieth General Assembly; along with issuing general denunciations of such policies as apartheid, it would issue a bill of particulars that listed specific abuses in a lawyer-like fashion (as Clarence Mitchell had done).

In conclusion Moynihan said that the United States still supported a worldwide amnesty for political prisoners, and he quoted a statement of Andrei Sakharov in support of that position. The Soviet Union, having seen an advance copy of Moynihan's speech, had asked him to delete the reference to Sakharov because the dissident was "an enemy of the Soviet people." Moynihan refused, and the Soviet delegation walked out of the assembly when he reached the passage.[44]

In the period following his near resignation in November, Moynihan's activities indicate that he felt greater freedom than previously to express his own views. Moynihan knew he had to make the most of what time

he had, so he spoke his mind. He sensed that his time at the United
Nations was limited; if he did not feel compelled to resign over one issue
or another, it was likely that he would be fired sooner or later. If Kissinger
wanted to keep American activities in Africa secret, Moynihan was
willing to tell a national television audience that the American people
had a right to know exactly what the administration was doing.[45] When
Moynihan concluded that oil shipping lanes were at stake in the fight
over Angola, he said so without determining first whether that was also
the State Department's interpretation.

What Moynihan was doing was not mere political opportunism.
Throughout the session he was coming to believe that the third world
nations, far from adhering to the variant of democratic socialism he had
described in his *Commentary* article, were becoming increasingly authoritarian and falling under the domination of the Soviet Union. Democratic socialism had "taken a brutal clobbering" in the last eighteen
months, and the world situation he finally faced in the United Nations
was much more grim than the one he had described in *Commentary*.
He now tended to regard the Zionism resolution as having been Soviet
sponsored rather than an Arab initiative. Incredible as it seemed, the
Soviets were engaged in a cruel campaign to link Zionism with Nazism,
and the Zionism resolution was just one step in that campaign.[46] Moynihan began to think that he had been naive in believing he could build
strong links to the democratic socialist nations through his opposition
strategy. That tradition was fading much faster than he had imagined,
and was being replaced by authoritarian and antidemocratic regimes that
were unvaryingly hostile—both politically and economically—to the
United States. The appropriate response, never specifically stated, was
for America to hit back with greater vigor.[47]

Moynihan's outspoken posture won him extraordinary attention in
the world press, giving him in effect the stature of a secretary of state.
Some members of the press, like Bernard Levin in the *Times* of London,
reacted warmly. Others were vitriolic and hostile. Tass, the Soviet news
agency, said that Moynihan had senatorial ambitions and was cynically
using the United Nations for the purposes of winning votes from Jewish
voters in New York. And in Africa the *New Nigerian* reported that
Moynihan and Vorster were trying to destroy Angola, and it called on

Africa to resist by doing everything—short of supplying arms—to help the MPLA.[48]

Although Kissinger, too, believed now that Moynihan was using the United Nations as a platform to advance his personal fortunes, he nevertheless found himself implementing a Moynihan policy recommendation early in January. After months of discussion Kissinger announced the establishment of a multilateral affairs desk in the Bureau of International Organizations to monitor the behavior in international forums of those nations with which America had bilateral relations. It was clearly a victory for Moynihan, and the press interpreted the announcement in that light.[49]

Moynihan's battle with the Soviets continued into 1976. He clashed with Ambassador Yakov Malik over whether the Security Council in November had invited the PLO to participate in a discussion on the Middle East. Moynihan had interpreted the vote to extend the mandate of the Golan Heights peace-keeping force as one that did not invite the PLO to participate; eleven nations on the Security Council came to the opposite conclusion. In making this determination, Moynihan said, established procedure was being subverted and an "extra-legal semi-secret" apparatus was now making decisions by fiat. The Security Council itself was moving toward "totalitarianism."

Malik responded by saying that while he agreed that totalitarianism was a terrible thing, it was no less terrible than gangsterism in politics. Then Moynihan intervened to say that while totalitarianism was bad and gangsterism was worse, capitulationism was worst of all, and it was something to which he would never succumb.[50]

By now Moynihan's style had become so distinctive that when he gave a low-key speech on the Middle East later that week in the Security Council, there was speculation that it had been written in Washington. However, his change of tone had little effect on the Security Council; the United States again had to exercise its veto on a resolution calling for the establishment of a Palestinian state. And behind the measured tones Moynihan used in the Security Council there was strong disagreement with Kissinger over the approach the United States should take. Because of the Palestinian presence Israel had decided not to participate in the debate, and the articulation of its position was left to Moynihan.

Kissinger, in Moynihan's view, was exhausted and no longer concentrating. The secretary of state wanted to mollify the Arab states and feared attacking the PLO. He hoped that the Geneva conference would ultimately be reconvened with all parties participating, and to anger the Arabs now would jeopardize that outcome. Worse, Moynihan concluded, Kissinger believed that United States influence had declined so far that it no longer had the power to influence world politics diplomatically. Moynihan had wanted to focus the debate on the PLO, but Kissinger stopped him. Sam Lewis and Joseph Sisco indicated that Kissinger did not want to upset the Arabs or the Russians and left Moynihan to deliver an innocuous speech after his own draft had been rejected.

Moynihan then sent all United States embassies a cable, "The Blocs Are Breaking Up," criticizing the foreign service and the State Department for failing to realize that his tactics were succeeding in breaking up the anti-United States voting blocs at the United Nations. Kissinger wanted to moderate the language of the cable but made no substantial changes in it. Moynihan said he did not expect State Department officials to change their minds; rather, he asked only that they "stop blabbing to the press what is not so." By sending the cable with the lowest security clearance — *"Limited Official Use"*— to every American embassy in the world, Moynihan was taking a substantial and perhaps intentional risk that it would be leaked to the press. And perhaps he did not in fact care what happened to it. He would make his feelings known, and if the media found out, he would not let himself be disturbed.

On January 27 the *New York Times* got hold of the cable just as Moynihan was leaving a meeting in which President Ford had told him he should stay on at the United Nations. Throughout the month Ford and his operatives had been working to keep Moynihan at Turtle Bay. Elliot Richardson had called Harvard President Derek Bok to learn whether Moynihan's tenure could be extended, and the president himself was willing to call Bok if Moynihan wanted him to. But there was no hope. Moynihan had stretched Harvard's rules to the limit by taking two years off to work for Nixon, returning to Harvard for only two years before going to India for another two years, and then—after only one term at Harvard—leaving again to go to the United Nations. Bok told callers he was sorry but it was impossible to grant Moynihan another

extension. Despite his differences with Kissinger and the State Department, Moynihan had told Kissinger early in January that he would stay on at the United Nations after his tenure at Harvard expired in February. But he had not formally told the president this, and he could wait until the last moment (early in February) to tell Harvard of his final decision. If he were going to stay on, he wanted to be assured of having the full support of the State Department.

Kissinger and Ford both issued statements of support for Moynihan after the cable leaked, and Kissinger termed the criticism of Moynihan "normal bureaucratic backbiting."[51] At this time Ford's support was probably the more self-interested and therefore genuine; he had to deal with the immediate electoral consequences in the upcoming New Hampshire primary. But Kissinger was tired of battling with Moynihan, and he believed his ambassador had deliberately sent the cable on low security clearance so that it would be leaked to the press. And his feeling was shared by most of those in the State Department and the United States mission, including a number of people sympathetic to Moynihan.

Two days later a newspaper column changed Moynihan's mind about remaining at the United Nations. James Reston wrote that Ford and Kissinger were obliged to support Moynihan in public but privately deplored him. Political constraints would not permit them "to tame him or repudiate him." Kissinger agreed with Moynihan's defense of American interests but was not satisfied with his style or his provocative rhetoric.[52]

When Moynihan read the *New York Times* article, he felt that it had left him "naked." He thought Kissinger had given the story to Reston just when Moynihan had surrendered his tenure at Harvard in order to embarrass him. There was only one thing for Moynihan to do; he still had five days before his tenure expired, and after reading the article he told his wife that they were returning to Cambridge.

The following day Moynihan called Henry Rosovsky, dean of the Faculty of Arts and Sciences at Harvard, to tell him he would return. "I've just informed the president I won't be coming back."

Rosovsky thought Moynihan was referring to President Bok (in Cambridge the title is generally reserved for the head of the university) and replied, "I'm so sorry."

Moynihan promptly corrected him. "I mean the president of the United States."

The resignation would not be announced until the following Monday in order to give President Ford a chance to consider Moynihan's resignation letter. Moynihan was particularly anxious that Leonard Garment not learn about the resignation before it was publicly announced. Garment was leaving for a human rights meeting in Geneva, and Moynihan knew that he would protest and might even cancel his trip if he knew what was happening. Moynihan told all the guests at a farewell lunch that he was resigning and swore each of them not to tell Garment. Dick Cheney tried to reach Garment during the luncheon, but Moynihan would not let him take the call.

On Monday, February 2, Moynihan's resignation was announced. In his brief letter Moynihan made no mention of the Reston column or his differences with the State Department. He cited only tenure considerations for his decision to return to teaching. Moynihan thanked Ford for being "unfailing in your encouragement and support." Ford replied that he accepted the resignation with "the deepest reluctance and regret," and added that Moynihan "elevated public discourse by puncturing pretense and by eloquently advocating the cause of reason."[53]

Because Moynihan had been nominated Security Council president for February, it was decided that he would continue in that capacity until the end of the month, commuting to Cambridge to teach one and a half days a week. But returning to Harvard did not mean he was closing the door on a political career. "I assume I will be back in government one way or another some time. I am going back to teaching now."[54]

11

The Big Gamble

If I thought I could win an election occasionally, I'd be delighted
to go into politics.

— Pat Moynihan, 1953

Pat Moynihan left the United Nations with a flourish. One of his last
press releases, for example, reports a statement he made in the Security
Council shortly before his departure, while exercising his right of reply
to an attack by Soviet Ambassador Yakov Malik. Malik had criticized
Moynihan and Kissinger for making slanderous charges to the effect that
Russia intended to colonize Africa. The United States should "take
care" when discussing Moscow's policies, Malik had said. Moynihan
struck back, as though to emphasize that whatever the exigencies of
American domestic politics, he would leave the United Nations with the
United States presenting a united front to the world.

> Now, gentlemen, the distinguished Ambassador may speak as any of you
> may speak, as he will, of this Ambassador. Do not, however, presume to
> speak of my Secretary of State in such terms. Do not address the Secretary
> of State in the language of a purge trial. We are not intimidated, we are
> not afraid. We will not "take care," we do not give a damn.[1]

His return to Harvard was almost as flamboyant. On February 12, 1976, he arrived in Cambridge to teach his graduate seminar on ethnic politics wearing a trench coat and the familiar Irish tweed hat and trailed by a dozen reporters and photographers. This was no ordinary professor of government come to meet his students. The university had taken the precaution of stationing two policemen outside the door of the seminar room in Sever Hall for security. And before the two-hour session ended Moynihan made unexpected use of them.

Moynihan began with a brief lecture on ethnic identification in American life and a statement of the requirements of the course. All students would be expected to write a long research paper, and anyone planning to stay in the class would have to turn in an outline of his or her paper the next day. Students at Harvard have two weeks to reach a final decision on the courses they will take that term, and usually the early meetings of a class attract far more students than will ultimately enroll. Moynihan's ethnic politics seminar drew 90 students the first day —about 75 more than would actually participate. The group was unruly, and Moynihan said that while he would excuse people for arriving late he would not tolerate people leaving early. And when he saw a student leaving the classroom midway through the lecture, he stopped and called out, "Sir. Sir. Someone bring that student back in here." A willing student went out, caught the fellow who had left (Harvard *Crimson* reporter Richard Weisman), and brought him back into the room of somewhat stunned undergraduates and graduates.

When the class session ended, photographers entered the room to photograph Moynihan, but he would not allow it. It was against university rules for the press to come into the classroom, Moynihan told the photographers, and he called in the two policemen to make sure that the rules were observed. Thereupon he left, trailed by eager photographers and reporters who asked him repeatedly if he planned to run for the United States Senate seat held by Conservative-Republican James Buckley of New York.[2]

Moynihan had told the members of the press who attended the first meeting of his seminar, "I don't know what all of you are doing here. I teach government at Harvard."[3] Yet it was clear that his role in American politics in 1976 would not merely be that of a mere spectator.

Just before returning to Harvard Moynihan had met with Democratic presidential aspirant Henry Jackson, who had taken to asking audiences, "Wouldn't it be great to have Daniel Patrick Moynihan as secretary of state?" Jackson, a strong opponent of Secretary of State Kissinger, had sought Moynihan's endorsement, and evidently Moynihan had responded favorably but said he would have to leave the United Nations before making a formal statement. The statement came in time for the Massachusetts primary; Moynihan campaigned with Jackson and helped him to win a narrow victory. Then Moynihan went to Florida to try to help Jackson win key Jewish support. But the results of the Florida primary confirmed Moynihan's suspicion that Jackson did not have much chance of winning the nomination. If Moynihan were going to return to government, it would probably have to be on his own.

Moynihan wanted to run for the Senate in New York, but a number of problems had to be resolved before he could make an announcement or authorize a committee to begin working on his behalf. He had told a national television audience that it would be "dishonorable" for him to run for the Senate upon leaving the United Nations, and he disliked having to reverse himself so blatantly. In addition a group of black leaders in New York had issued a statement saying that he was an unacceptable candidate for the Senate because of his "benign neglect" memorandum and his association with Richard Nixon.[4] Moynihan was sensitive about his poor relationship with black leaders, and he had little inclination to fight old battles again in public. Governor Hugh Carey was not eager to see another powerful Irish politician in New York State and thus was hesitant at first about encouraging Moynihan. Moreover, Moynihan did not enjoy campaigning and was unsure that he could endure the rigors of a long campaign. A loss would undercut the popularity he had won at the United Nations and thereby weaken his political standing. Finally, there were already several potential candidates for the seat—Bella Abzug, Paul O'Dwyer, Ramsey Clark, Andrew Stein, Abraham Hirschfeld—and Moynihan well knew that anything can happen in a crowded Democratic primary.

These doubts were so strong that Moynihan resisted the efforts of his lawyer, Arthur Klebanoff, and a close friend, Midge Decter, to organize a committee to assess his support around the state and to raise the money needed to get a campaign off the ground. Nor was he very good about returning calls from prospective supporters in New York. Part of the problem was that he was understaffed, but his lack of commitment to the idea of running often led him to ignore invitations from possibly crucial New York backers. However, he did take the opportunity to go before the electorate as a candidate in the New York primary for delegates to the Democratic convention, and here he saw a dramatic demonstration of his drawing potential.

Moynihan was still testing the waters for a Senate race in mid March when the final slates of delegates were completed for the New York presidential primary. At the last possible moment the Jackson forces added Moynihan's name to the list of candidates in the 22nd Congressional District in the Bronx, which includes Co-op City, a large housing development populated principally by elderly Jews (who were presumed to be most sympathetic to him). A problem arose when Moynihan's substitution form reached Albany two days late. However, Secretary of State Mario Cuomo was willing to take Moynihan's word that the form had been mailed on time. This generated some ill will because the representative of the district, Jonathan Bingham, was heading the rival Udall slate and had not been informed of the change by Moynihan. As Moynihan's former political patron, Bingham thought that common courtesy required some advance notice.

Moynihan ran far ahead of the rest of the Jackson slate in the district, winning handily and helping his candidate to capture all but one of the delegate spots—that won by Bingham. The brief campaign had given Moynihan the opportunity to stump with Jackson throughout the state and to assess the political climate. One trip won him page-one coverage in the *New York Times*—a demonstration of how seriously his Senate candidacy was being taken.[5]

After the presidential primary Moynihan began to look more like a Senate candidate. He made a low-key tour of the state, conferring with political leaders and potential supporters such as Erie County chairman Joe Crangle, with whom he had dinner in Buffalo. Moynihan told Crangle only that he was considering running, and the two agreed to speak further. Crangle was in touch with labor leaders in New York and Washington who could generate pressure. Lane Kirkland, the secretary-

treasurer of the AFL-CIO, and Al Barkan, the union's political operative, urged Moynihan to run and implied that financial support would
be available if he made the race. On a number of occasions New York
builder Richard Ravitch entertained Moynihan in an effort to draw him
into the race.

In May Moynihan was gradually persuaded that he should become a
candidate. By the middle of the month he was almost certain of running,
and there was speculation that he would announce early in June. Then,
toward the end of the month, he suddenly had reservations. Late in May
he met in Washington with part of the New York Democratic congressional delegation and came away with mixed reviews. Then Representative Edward Koch, now mayor of New York City, said after the meeting
that Moynihan had not made the "kind of presentation of which he is
capable." Representative Matthew McHugh said Moynihan's manner
was better suited to a dining room or the United Nations than it was
to a statewide campaign. It was the sort of appearance that Moynihan
did not enjoy, and he realized there would be many more of them if he
decided to run. The prospect made him uneasy; close friends recall that
they had never seen him as nervous as he was at this time.

When New York County Democratic leaders decided to support Paul
O'Dwyer, Moynihan's doubts grew. Crangle and Ravitch then had dinner with Moynihan in a final effort to get him to run, and Crangle
promised to go down the line with him. On June 10 Moynihan announced his candidacy.

Looking back on his decision to run, Moynihan sees two factors that
helped him to reach that decision. The first was the threatened closing
of City College because of a shortage of funds; Moynihan, who had
attended City College, believed that a free university symbolized what
was right about New York. The second, more significant, reason was that
Moynihan did not want to feel that at forty-nine years of age he had
passed up his chance to be a United States senator.[6]

Moynihan had no campaign manager—much less a campaign staff—
when he announced in mid June. Former aide Richard Blumenthal
agreed to serve as interim campaign manager, but he was no campaign
technician. Moynihan's first press conference was not well organized. No
one in Moynihan's immediate circle of friends had met Al Slaner, a key

fund-raiser, before the announcement, and Moynihan had trouble reaching him. He had not even signed the papers that would authorize a committee to be formed on his behalf—an act that was required by the time of his announcement.

At the press conference with Moynihan were Crangle, Ray Corbett (head of the state AFL-CIO), and black leaders Bayard Rustin and Bernard Gifford. The participation of Rustin and Gifford would demonstrate that Moynihan could attract at least two prominent blacks to his campaign team. To be sure, neither of them was in the mainstream of New York black leadership, but their very presence made Moynihan feel better. In fact Gifford was standing at the back of the room when Moynihan began to speak, and Moynihan made a point of having him come to the front of the room.

Following the announcement, Moynihan traveled around the state to repeat his statement at a series of press conferences, using an airplane hastily chartered for him by a contributor, Daniel Rose. The next day's newspapers captured Moynihan's theme: he was the only Democrat who could win in November.

To qualify for the New York primary ballot a candidate must collect at least 50,000 petition signatures statewide or receive 25 percent of the vote at the State Democratic Committee endorsement meeting. While Moynihan and Crangle were not eager that he be identified closely with the party leaders (and thus open Moynihan to charges that he was the bosses' candidate), they did not want to have to obtain the petition signatures. Crangle determined that the ideal way to qualify for the ballot would be to get more than 25 percent of the vote but not enough to win the endorsement.

On the first ballot Moynihan, Abzug, and O'Dwyer each received over 25 percent of the vote and Ramsey Clark had less than 10 percent. On the second ballot Crangle threw his upstate support to Clark in order to get him on the ballot and thereby further divide New York's liberal Democrats, who were already split between O'Dwyer and Abzug. On the third ballot Crangle supported O'Dwyer, helping to give him the party designation. It was a triumph of sorts for Moynihan, yet for the first time he saw the type of attack he would have to face in the campaign. Abzug circulated a flier that showed Moynihan with Nixon and asked, "What kind of Democrat do you want for your Senator?" Moynihan was also heckled when he spoke; his foes interrupted him to ask hostile questions about his attitude toward blacks.[7]

Once again Moynihan was a candidate, and once again the process took its toll. Little was being done to organize the campaign, and Moynihan had only his wife to help monitor the increasingly heavy demands on his time. He began to make mistakes. He failed to keep a luncheon appointment in Washington to discuss his Senate candidacy with a group of twenty-five reporters. Contacted afterward, Moynihan said he had been in a daze and had simply forgotten it.

Moynihan's brain trust (Leonard Garment, Norman Podhoretz, Arthur Klebanoff, Dick Blumenthal, and Joe Crangle) wanted an advertisement in the *New York Times* announcing Moynihan's candidacy and asking for contributions. It was left to Moynihan to prepare the final text, so he sat down at his typewriter and came up with the slogan, "He spoke up for America. He'll speak up for New York State." The photograph he selected showed himself in an assertive posture, voting at the United Nations. Rather than follow the usual procedure of having an advertising agency design the ad and refine the copy and the photography, Moynihan himself took everything to the *New York Times* advertising office on West 43rd Street and asked for space in the Week in Review section for Sunday, June 27. He handed a shocked *Times* employee the photograph and the copy he had written, paid for the ad, and strolled off toward Times Square. The employee had still not recovered from Moynihan's personal visit when Dick Blumenthal arrived to look over and approve the appearance of the ad. The *Times* advertisement was noticed, bringing a torrent of telephone calls to the makeshift Moynihan-for-Senate office and spurring a number of early contributions. Thereafter almost all the basic Moynihan campaign materials included the slogan Moynihan had composed and the photograph of him voting at the United Nations.

The campaign had acquired a degree of organization by late June when a permanent campaign manager was hired after Dick Blumenthal took a job with a law firm in Connecticut. Meyer (Sandy) Frucher, a veteran of New York political campaigns, was a close ally of Erie County leader Joe Crangle. Frucher had ties to the regular party organization yet was comparatively young and had spent a year at Harvard's Kennedy School of Government. Blumenthal thought Frucher would be able to work well with Moynihan. This proved to be a miscalculation.

Moynihan went to Israel over the July 4 weekend to receive an honorary degree from Hebrew University. The trip to Israel is something of a tradition for New York politicians at the start of a campaign, and for Moynihan the timing was particularly fortuitous. That happened to be the weekend of the Entebbe raid in Uganda, and although no Israeli leader discussed the raid with him in advance, he could share in the general euphoria that followed its successful execution. On his return to New York Moynihan held a well-attended press conference at which he called for new sanctions against international terrorists. He also wrote an account of the weekend for *New York* magazine.

Surprisingly, foreign policy did not preoccupy Moynihan during his campaign. Moynihan did not duck foreign policy issues, and he wanted to demonstrate that he was not a one-issue (Israel) candidate. But he spent at least an equal amount of time talking about New York State's economic problems and national domestic issues. The themes he stressed were those he had stressed throughout his years in government: family stability, welfare reform, unemployment measures, and financial relief for depressed urban areas (particularly New York City). In a sense the campaign served to tie together the various strands that had always been present in Moynihan's world view.

The late start of Moynihan's campaign meant a serious lack of money at a crucial stage. To reach New York voters effectively a candidate must buy substantial amounts of expensive television and radio time. One cannot hope to meet even a small fraction of the electorate by campaigning at well-traveled locations. Thus Moynihan spent a disproportionate amount of his time speaking at breakfasts, lunches, cocktail parties, and dinners in search of funds. The typical party would be held on the East Side of Manhattan; affluent couples would have drinks with Moynihan, listen to a brief speech, and then write checks in amounts of up to $1000 (the federal limit for individual contributions). The limit certainly hurt Moynihan, for there were a number of wealthy New Yorkers who were prepared to give substantially more. It also put a premium on his reaching out to as many people as possible. In July Moynihan's heavy schedule led Sandy Frucher to remark, "Pat is spending so much time at breakfasts, lunches, and dinners with contributors that we'll have the fattest candidate around."[8]

A number of prominent New Yorkers, among them journalist Theodore White, opened their homes to Moynihan and his campaign staff for fund-raising parties. Events of this nature were well attended but often failed to raise much money, for many people would come simply to sip white wine with Bess Myerson and other celebrities and to see what kind of house Teddy White had. While Bess Myerson was a great drawing card and Teddy White's brownstone lived up to expectations, the crowding of hundreds of people into comparatively small areas only made everyone hot and uncomfortable. Many guests had to watch the festivities from awkward vantage points such as a hall staircase. The Moynihan staff had difficulty monitoring large crowds, and many people got away from such parties without making a contribution. Others made only token contributions of $25 or $50.

Moynihan raised about $175,000 through his efforts, however, enough to fund a modest media campaign. But relations between Frucher and Moynihan had begun to sour, and within the campaign staff itself there was dissatisfaction with Frucher's managerial abilities. A parallel campaign was started by Bernard Gifford and Herbert Rickman, another veteran of New York Democratic campaigns. Gifford and Rickman organized a citizens' committee and opened their own office on the West Side to coordinate its activities. Liz Moynihan, frustrated with Frucher, began working closely with Gifford and Rickman. Much of the campaign's street activities were managed in the citizens' committee office; so was much of the recruitment of surrogates to speak for Moynihan when he was unable to accept an invitation.

In August Joe Crangle came down from Buffalo to give Frucher a hand with the main campaign organization. There was a certain measure of risk in this move; Moynihan counted on Crangle to bring out a big vote in upstate New York, and for Crangle to leave his home base in the month before the primary meant that the Moynihan campaign there might be less well run than it would have been otherwise.

The emphasis on fund-raising drew attention away from issues and personalities, and, therefore, at first it was a dull campaign. The television commercials, which proved to be the most significant part of the campaign, did not begin in earnest until the first half of August, after Frucher pressured the rest of Moynihan's advisers to spend money they had intended to save for a blitz in the final weeks of the campaign. The decision was an important one, for Moynihan's own polls early in August showed him trailing. Gradually the media began to focus on the two people they considered to be the front runners: Pat Moynihan and Bella Abzug. And as attention turned to the two of them, they began attacking one another. Moynihan criticized Abzug for opposing the Family Assistance Program and supporting massive cuts in the defense budget. Abzug said she would not support Moynihan if he won the primary. "I don't see any reason for me to support anyone who continues Ford-Nixon policies."[9]

Then Abzug ran into difficulties. Thirty-three Democratic county chairmen responded to her statement by urging her to change her position.[10] And a radio advertisement that she had sponsored, which began, "The following tape comes to you from the Nixon White House," and which was intended to demonstrate the link between Moynihan and Nixon, had to be withdrawn when it was learned that the recording had originated in the Hotel Pierre in New York.[11]

If there was a sympathy vote in the race, Moynihan won it late in August. While he was campaigning one Saturday on the lower East Side a member of the Youth International Party ran up and hit him in the face with a pie. Moynihan was stunned momentarily, but there was no serious damage. The one photographer on the scene, who worked for a foreign newspaper, captured the event, and Moynihan staff members took his photograph to all the major newspapers. The following day Moynihan's pie-faced picture was on the front page of the *New York Times*. One can only wonder how Moynihan must have felt, having begun the year debating world affairs with Soviet Ambassador Yakov Malik in the United Nations Security Council and now fending off attacks from Yippies with banana cream pies.

In the closing days of the campaign the two morning newspapers, the *New York Times* and the *Daily News,* endorsed Moynihan's candidacy. The *News* had a heavily Catholic readership in the four boroughs outside Manhattan, and the *Times* reached upper middle class Protestants and

Jews in Manhattan and suburban New York. The two newspapers rarely
endorse the same candidate, so winning the support of both was quite
a coup.

The *Times* endorsement was a story in its own right, coming as it did
only after a bitter fight between John B. Oakes, then editorial page
editor, and Arthur Ochs Sulzberger, the publisher. The editorial board
had voted to endorse Abzug, but Sulzberger vetoed their decision and
threw the paper's enormous prestige behind Moynihan, whose endorsement Oakes adamantly opposed. The editorial itself stirred further ill
feeling, for it sought to woo Abzug's supporters by minimizing the
considerable political differences between her and Moynihan while emphasizing his superior chances of winning. The outraged Oakes then
stated his own position in a letter to the editor, a truncated version of
which the paper agreed to run.

As the campaign wound down Moynihan became more and more the
target of the other four candidates' attacks. There was a series of rather
acrimonious debates, but the major development of the last week or ten
days was the loss by Paul O'Dwyer of a substantial amount of support
among regular Democrats, who began defecting to Moynihan. The
defections were particularly pronounced among the Catholic voters who
had been O'Dwyer's core group. In late August O'Dwyer had been
winning the Catholic vote over Moynihan, 29 percent to 26 percent; by
primary day polls showed Moynihan was carrying Catholics over O'Dwyer, 34 percent to 17 percent.

Early returns on the night of the primary indicated that the election
was going to be very close. Throughout the night Moynihan managed
to hold a narrow lead of one or two percent, a lead that never seemed
to widen. Moynihan awaited the results with a few close friends at his
apartment on East 78th Street. By 1:00 A.M., with Abzug unable to cut
into his lead, it began to appear that he would win narrowly. Moynihan's
final margin was 10,000 votes; he had 37 percent of the vote to Abzug's
36 percent.

Moynihan carried New York City, its suburbs, and upstate New York.
Abzug did well in parts of the upstate area, winning Crangle's Erie
County and Monroe and Niagara counties. She won Manhattan and the
Bronx, and also she carried Westchester and Suffolk counties. Moynihan

won Brooklyn, Queens, and Staten Island, and Nassau and Rockland counties. Upstate he won Albany, Broome, and Onondaga counties. Moynihan defeated Abzug decisively among Catholic and Jewish voters but lost to her overwhelmingly among black and Puerto Rican voters. Abzug also won a large plurality of the women's vote.

In the first days after the primary the tone of the general election campaign was set. Despite the fact that Moynihan had clearly been the most conservative candidate in the Democratic primary, Senator Buckley was sufficiently conservative to tie him to the left wing of the Democratic party. Moynihan, Buckley said, "would be a flamboyant Senator who would lead the charge in the wrong direction." He was nothing but a liberal professor who was out of touch with the concerns of most New Yorkers.[12]

Moynihan has always been more comfortable dealing with criticism from the right rather than from the left, and he handled Conservative-Republican Buckley with ease. He portrayed himself as a moderate and his opponent as an extremist who was outside the mainstream of American politics. After all, Buckley had been elected on a third-party line and had not been welcomed as a full-fledged member of the Republican party. While Moynihan may not have looked like an authentic member of the working class, Buckley's patrician manner did little to convince the electorate that he was any closer to the people than Moynihan. As Moynihan pointed out, Buckley had attended the exclusive Millbrook School in upstate New York while Moynihan went to public schools in New York City and worked on the docks.

There was a sharp difference between the two on the degree of federal aid that should be offered New York City. Moynihan favored massive assistance—a position naturally supported overwhelmingly by the New York electorate. As senator, Buckley had done little to help during the fiscal crisis of that year. Indeed, Buckley suffered from the fallout of a headline in the *Daily News* the previous winter that read: FORD TO CITY: DROP DEAD.

Early polls gave Moynihan a lead of more than 10 percent, but he had problems organizing his campaign. His staff was in disarray, he and Frucher were barely on speaking terms, and Crangle was no longer held in high esteem after the loss to Abzug in Erie County. There was an effort to remove Crangle entirely from the campaign and vest formal control of the campaign in Edward Costikyan, and there was also an effort to make Frucher press secretary. But Frucher refused to go along with a plan which would have undermined his patron Joe Crangle and ultimately the idea was abandoned. Frucher stayed on as a sort of figurehead while most of the day-to-day details of the campaign were decided at the citizens' committee headquarters. Campaign strategy was conceived by Moynihan's close friends Leonard Garment, Arthur Klebanoff, and Norman Podhoretz, with Liz Moynihan serving as coordinator of the ad hoc group. Little was done on a grass roots level during the campaign, but by then there was not much need for a significant organizational effort in that direction.

The election campaign, like the primary campaign, was desperately short of money. A $100,000 debt remained from the primary, and Moynihan had to reach into his own pocket to finance the final weeks of the general election campaign. In a sense, however, the disorganization of the campaign was a hidden blessing: had much money been available, it might only have been wasted by Moynihan's disorganized staff.

Another problem concerned the Liberal party. The Liberals in New York State traditionally nominate a stand-in candidate before the Democratic primary is held and afterward substitute the name of the Democratic winner. In 1976, however, there was feeling that Moynihan was too conservative and that the Liberals should nominate another candidate. Overtures were made to Bella Abzug and former mayor John Lindsay, but both refused to run in the general election. Ultimately Governor Hugh Carey went before the Liberal party policy committee to plead Moynihan's case and convinced the party to give the Democratic standard-bearer its line. Thus Moynihan had the Democratic and Liberal party designations and Buckley designation of the Republican and Conservative parties. The only Democratic groups that did not support Moynihan were minority groups and the party's reform New Democratic Coalition. Although blacks and Puerto Ricans offered little support, at least there were few public demonstrations of opposition; one such demonstration did, however, come from psychologist Kenneth Clark, who backed Buckley. Liberal reform Democrats were similarly reluctant to support Moynihan but did not campaign actively against him.

Moynihan's most far-reaching problem was deciding what to do with his Harvard professorship. The university would not grant him another leave of absence, and virtually all his colleagues in the government department wanted him to resign. But if he resigned and then lost the election, he would be unemployed. Even though his election was considered a safe bet, he was unwilling to give up the position for which he had worked for most of his adult life. And despite his prominence Moynihan was not convinced that he could obtain a similar post if he lost the election. When friends sought to reassure him, Moynihan cited the case of Arthur Schlesinger, Jr., who had been prominent during the Kennedy years but had later fallen into what Moynihan described as relative obscurity at the Graduate Center of City College.

Moynihan also believed he needed the money. He described his situation during the campaign. "My primary campaign ended $146,000 in debt. I signed personal notes for $50,000 of that, which is half the money I've been able to save in nearly 25 years of working in Government, teaching, writing, and lecturing. I've got two kids in school and I've already taken enough chances this year."[13] There may have been some exaggeration in this statement; in 1976 he actually earned $43,000 in salary from his United Nations and Harvard posts and an additional $152,000 in lecture fees.

So, despite the objections of such close friends as Professor James Q. Wilson, Moynihan decided to commute to Harvard two days a week to teach his two courses. One of the courses, Social Science and Social Policy, was an undergraduate lecture course to which Moynihan was supposed to lecture twice a week; here he was fortunate in having three very good teaching assistants (Nick Eberstadt, Bob Katzman, and Bill Kristol) who could fill in for him when he was unable to prepare a lecture. His other course, the seminar on ethnic politics, required little preparation, yet he occasionally surprised members of the class with a discussion of academic articles he had somehow found time to read while ostensibly campaigning full time in New York.

Moynihan may not always have been able to prepare conscientiously for his classes, but he fastidiously avoided discussing electoral politics in the classroom. With annoyance, he brushed off questions about his campaign, insisting that he was at Harvard to teach and not to discuss his race with Buckley. To add to the general discomfort of teaching responsibilities heaped on a full-time campaign schedule, Moynihan strained his neck when his plane hit turbulence during a trip around New York State.

Moynihan campaigned with Jimmy Carter and Walter Mondale on a number of occasions, and he continued to brand Buckley an opponent of traditional New Deal liberalism. As the two men generally agreed on foreign policy, economic issues created the only real differences between them. And with Moynihan holding a substantial lead in the polls, Buckley had to resort to ad hominem attacks to try to catch up. He criticized Moynihan for campaigning after having said it would be dishonorable to leave the United Nations to run for office, and he accused Moynihan of altering his positions for political gain. Constantly referring to Moynihan as "Professor," Buckley played on the electorate's presumed anti-intellectual bias.

Moynihan struck back by labeling Buckley a "radical of the right"— a charge that Buckley denied heatedly. Moynihan, Buckley said, was using the big lie technique of Joseph Goebbels. A supporter of Buckley wrote President Bok of Harvard to say that the university's reliance on federal funding might make it illegal for Moynihan to be on the payroll and run for the Senate. Buckley's aides told the press that Moynihan had left substantial debts behind when he left India. Moynihan responded by calling these campaign tactics "cruddy and Neanderthal" and asked what any of it had to do with the Senate race.

Buckley was not deterred. In the final weeks before the election he sponsored television ads that quoted Moynihan as saying that black Americans should be treated with benign neglect and that anyone who starved in America was an idiot. Apparently Buckley had decided he could not win the election on the issues and could succeed only if he attacked Moynihan personally and distorted the record.[14]

Moynihan's rhetoric in turn became more personal as the campaign drew to a close. He called Buckley "an eccentricity that New Yorkers can ill afford in the United States Senate." He said Buckley's voting record was "so consistently uncaring, so consistently arrogant toward us, that if it did not exist, it would be impossible to invent it."[15]

Moynihan won comfortably. The victory was obvious early in the evening, and Buckley conceded an hour and a half after the polls closed. Moynihan attended a few victory parties and celebrated long into the night. Not only was he pleased at having beaten Buckley, he felt largely responsible for Carter's victory in New York State. Moynihan had run some 300,000 votes ahead of Jimmy Carter, and without his own presence on the ticket, Moynihan reasoned, many moderate and conservative Democrats might have defected. With a Democratic candidate like Bella Abzug the defections might have been so substantial that Gerald Ford would have defeated Carter.

The next morning senator-elect Moynihan flew to Harvard to meet his Social Science and Social Policy class. Again he was trailed by reporters. Having had no sleep the night before, Moynihan was irritable. When a reporter asked when he had prepared the day's lecture, he answered, "None of your business." Asked if he had mentioned the election in his class, he was indignant; of course not, he said, it had nothing to do with the class. At his campaign headquarters in New York the following day he was still irritable when a reporter asked him to detail the welfare reform proposals he would give the Carter administration. "It's not something for the simple-minded, I'm afraid."[16]

Yet Moynihan was elated by his triumph; he had taken the biggest gamble of his career, and it had paid off handsomely. Only his financial situation was of serious concern, and to alleviate that he decided to go on the lecture circuit for a couple of months. The attention he had received while in the United Nations, combined with his recent election victory, made him a hot commodity; he could now demand as much as $5,000 for a speech in such places as Loma Linda College in California. A few weeks of exhausting travel would help to pay off most of the $50,000 personal debt he had assumed in the primary.

At Harvard there were those who were happy about his triumph for a different reason—he would finally be leaving Cambridge. One high university official told a law student sitting beside him on a flight to New York the day after the election that "both institutions [Harvard and the United States Senate] would profit from Moynihan's victory." The government department congratulated Moynihan on his victory at the first departmental meeting he attended following the election, even though most if not all of the members believed he had abused his position by having stayed on after winning the Democratic primary.

Harvard had its little revenge on Moynihan at the end of the year. When he submitted his resignation in mid December, he was not allowed to keep his office until the term ended in mid January. Thus Moynihan had to work out of his home on Francis Avenue for the remainder of the month before moving to Washington. Later the students in his graduate seminar would have to mail their research papers to him in Washington in order to be graded in the course.

12

A New Year in the Senate

Being in the Senate is the highest honor you can get in this republic
other than the presidency. It means that you must be just absolutely
fearless and try to be intelligent. I expect to be a good Senator.
—Pat Moynihan, 1976

Foreign policy may have put Pat Moynihan on the political map in New
York State, but in the everyday life of a politician fiscal questions are
more important. And when a senator's home base is a New York City
teetering on the brink of bankruptcy, he will have a good idea of what
he must do. Asked during the primary campaign what Senate committee
he hoped to serve on, Moynihan answered without hesitation: finance.

Finance is where the money is, Moynihan had said emphatically
during the campaign, and now he began an aggressive public and private
drive to win appointment to that committee. In public he made the case
that it had been at least a hundred years since a New Yorker had served
on the committee. In private he saw his vote for Senate majority leader
as a bargaining chip in winning the committee assignment. When it
appeared that Hubert Humphrey had a chance to win the leadership
post, the betting in Washington was that Moynihan would support him.

Then, as Humphrey's chances faded and the election of Robert Byrd became more certain, Moynihan made it clear that he planned to support the likely winner. On the day the Senate convened to choose its new leadership, the front page of the *New York Times* carried a photograph of Senator Moynihan conferring with Senator Byrd. Moynihan's support of Byrd outraged Edward Kennedy and other liberals who had counted on his vote for Humphrey, but Moynihan maintained that he had never given Humphrey a commitment and had always planned to vote for Byrd. In February 1977 Moynihan was appointed to the Finance Committee.

There was a measure of irony in the appointment. The Senate Finance Committee, chaired by Russell Long of Louisiana, was the body that was largely responsible for killing the Family Assistance Program on which Moynihan had labored for two years in the Nixon White House. And it was the body that would shape and refine the Carter administration's own plan to reform the welfare system. When Long named Moynihan chairman of the committee's Public Assistance Subcommittee, New York's new senator knew he would be at the center of the discussion of welfare reform.

Moynihan's other assignments were to the Environment and Public Works and Intelligence committees, and on both committees he would make substantial contributions during his first two years in the Senate.

The United States Senate is a very different place from the United Nations. At the United Nations Moynihan felt surrounded by hostile forces and believed it important to champion the American position without regard for whom he offended. In Washington, however, Moynihan did not face the enemy. Heeding Sam Rayburn's old adage that to get along you have to go along, Moynihan began to court the people who would determine how well he would make out for New York State: his ninety-nine colleagues, especially Chairman Long of the Finance Committee and Chairman Jennings Randolph of the Public Works Committee. His strategy showed early signs of success as he won praise from his New York colleague Jacob Javits, from Daniel Inouye, chairman of the Intelligence Committee, and from Long and Randolph. Moynihan's reputation for an ability to polarize and divide began to give way to his ability to flatter, cajole, and persuade—skills that he has used with substantial success in the Senate.

Moynihan's first test came in February 1977 when he led the fight to block an amendment to public works legislation that would have mandated the uniform allocation of federal funds to the states. Had it passed, the amendment would have cost New York $136 million in aid. Just as Moynihan joined the committee the amendment came before it, and one of the new senator's first acts was to persuade Randolph and the ranking Republican member, Robert Stafford, to introduce a new formula that would give more assistance to states with high unemployment —such as New York. The initial proposal for the uniform allocation of funds (introduced by Senator John Heinz of Pennsylvania) was defeated in committee, and Moynihan's proposal was accepted in its place.

The battle had only begun. Since Moynihan had raised the issue, Randolph left it to him to lead the floor fight for his own plan. He lobbied assiduously, demonstrating to senators from small states that had previously been given equal benefits that his revised plan would give them a minimum of $20 million, $10 million more than they would get under Heinz's proposal. The Heinz plan was defeated in the Senate, and in April the House and Senate conferees accepted the Moynihan formula, which gave New York the maximum grant of $500 million. Moynihan's first victory in the Senate proved that he was just as skilled at quiet diplomacy as he had been in public debate at the United Nations.[1]

Moynihan has been careful not to offend his colleagues in the Senate, but he has shown no such caution with regard to the Carter administration. Given the age-old tension between the legislative and executive branches, Moynihan risked losing no friends in the Senate by taking on the administration. Since he had played a major role in drafting the 1976 Democratic platform and sensed that his substantial victory had helped Carter to carry New York, he believed he had a special responsibility to see that his policies were implemented.

One of the major themes of Moynihan's Senate campaign was that he would work to bring additional federal revenue to beleaguered New York City and State. And in the first months of his Senate term he was criticized for taking an excessively parochial view of national issues, focusing only on their impact on New York State.

In June Moynihan issued a report with a follow-up letter to the president on "The Federal Government and the Economy of New York State," which maintained that "Washington is directly accountable for a major proportion of the state's economic problems." The report made three principal arguments. First, far more money leaves New York in taxes than returns in revenue; at present the gap is about $17.1 billion annually. Second, national environmental policies are so strict that it is difficult for New York to maintain its current levels of economic activity, much less expand. Third, international free trade policy had greatly damaged the garment industry, the largest in New York City. Now it was up to President Carter to repair this state of affairs. An emergency revenue-sharing program to close the gap between what New York receives and what it pays out was needed; if Carter would not propose one, Moynihan would do it as a member of the Senate Finance Committee.[2]

It was not until mid September 1977 that President Carter responded to Moynihan's letter and report, and while the senator characterized the president's reply as "positive," it was clear that he was far from satisfied with it. The president wrote Moynihan that he would direct the Office of Management and Budget to study the government's capability for monitoring the effect of taxing and spending policies on individual regions and states. "The federal government," Moynihan said, "does not know if it is devastating the economy of New York, and what is more it can't find out." And if the federal government could not do its work, it was up to New York State to prepare economic analyses for the president. The president also asked Charles Schultze, chairman of the Council of Economic Advisers, and Stuart Eizenstat, his chief domestic policy adviser, to prepare an analysis of Moynihan's report.

While Moynihan had a number of disagreements with their report to the president, he noted that they seemed to share his view that New York had received only $26 billion in federal expenditures in 1976, not the $40 billion that the government claimed. The difference of $14 billion consisted largely of interest payments on the public debt that had been made by the Federal Reserve Bank in Manhattan and could not legitimately be considered an expenditure in New York. Agreement on this interpretation would not result in a windfall to New York State but would help to change the nature of the discussion of the state's fiscal status. Instead of the Community Services Administration's reporting that New York received $40 billion and paid out $36.9 billion in taxes, the revised figures would be $26 billion received and $36.9 billion paid out. Thus New York's representatives could maintain that the federal government collected $10 billion more than it returned—thereby making a stronger case for fiscal relief from the federal government. In mid January the Community Services Administration wrote Moynihan that they accepted his analysis of federal expenditures.[3]

The victory over the reporting of federal outlays was an isolated one and did not immediately result in more aid to New York. And early in 1978 Moynihan's efforts on behalf of New York City took on a renewed sense of urgency after William Proxmire and Edward Brooke, the ranking majority and minority members of the Senate Banking Committee, wrote President Carter to oppose the renewal of federal loans to New York City. Subsequently Moynihan offered the president a proposition that he conceded was outlandish on first reading—but insisted was self-evident on reflection.

> The proposition is as follows. The single object of urban policy in the United States in the years ahead must be to prevent the bankruptcy of New York City. . . . For if New York City goes bankrupt, nothing else will be noted, nothing else will be remembered. . . . It would change the culture. It would be the only thing this Congress and your Administration would be remembered for.[4]

In February he returned to this theme at a White House Conference on Balanced Growth and Economic Development. He argued that the administration should avoid all efforts to politicize the issue of regional imbalance and should provide guarantees to the State of New York if it agreed to refinance the city's debt obligation. A couple of weeks later, after the Senate Banking Committee indicated preliminarily that there should be no more loans to New York City, Moynihan told the New York State Bankers' Association that "the time is at hand to hear from the President. It is no longer enough for him to say that he will not allow bankruptcy. The time has come for him to state how he will prevent it."[5]

In mid March Moynihan told an audience he was in a "black mood" about the possibility of staving off bankruptcy before the July 1 deadline for the enactment of new legislation.

Ultimately the administration proposed a New York City Loan Guarantee Act that authorized the secretary of the treasury to guarantee loans of up to $2 billion to cover the city's debt obligations. Senators Moynihan and Javits introduced the legislation. With vigorous lobbying efforts by the administration and Moynihan, congressional approval of the legislation was achieved and the city's bankruptcy was again averted. In July 1978 Moynihan released a study showing that federal payments to New York had increased by almost $8 billion in fiscal 1977. His accompanying statement did not discuss his own role in gaining more assistance for New York, yet it did imply that he had played his part.

Although the question of aid to New York City raised the possibility of a split between Moynihan and the administration, two other domestic issues—welfare reform and tax credits to fund parochial education—brought out the most pronounced differences between New York's junior senator and the president.

Late in April 1977 Moynihan denounced the administration for delay in submitting its welfare reform legislation so that it could not take effect until fiscal year 1981. "You can draft the bill in a morning," Moynihan said.[6] Whether or not the administration was going to proceed promptly to introduce the legislation, Moynihan would not be deterred from holding hearings on the subject in his Subcommittee on Public Assistance. When the hearings were convened, Moynihan took exception to the administration's belief that large numbers of people could be taken off welfare and put to work. Secretary of Labor Ray Marshall testified that welfare recipients could do weatherization work and remove lead paint from apartment buildings. Weatherization was something for skilled carpenters, Moynihan said, and when Marshall disagreed, the senator told him, "You'd better be [skilled] when you're on a fourteen-foot ladder." When Marshall said that lead paint removal was potential employment for welfare recipients, Moynihan asked him pointedly how many jobs were involved, how much skill it required, and how long it took to learn. He was skeptical, and he was not going to let the administration off the hook easily.[7]

In general Moynihan and the Carter administration have never consistently agreed on a welfare reform plan. Moynihan has disagreed with the administration on the issue about as often as he has agreed with it. In September 1977 the administration lobbied to block in the Senate Finance Committee a Moynihan plan that would provide $1 billion in fiscal relief to cities and states for welfare costs. The administration's own plan for fiscal relief was attached to legislation that would overhaul the entire welfare system; thus it opposed Moynihan's more limited reform package. For his part, Moynihan was skeptical about the prospects for passage of the administration bill even though he was willing to introduce it in September. He was angry that it would not go into effect until fiscal year 1981, and he cited twelve potential problems in the legislation.

Moynihan was particularly hard on administration spokesmen who he thought came before his subcommittee unprepared. He once criticized Secretary of Health, Education and Welfare Joseph Califano for being "naked of fact," and upbraided Califano's department for its "dumb insolence" before the committee.

By the summer of 1978 it appeared that Moynihan's worst fears about the fate of the administration's welfare reform legislation were to be confirmed: the bill was all but dead in Congress. The issue of whether the federal government would assume local welfare obligations was still unresolved. To remedy the situation Moynihan introduced his own "no frills" $5 billion welfare reform legislation, which provided for federal assumption of all local welfare costs. The president did not support Moynihan's legislation, and Moynihan accused the administration of trying to sabotage the bill by asking editorial writers at the *New York Times* and the *Wall Street Journal* to oppose it. "It was as if they thought the welfare problem would be resolved through intrigue," Moynihan said. It was "nonsense" to believe—as the administration apparently did—that his legislation would upset the chances of passing major reform legislation in 1979. The administration's behavior on the question was "kind of dumb."[8]

One Moynihan-sponsored domestic initiative drew much more broad support than his proposals for assuming New York's welfare costs and guaranteeing its loans. And again he found himself in conflict with the administration. With Robert Packwood of Oregon, Moynihan introduced legislation late in 1977 to give tax credits to parents of children attending parochial elementary and secondary schools.[9] Early in 1978 the Carter administration introduced its own tuition assistance legislation to broaden the eligibility of middle income families for direct grants for college education. The Carter proposal, directed at college students, aimed to provide assistance only to families whose annual income is less than $25,000; the Moynihan-Packwood plan included all taxpayers, regardless of income. In announcing his program Carter made it clear that the two proposals were mutually exclusive. Moynihan's plan won broad-based support in Congress but failed to win approval in 1978.

The proposals again put the president and Moynihan on different sides of an issue. Moynihan charged that the president was reneging on his campaign commitment to provide tuition assistance to children attending nonpublic schools. He said he found it "increasingly difficult to understand why [the administration] opposes our proposal with such vehemence and sometimes violent emotion. It is unbecoming and a bit alarming."[10] Moynihan tried to mute direct conflict with the White House by arguing that the Department of Health, Education and Welfare—and Secretary Califano in particular—was responsible for the president's change in position. When it was clear that the president's proposal would not include aid to children attending parochial schools, Moynihan said, "Nothing seems more clear than that Secretary Califano on his own has gotten the President into the untenable and surely unwelcome situation in which he appears to be repudiating a solemn commitment. This is not like our President. He should be better served."[11]

Moynihan's major differences with President Carter came over foreign policy. He joined the Senate believing that he had an obligation to see that the foreign policy positions he advocated were not ignored; after all, Moynihan had had much to do with popularizing concern for human rights long before Carter began talking about the subject. And whatever his concerns as a senator from New York, the continued stability of the American democracy would always take precedence. Certainly his anxiety over the expansionist tendencies of the Soviet Union had grown stronger.

At the outset Moynihan and Lane Kirkland, secretary-treasurer of the AFL-CIO, were disappointed that Carter's appointments to high-ranking posts in the White House and the State Department included no one who shared their views on foreign policy. Consequently Moynihan decided that if there were to be no dissent on foreign policy in either the executive branch or the State Department, it would have to come from the Congress. Thus he often vehemently voiced his disagreement with the president and with Secretary of State Cyrus Vance whenever their views deviated from his. That Moynihan did not receive greater attention in this regard was more a function of the ways in which the national media treat a first-term senator than of any move toward moderation on Moynihan's part.

Moynihan opposed Paul Warnke's nomination as chief negotiator at the Strategic Arms Limitation Treaty talks because he believed that Warnke failed to realize the extent of the Soviet threat and advocated unwise cuts in United States defense commitments. When Carter delivered his first comprehensive statement on foreign policy in the spring of 1977, Moynihan delivered a stinging rebuttal. While accepting Carter's general commitment to human rights, Moynihan questioned whether "he fully intends what he plainly proposes." Instead of focusing on the opposition between the totalitarian states of the East and the democracies of the West, Carter spoke of the relations between the industrial North and the developing South. In doing so, and by including the Soviet Union among the Northern nations that must help the South, Carter was ignoring the current major political battle. "It is as if—with no further consideration—we should divert our attention from the central political struggle of our time—that between liberal democracy and totalitarian Communism—and focus on something else."[12]

Moynihan expanded his argument in "The Politics of Human Rights" in the August 1977 *Commentary*. As an essential component of American foreign policy, human rights must occupy the same position in American policy that Marxist-Leninism does in the Communist nations. But to Moynihan the Carter-Vance approach—as articulated by the secretary of state in his Law Day speech in April—"bodes disaster." The speech missed the point altogether by asserting that human rights was an individual humanitarian aid program rather than an essential element of American foreign policy. A coherent human rights policy meant attacking rights violations wherever and whenever they occurred, not just making symbolic gestures such as receiving Soviet dissidents at the White House. Moynihan said the administration was backing away from attacking the Soviet Union for rights violations. Because the Soviet Union is the most powerful opponent of liberty, it must be challenged constantly.[13]

Before Egyptian President Anwar el-Sadat went to Jerusalem in November 1977 Moynihan criticized the Carter administration for accepting what he said was a Soviet-inspired document calling for the reconvening of the Geneva Conference on the Middle East. The Soviet Union did not want peace in the Middle East; their interests were best served by upheaval and war. Because the document did not explicitly require all parties to accept Israel's right to exist, and because Carter told the United Nations General Assembly on October 4 that "the legitimate rights of the Palestinians must be recognized," Moynihan charged that Carter's support for Israel was "softening."

Moynihan was particularly harsh on the president. "What we cannot accept is a pattern of novel twists of policy sprung upon us without warning, without consultation, and without seeming consideration of their potentially weakening effect upon the diplomatic position of the United States." When Carter told the General Assembly that the legitimate rights of the Palestinians had to be protected and that Israel had some responsibility for protecting those rights, Moynihan said that the president was allowing totalitarian thinking to pervert his language. The issue is not whether Israel should be equated with the PLO as a violator of human rights; rather, "the issue is nothing less than a continued recognition of Soviet totalitarian ambition on the one hand, and the solidarity of the world's democracies on the other." Nothing is more important than recognizing this point, Moynihan said, and he quoted ominously from Winston Churchill: "Let us not resume the follies which so nearly cost us our lives."[14]

In April 1978 Moynihan acknowledged what had long been obvious, that he had "a profound disagreement with those responsible for our

Middle East policy" in particular and for American foreign policy in general. According to Moynihan, the government had come to accept as fact that the Soviets were not only the equal of the United States in military power but were destined to surpass it. Throughout 1977 and 1978 the administration "has quietly given in to the long sustained efforts of the Soviets to depict Israel as an outcast nation, an illegitimate nation, a nation whose very existence violates the standards of the international community."[15] Moynihan feared that the administration would offer a Strategic Arms Limitation Treaty that would accommodate the trend toward dominant soviet military power, and he said that he and a majority of the Senate would never support it. When Secretary of State Vance later indicated he would go ahead with the SALT talks despite the trials in the Soviet Union of two prominent dissidents, Anatoly Shcharansky and Aleksandr Ginzburg, Moynihan joined with Senator Jackson to criticize the decision to proceed.[16] But since then Moynihan has not really had occasion to criticize the administration's foreign policy. The Camp David accords have (at least temporarily) removed the Middle East from the arena of partisan debate and as of this writing the Senate has not yet considered the SALT agreement.

Moynihan's criticisms of the president did not go unnoticed by the administration. Carter's antagonism surfaced first when Moynihan advocated tighter monitoring of Soviet efforts to tap American telephones. The president responded with an ad hominem attack that did not even address Moynihan's argument. He said that Moynihan, as a high-ranking member of the Nixon administration, was well able to judge at least the knowledge that *that* administration had developed about such activities.

Another indication of the president's feelings toward Moynihan can be gleaned from a review of some of the comments White House staff members have made about him. Some have been analytical. One staffer has commented that Moynihan, "has a national constituency, he has the ability to raise money, he is articulate, and he doesn't have to run for the Senate again until 1982," indicating a fear that Moynihan might well become a challenger of President Carter. But not all see Moynihan's opposition in totally political terms. "I wouldn't consider him an administration loyalist, but I don't think he's an adversary either," another staff member has said. "Hell, it's almost an adventure every time you talk with Pat because you never know where he's coming from." One simply dismissed him as "an unguided B-1."

In November 1977 a presidential aide told a *New York Times* reporter that Carter did not like Moynihan's approach.

> Moynihan is an arrogant man. His method and style rankle. The President is annoyed. Moynihan has teed everyone off here because of his style that he knows the answer to everything and because he goes public, figuring that criticism can move the President. If he'd call up and say he'd like to come over and talk about welfare reform and more economic help for New York it might be different. But he has worn out his welcome with demands and he has to crow about everything he does.[17]

The White House was so sensitive about the comment that press secretary Jody Powell went to great lengths to disavow it, maintaining that there were no irreconcilable differences between the two men. And this may be true: Moynihan has supported the administration on energy legislation and the Panama Canal treaty and has repeatedly—if erratically—said complimentary things about the president.

Nevertheless, Moynihan's behavior on a number of issues important to him—welfare reform, attitudes toward the Soviet Union and the Middle East—leads one to conclude that he would be willing to break with the president if he believed the administration were really on the wrong track. Moynihan may be a skilled political operator who is equally comfortable before crowds and in back rooms, yet he holds firmly to a set of identifiable principles. While he does not lack a willingness to compromise or bargain, there are issues on which he is adamant. If the administration were to make what he considered overly favorable concessions to the Soviet Union, or accepted the creation of a Palestinian state governed by the PLO, or abandoned welfare reform and fiscal relief for the Northeast, Moynihan might begin to speak out stridently—and consistently—against Jimmy Carter.

Would Moynihan himself run against Carter? He has said on a number of occasions that he will not be a candidate in 1980, and there is no reason to doubt him. Nevertheless, things happen so quickly in politics that significant differences with the administration or the absence of strong candidates of like mind could conceivably draw Moynihan into such an effort.

Regardless of whether he runs for president in 1980, Moynihan will certainly be a strong contender in the future. Today, at the age of fifty-two, he can look forward to a candidacy in 1984, 1988, or even 1992. He has a number of assets that most first-time contenders for national office do not. His term as ambassador to the United Nations gave him national recognition, and he is taken seriously by the national media on the basis of his diverse experiences in the last five administrations. Politically, Moynihan has a strong potential base of support in the Northeast, particularly among urban Catholics and Jews. He is close to the leadership of organized labor and could be expected to win the support of the AFL-CIO. And his hard-line anti-Communist posture would probably bring substantial support from the growing number of Americans who fear the buildup of Soviet military power.

No consideration of Moynihan's prospects for national office should obscure the fact that he is working to establish a strong record in the Senate. In the long term he seeks to prove that in addition to speaking out for principles in which he believes he can also do the nitty-gritty job of passing legislation. Thus he has sought to integrate himself into the power structure in the Senate—to the degree that some senators now criticize Moynihan privately for being too closely allied to Robert Byrd and Russell Long.

Senator Henry Jackson's two defeats in 1972 and 1976 have virtually eliminated him as a future presidential candidate, and Moynihan could well become the leading spokesman within the Democratic party for the center-right position, which emphasizes firm anti-Communism along with New Deal liberalism.

In any campaign for national office some effort will be made to evaluate Moynihan's impact on American politics during his nearly two decades of service in Washington. Since 1960 he has been in either the Cabinet or the subcabinet of four presidents, and when the fifth took office in 1977, Moynihan was a member of the Senate. The press will ask, and voters will want to know, whether Moynihan has made a lasting impression on the development of American policy.

13

Moynihan in Opposition?

> In Washington I learned as an adult what I had known as a child,
> which is that the world is a dangerous place—and learned also that
> not everyone knows this.
>
> —Pat Moynihan, 1978

Soon after he joined Averell Harriman's administration, Pat Moynihan became friendly with Mark McCloskey, a member of the governor's circle of advisers. McCloskey, then in his mid fifties, had a background roughly similar to Moynihan's own. He had grown up poor in Hell's Kitchen, worked his way through Princeton, and gone on to a distinguished career in government. McCloskey loved telling stories about his boyhood in Hell's Kitchen, and Moynihan, who had tended bar there during his college years, quickly developed a sort of father-son relationship with him. The bond between them lasted long after Moynihan left Albany. Moynihan named his second son John McCloskey Moynihan. And Moynihan may well have drawn on McCloskey's accounts of his boyhood for the stories he told journalists about his own youth.

The eulogy Moynihan delivered at McCloskey's funeral in 1977 offers a clue to understanding why Moynihan has taken some license with the events of his youth. McCloskey, according to Moynihan, had the great gift of being able to "make connections" between different people and places. McCloskey could sense that the world was becoming disjointed, that traditional institutions were breaking down. New York City was suffering from "anomic disintegration" and was filled with the "dust of individuals."[1] Making connections was McCloskey's self-appointed goal; giving others something to hold onto was the cause to which he dedicated his life. He had gone to Princeton and entered government service, but he had still remembered that he came from Tenth Avenue in Hell's Kitchen. This was his way of telling others that you must connect. In the end Moynihan was not certain that the Hell's Kitchen McCloskey had described really existed; in a sense it did not matter.

Throughout his life Moynihan has emphasized his origins in the working class—and specifically in the archetypically tough neighborhoods that novelist Ayn Rand and others have used as the starting point of such rags-to-riches odysseys as that of Gail Wynand in *The Fountainhead*.[2] If there has been a common thread running through his early years—perhaps even into his later life—it was the sense of being an outsider. Moynihan has never really "connected" in the way that he perceived McCloskey had. To compensate for this he has constantly emphasized to reporters, his staff, and his readers that his background has given him special insight into the problems of poverty and urban affairs.

A quick review of his life demonstrates how constant his position as an outsider in various social groups and government institutions has been. As a child he was buffeted from neighborhood to neighborhood, city to city, after his father left the family in the mid 1930s. Despite his mother's best efforts, he never knew a stable family life, and a life without structure or reinforcement is an isolated, lonely experience. He was a loner during two years of high school in Westchester, and he was the only Irishman in his class at Benjamin Franklin High School in his junior and senior years. Nor was he able to establish roots in college; the war intervened after one year, and off he went to Middlebury and then to Tufts. At Middlebury Moynihan was the only youth from modest circumstances in a group of relatively well-to-do young men who had largely been educated at prep schools, and he was uncomfortable in a way that his friends could never imagine. His education at Tufts was disrupted by a tour of duty in the navy, and in spite of his gregariousness he made few lasting friends during his undergraduate years. In England Moynihan was an outsider on two counts: as an American in British society and as an Irishman where people from Eire were looked down on.

Back in the United States, Moynihan found that he did not fit comfortably into any faction in New York City Democratic politics. Regular Democrats and reform Democrats both distrusted him, each considering him a member of the other group. He considered himself a strong Kennedy Democrat, but the people he thought were his natural allies rejected his social policy approach in the 1960s in his two major areas of concern, the poverty program and the black family. After 1963 his work in the Labor Department was done with almost total independence. Nor did Moynihan feel comfortable at Harvard. Traditional social scientists did not really accept him as one of theirs. He lacked the training in quantitative methods that would enable him to interpret the complicated statistical studies that were becoming increasingly important to scholars who were trying to analyze complex social phenomena. When he joined the Nixon administration, the Republicans were no more willing to embrace him completely. Enemies in the White House sabotaged him through the selective leaking to the press of his more controversial memos to the president, and the Nixon administration would not put its full prestige and influence behind the Family Assistance Program. As a diplomat in India, Moynihan fared no better. He was never comfortable with State Department officials, and his relationship with Indian officials was only distantly cordial. His turn to foreign policy in 1973 was perhaps the consequence of his having become an outcast in American domestic policy.

His "opposition" strategy at the United Nations quickly brought him into conflict with the vast majority of diplomats—and there he was also pretty much on his own because many considered his style undiplomatic and unseemly. In the Senate he has made alliances, particularly among the Democratic leadership, but he is by no means a deferential junior colleague.

Knowing that he came from a broken family has given Moynihan a perspective that few major political figures, rich or poor, have shared. The sense of rootlessness that he experienced so intensely during his childhood helped to inspire the black family report—and perhaps explains in part why he reacted so intensely when the report was attacked by civil rights activists. His stories of Hell's Kitchen are his attempts to create through fable connections in his life—connections that have never really existed.

Moynihan's feelings of rootlessness probably helped to create in him a sense of existential vulnerability. Despite his extraordinary talents and abilities, he has never been comfortable with the fact that he has scaled the heights of the political world. He continues to fear that a single wrong move could result in his being discredited and placed in financial jeopardy. True, there have been periods when segments of the liberal elite tried to dismiss him, but for the last thirteen years or so he has enjoyed a firm position as one of America's leading social commentators and policy makers. Yet throughout the Senate campaign he held tenaciously to his chair at Harvard for the personal and financial security that it provided. His closest friends were struck by his apprehension that if he lost the Senate race he would become a forgotten man who could command only a low-salaried post at a third-rate university. Certainly he exaggerated his situation; his desirability as a speaker alone brought him over $150,000 on the lecture circuit during 1976, and surely he would have had a wide choice of positions in government or in education if he had lost the election.

Moynihan's vulnerability extends to his acceptance of criticism: he has never taken it well. The latest critical comment in the morning newspaper will often send him to the telephone to charge editors with unfairness. At times he has adopted an "us against them" view of the world, in which his critics are seen as demons bent on his destruction. In some cases, undoubtedly, he has been justified; yet one is drawn to the conclusion that he has occasionally overstated the case.

Moynihan's personal vulnerability has also informed his view of history and the formation of social policy. Unlike some high-ranking policy makers, he worries that something apocalyptic will happen to America, that America may not be able to muddle through every crisis it faces. And Moynihan was virtually alone among Kennedy administration offi-

cials in seriously believing that Lee Harvey Oswald might be killed. He
sensed then that the "over-educated" people in authority did not understand something that people from his own rather ordinary background
knew well—that awful things do happen.

Four or five years later Moynihan was one of the leading exponents
of the view that liberal institutions might crumble under the pressure
of black riots and student protests. His warnings came at a time of
turmoil, when most liberals believed that the principal danger to democratic institutions came not from the left but from the right alone. Today
Moynihan is a leading exponent of the view that America faces a grave
threat from the Soviet Union in spite of—perhaps even because of—
détente. Again he has pointed out that many sophisticated and well-
educated people believe they *know* there is no real danger. Yet Moynihan feels the threat keenly. As he has learned in his own life and as he
has found in politics, "not ever being frightened can be a formula for
self-destruction."[3]

As a result of his personal experience, Moynihan has made reinforcing
and rebuilding traditional community and family institutions a major—
if not his paramount—political goal. Following in the path of a long line
of social scientists, Moynihan believes that people need to have a sense
of community. Local institutions act as a buffer between individuals and
the power of the state and satisfy the population's psychological needs.
The task of social policy makers is to try to reinforce the traditional
institutions of community—family, neighborhood, church—in order to
prevent people from becoming alienated and rootless. Accordingly,
Moynihan advocates social policies which would accomplish this goal,
together with a wide variety of programs (job creation, family allowances,
welfare reform) which would enhance family stability. At the same time
he has opposed programs that would undermine local institutions
through the creation of new government programs (e.g., the community
action program).[4]

Here Moynihan's thinking is fully in accord with traditional Catholic
social thought. Following the argument of Pope John XXIII in his
"Pacem in Terris," Moynihan seems to believe that the state's interests
should be served only after the rights of the individual are protected.
This notion, central to Moynihan's thought, underlies his advocacy of

freedom and liberty in international politics. Moreover, the encyclical held that it was a mistake to take away from individuals and give to larger collectives those functions which the individuals themselves can perform. It was an "injustice" and "a grave evil and a disturbance of right order" to give to larger bodies tasks that could be performed by "lesser and subordinate bodies." Rather than encourage the state to take over individual functions and to absorb the functions of "lesser and subordinate bodies" such as the family, church, and neighborhood, the government should pursue the opposite path.[5]

It would be a mistake to try to understand Moynihan's thought solely in terms of his personal life, however. Such an approach—while useful —is in the end too narrow to provide a complete picture of the complexity of his thought, especially in its development throughout the 1960s and 1970s. In his early teens Moynihan was at the far left of the political spectrum, but his thinking then was never clearly articulated. As he matured he became a strong partisan of the Democratic party, enthusiastically supporting Roosevelt and Truman and—somewhat less enthusiastically—Adlai Stevenson in 1952. The Harriman administration in 1955–58 anticipated some of the New Frontier and Great Society programs of the 1960s, and there is no indication that Moynihan was not in complete sympathy with the governor's initiatives. At his arrival in Washington in July 1961, there was no evidence that Moynihan was anything but a strong Kennedy Democrat committed to federal intervention to improve the social and economic position of less-advantaged Americans. He was confident of the government's ability to restructure the social order even as he felt a strong commitment to protecting traditional community institutions. The two policies did not necessarily conflict—in fact, the first might strengthen the second—but in the course of the 1960s they came to be set against one another. And as the conflict between them developed, Moynihan became less confident about the ability of government (and social science) to solve domestic problems. His strong commitment to the preservation of traditional neighborhood and family ties did not, however, decline.

At first Moynihan supported programs that would implement both policies. His advocacy of massive job programs and a family allowance were designed to put the federal government in the forefront of the struggle to improve the economic position of disadvantaged Americans, while at the same time providing incentives for the nuclear family to stay together. Families were less likely to break up when the husband had a job and the family had an adequate income, Moynihan reasoned. But he opposed programs that might hasten the disintegration of local institutions. When the concept of community action programs was proposed, Moynihan quickly warned that their establishment would hasten the breakdown of urban political machines by usurping their functions. During the 1960s liberals became quite fond of social engineering, and with each new proposal Moynihan worried that the newly created agency or department would take over the work of traditional local institutions.

Moynihan also became more and more skeptical about the federal government's ability to solve urban problems at all. The experience of the 1960s taught him that the "federal government is good at collecting revenues, and rather bad at distributing services." The services strategy of the Johnson years had largely failed, Moynihan concluded, and what was needed was for government to turn to an "income strategy where federal revenue should be redistributed between different levels of government, regions, and different classes of people."[6] This conclusion led him to advocate revenue sharing and an income maintenance program that would redistribute income to the poorest members of American society. It became important for policy makers to recognize the distinction between what government can and cannot do. To seek to do the impossible "with the passionate but misinformed conviction that it can be done is to create the conditions of frustration and ruin."[7]

Another reason for Moynihan's growing caution during the 1960s was the problem of knowledge. He was coming to believe that social scientists were often recommending to government officials social policies that were based on inadequate or even faulty research. Much liberal advocacy of increased spending for school facilities seemed to reflect a mistaken assumption that additional expenditures alone could improve academic achievement. Still worse was the tendency of many policy makers to simply assume that they had adequate knowledge when in fact they did not. Traditionally there had been a close relationship between social science research and the advocacy of social change; but social scientists must not forget how little they actually know about most problems. Since understanding the past is likely to be more successful than predicting the future, Moynihan has recommended that social scientists confine themselves to evaluating existing programs rather than advocate new ones. Social scientists can only present data to government officials; it is the officials who must make the political choices between competing options.[8]

In government Moynihan has always considered himself a politician rather than a social scientist, which has allowed him to make recommendations (e.g., to continue the Model Cities programs early in 1969) even though as a social scientist he might have doubted their usefulness. Thus, Moynihan long argued—without strong evidence—that income maintenance programs would enhance family stability by providing the head of the household with enough income to support his family. Yet persuasive evidence now indicates that it has precisely the opposite effect. Moynihan has acknowledged these findings publicly, called for further research, and indicated that the new evidence must be taken into account in structuring future welfare reform legislation.[9] This lack of knowledge about complex social issues necessitates a caution in policy makers, one that was noticeably absent as political tension increased in the late 1960s.

Another factor that has contributed to the growing cautiousness of policy makers in the 1970s has been the natural tendency for many in America to believe that when a policy recommendation fails to achieve its desired result, someone or something is to blame. Americans need a villain. Expectations should not be raised indiscriminately, Moynihan has said, for if the desired result is not achieved, society will inevitably blame the policy makers. And this is dangerous for the country at large and for the legitimacy of the public servants who are attempting to do their jobs. Policy makers have to recognize that problems are becoming more difficult; caution, recognition of complexity, and lowered voices have become the order of the day.

Both the political inability of government to solve complex problems and the lack of relevant knowledge have reinforced Moynihan's sense of the inherent limits of the ability of politics to resolve ethical and moral problems. Government is doomed to fail if it must impart ethical and moral values to people who are without them. That is the task of moral philosophy. Expanding the realm of politics will inevitably lead to the statement of problems in such a fashion that they can not be solved. And, citing Georges Bernanos, Moynihan has held that "the worst, most corrupting lies are problems poorly stated."

An evaluation of the development of Moynihan's thought would be incomplete without a consideration of his attitude toward blacks. In making such an evaluation one must remember that his analysis of the structural weakness of the black community is related to, yet distinct from, his social policy views. Examining the black community as a whole, Moynihan concluded in his 1965 report that it was in fact split into two groups. One was a stable middle class population well on its way to achieving economic parity with its white counterpart. The other was a large underclass that lay outside the mainstream of American life. The fundamental problem of that underclass, according to Moynihan, was that it did not have stable family structures; the consequence was a tangle of pathology involving unemployment, high crime rates, and low educational achievement. Since the report was issued, Moynihan has marshaled evidence to show that this division in the black community has persisted and that the situation of the middle class has improved while that of the underclass (whose family structures have continued to crumble) has become progressively worse.[10]

Moynihan has written extensively on demographic trends in the black community; at the same time, his social policy recommendations have always focused on improving the position of all poor people rather than that of a specific ethnic or racial minority. Part of the reason for this focus is strategic. While the black family presents special problems and requires special attention, it is far easier to pass legislation that will benefit all poor families instead of poor black families alone. And there is more to this decision than political expediency. Moynihan, who supported income distribution, came to believe in the late 1960s that it was important to advance social programs that emphasized the unity in American society rather than the divisions. This is best accomplished by social policies that will have a *class* effect rather than a *racial* effect. Job and guaranteed income programs cut across the entire spectrum to help all poor people—and hence de-emphasize the increasingly polarized nature of American society. Such programs will not set blacks against whites—as did those which gave funds to specific black neighborhoods or to projects in black communities, to the exclusion of projects in white communities.

Out of this Moynihan came to be viewed by a wide spectrum of black leaders and white intellectuals as a racist. The cause of this state of affairs was three-fold: timing, semantics, and personality. The black family report had been well received by the Johnson administration and was used as the basis for the president's speech at Howard University in June 1965. But the report was released just after the Watts riot, at a time when black leaders were sensitive to any criticism of their community. And Moynihan's report was read by some as an indication that the administration believed that the black community's weaknesses lay not with white racism but with internal, self-created problems that had their roots in a loose sense of morality.

The policy implication of this view—which was fueled by press analysis—was that only through self-help could the black community improve itself; white America was guiltless. Such a view missed Moynihan's points about the tangle of pathology and the degree of responsibility of white racism. Weak family structure both led to and stemmed from unemployment and low economic status. Moynihan's report pointed out the larger forces that undermined black family stability, such as discrimination, but in the aftermath of the riots this point was missed. Consequently he came in for a great deal of personal abuse, and as he and the report became virtual symbols for white racism, the Johnson administration dissociated itself from his approach. Moreover, the subject of family structure is itself so controversial that almost anything that is done in the area will offend someone. President Carter and HEW Secretary Califano learned this during the summer of 1978, when their plans for a White House family conference in 1979 collapsed abruptly after a contentious dispute over staffing.

Moynihan's "benign neglect" memorandum created somewhat different problems. It came at a time when many people were suspicious about the administration's commitment to the black community—and here was Moynihan, seemingly arguing for a period of neglect. In the ensuing controversy Moynihan's message was almost totally ignored or perverted.

Because he believed that progress was being made in improving the social and economic positions of blacks, and that that progress was being retarded whenever extremists on the right or the left opened their mouths, he cautioned the president to avoid polarizing rhetoric of the type Vice President Agnew employed and instead allow progress to continue. Such advances came in periods of quiet; at times of intense divisiveness attention was often diverted from the serious analysis of real problems within the black community—as had happened in 1965 in the wake of the black family report.

To be sure, a number of serious objections were raised about the memo's argument. Many thought that enough progress had not been made and that the federal government had to take a more active role to improve the economic status of blacks. But much of the criticism turned on the expression "benign neglect" and the growing belief that Moynihan was advising Nixon to ignore the black community altogether. Such criticism represented an almost total reversal of what Moynihan had intended—and it was his very unfortunate choice of words that got him into trouble here. The "benign neglect" memo was also the last straw as far as many influential civil rights leaders were concerned; whatever support Moynihan had enjoyed among them now disappeared as men like Kenneth Clark and Thomas Pettigrew became disenchanted with him.

The late 1960s were a time when white liberals and black activists were deeply suspicious of anyone who said anything critical about the black community. The very nature of Moynihan's message, especially in the black family report, was alone responsible for generating a certain amount of resentment. Yet Moynihan's problem lay deeper; his sensitivity to criticism alienated him further from the black community. Moynihan recognizes that he does not have a conciliatory personality and that by the late 1960s he was either unable or unwilling to engage in the sort of rhetorical niceties that might have appeased black leaders. Yet criticism of the black family report hurt him so deeply that he found it hard to remain composed. In 1965 he had been able to discuss the black family report without lashing out at his critics, but he became increasingly sensitive about his treatment by the black community, and by the late 1960s he was less able to take harsh attacks without responding. The years before he joined the Nixon administration were difficult for Moynihan in his relationship with the black community, and when the "benign neglect" memo surfaced, his sensitivities were heightened. Moreover, the "benign neglect" memo was more susceptible to rhetorical attack than the black family report had been. The 1965 report was a serious document that presented a quasi-academic analysis of a social policy problem; the "benign neglect" memo was purely political, written for the president alone, and not intended as profound, detailed analysis. To be effective, presidential memos must be written artfully; the creative language meant for the president's eyes backfired when seen by a wider audience.

The memo made Moynihan still more hostile to criticism from the black community. In the early 1970s he took strong exception to people who referred to it cryptically, using the phrase "benign neglect" as a sort of shorthand for his argument. On one occasion he summoned a Harvard *Crimson* reporter to his home in Cambridge to explain his memo after the reporter had written that Moynihan had advocated a policy of "benign neglect" during his time in the Nixon administration.

Thus, although Moynihan's views have not changed markedly throughout the 1960s and 1970s, he has developed a certain defensive contentiousness as a result of the barrage of criticism he faced in the eight-year period from 1965 until his departure for India in 1973. He has few allies among black leaders, and some of their unfriendly attitudes have penetrated to the mass level. He won only a small portion of the black vote in the senatorial primary in 1976, when his opponent was Bella Abzug (though he did win 80 percent of the black vote in the general election, when his opponent was the more conservative incumbent, James Buckley). The early polls on his job rating after taking office showed him weakest with blacks. But early in his second year his rating in the black community had come up nearly to the level of his rating in the white community. A poll of New York City voters in November 1977 showed that white voters were satisfied with Moynihan's performance, 54 percent to 23 percent, while blacks were satisfied, 34 percent to 30 percent. By

March 1977 the figures for whites were 63 percent to 19 percent; for blacks, 48 percent to 23 percent.

Analyzing Moynihan's foreign policy thinking is more difficult than examining his thinking on domestic policy, for he had comparatively little to say on the subject between the early 1950s and the early 1970s. Nevertheless, a clear development is discernible. Since his first published work—a letter to the *New Statesman* in 1951—Moynihan has aggressively defended American democracy against the onslaught of totalitarianism. In 1951 he was more vocal about the urgency of preventing another world war than about the need to advance the moral superiority of the United States' position. His views anticipated the posture that Secretary of State Henry Kissinger took in the late 1960s and early 1970s.

For Moynihan the overriding moral objective was the prevention of mass annihilation. When anyone in Britain attacked America, Moynihan responded quickly. He emphasized that the United States was a free country while Red China was not; he answered attacks that labeled the United States an aggressive imperialist nation with the same sort of fervor he would demonstrate at the United Nations. Throughout the 1950s Moynihan appeared to embrace a relatively orthodox cold-war anti-Communist line that was in keeping with the approach John F. Kennedy would articulate in his inaugural address.

During the Vietnam War Moynihan began to advocate a more cautious policy. It was important, he believed, that America recognize the limits of its power; it could not export democracy to Southeast Asia. Domestic turmoil had stagnated virtually all initiatives in the area with which he was most concerned—domestic policy making—yet he never advocated unilateral withdrawal. It was important that the antiwar movement not be identified with those forces that were trying to use the enterprise in Southeast Asia as an excuse to discredit American society in general. In winding down the war, policy makers had to be conscious of the need to preserve the prestige of our armed forces. Early in 1968 Moynihan joined Negotiations Now in advocating a cease-fire and a peace conference that would involve all parties, including the National Liberation Front, as a prelude to democratic elections in South Vietnam. When Richard

Nixon took office and Moynihan joined him as a chief domestic policy adviser, he ceased making specific policy suggestions on Vietnam and resigned as a co-chairman of Negotiations Now. But he warned Nixon that if he did not find a way to end the war, it would be his political downfall.

Moynihan returned to foreign policy when he was appointed United States representative to the United Nations Third Committee in the fall of 1971. He was shocked by the 1971 Report on the World Social Situation's portrayal of life in totalitarian and capitalist nations: the absence of dissent in totalitarian nations was seen as an indication of a harmonious society; only unrest was treated as evidence of discontent. The essence of a democratic society, Moynihan argued, was the encouragement of criticism. Active dissent was one sign of a healthy society, quiescence an indication of a repressive regime. Yet few responded with this kind of defense of American society; Americans had had little experience in abstracting from their own experience with democracy in order to describe it to the rest of the world. This was one weakness in our foreign policy that had to be corrected. Moynihan hoped that an international dialogue could be conducted in the same way that domestic policy should be discussed—quietly and in a reasoned manner. He had argued that good domestic social policy could not be developed if the administration became ensnared by the rhetoric of its foes; on the international plane he came to believe the situation was very different.

At first his hope for constructive discussion in international politics was based on his analysis of the politics of the third world nations. These nations, coming out of the British social democratic tradition, were generally hostile to the United States on ideological grounds. To prevent their falling into the totalitarian camp America had to present its case forcefully—by going into "opposition." America had to refute the argument that capitalism and Western exploitation were directly responsible for poverty. International liberalism had done much good for the world; so had capitalism. America should not be ashamed to speak out for liberty and freedom, and in speaking out America would provide its own response to the distinctive ideological approach of the third world. There *was* an ideological rationale for American society, and the United States should take pride in presenting it to the world.

There were also domestic policy reasons for Moynihan's belief that the United States should respond aggressively to the third world. He had opposed the Vietnam War in part because it had paralyzed the Johnson administration's domestic program; now he advocated an aggressive posture in world affairs to rid America of the legacy of Vietnam. For America had become guilt-ridden and accepted the argument of the radical antiwar critics that the country was a bloodthirsty imperialist nation. Such a mood had to be eradicated, and the best way to do this was to stress America's strongest assets, its protection of freedom and liberty.

Many critics of Moynihan's analysis thought it unnecessarily defensive, yet he believed that if the United States recognized that a distinctive ideology was at work, it would be able to work constructively with the third world and keep its nations out of the totalitarian camp. However, his service in the United Nations made him much more pessimistic. The Zionism resolution and other episodes convinced him that the totalitarian nations—particularly the Soviet Union—had a much greater hold over the third world nations than he had thought. The Russians had inspired that resolution and had put up third world countries to sponsor it. Thus the struggle in world politics was squarely between the United States and the Soviet Union, and it was a struggle that the United States was losing. Democracy was in danger in Europe through the advances of Eurocommunism, and the Russians were seeking to extend their influence in Africa through their Cuban surrogates. He realized sadly that the social democratic tradition in Africa was much weaker than he had thought; heads of state there were not at all interested in protecting the democratic processes and the liberties that were a legacy of the British socialist tradition. And the United States had to take a more assertive posture in world affairs not only for ideological reasons but for security reasons. The Soviets had an expansionist, imperialist, totalitarian regime that had to be checked at every juncture.

Throughout his career Moynihan has served as a sort of honest broker between the academic community and the political world. His greatest skill has been not in defining radical new solutions to contemporary social problems but in bringing into the public realm the research that others have done. In using this research to develop political approaches to complex problems Moynihan's influence has been considerable.

In the late 1950s Moynihan was one of the first to popularize the now commonplace notion that the proper way to reduce traffic injuries was to make the automobile safer. Researchers had long known that little was to be gained in trying to influence driver behavior, yet the discussion of highway safety had largely been conducted out of the public eye in technical journals. Moynihan (and Ralph Nader) brought the issue before the public and helped to focus attention on designing safer cars. He also helped to popularize the idea of no-fault auto insurance during the mid 1960s.[11] Much of Moynihan's success in this area resulted from his close collaboration with Dr. William Haddon, who now heads the Insurance Institute for Highway Safety.

Similarly, Moynihan's concern with the family structure in social policy formation drew heavily on scholarly literature, which he used to demonstrate to the Johnson administration how important a strong family structure was in the improvement of the economic and social position of black Americans. Insofar as his black family paper had an impact, Moynihan deserves credit for bringing the issue to the attention of the White House and persuading the administration to focus on the issue as an important part of the civil rights revolution.

Welfare reform was another area in which Moynihan advanced ready ideas rather than developed new proposals. Clearly Moynihan deserves credit for getting the Nixon administration to commit itself to a Family Assistance Program in 1969. But Moynihan had not joined the administration with a set program for welfare reform that he wanted to see implemented. In the mid 1960s he had been an advocate of family allowances, a device used in most Western European democracies. When it appeared that the best that could be expected from Richard Nixon was minimum national standards for welfare payments, Moynihan supported that enthusiastically. When FAP was offered, he quickly abandoned minimum standards and gave his attention to the new proposal. While he had initially wanted more costly family allowances, he had no trouble deciding that FAP—in effect a negative income tax proposal—was infinitely preferable to the present patchwork system. So he became the program's major advocate within the administration, and he managed to sell the president on the idea. The legislation never passed, but Moynihan is now chairman of the Senate Finance Committee's subcommittee on public assistance, which will shape the Carter administration's welfare reform legislation. Meanwhile, minimum federal support for the poor, aged, blind, and disabled has been enacted, and Moynihan deserves some measure of credit for that.

Moynihan was also a prominent advocate of decentralized decision making. By 1967 he was telling liberals what many conservatives and radicals had long been saying—that power had to be redistributed from the federal government to local governments. Whether decentralization would result in additional influence for the left or the right would depend on who was given power. Nevertheless, Moynihan's was a clear voice in favor of the idea of decentralization in the late 1960s, a time when many were beginning to realize—albeit slowly—that all answers did not lie with the federal government.

In foreign affairs Moynihan again deserves credit for focusing attention on the real nature of the debate. As United States ambassador to the United Nations he introduced human rights into the national political dialogue. To be sure, the concept could be traced back to Woodrow Wilson (as Moynihan himself pointed out), and international organizations such as Amnesty International had helped to keep it alive. Moynihan's contribution was to give the concept wide currency. No doubt he was in no small part responsible for Jimmy Carter's approach to human rights in his campaign and in the early days of his administration. And while Moynihan may have momentarily angered some career diplomats with his blunt rhetoric at Turtle Bay, he struck a responsive chord in America. The American people, regardless of age, education, or political persuasion, thought that Moynihan was right to speak up as he did at the United Nations. A Harris poll completed late in 1975 showed that almost three-fourths of those questioned in a national sample approved of his performance (only 15 percent disapproved). And the support that Moynihan won went beyond simple approval or disapproval; those who agreed with Moynihan often believed passionately that he was speaking up for the nation at a time when few were defending it. Accordingly, in late 1975 and early 1976, wherever he went he found himself mobbed by people wanting to congratulate him.

Intellectually, Moynihan's major contribution has probably been the introduction of the concept of ethnicity into discussions of social policy. Moynihan and his colleague Nathan Glazer challenged the Marxist assertion that class relations were the basis of societal organization; they maintained that ethnic and racial relations have an independent and powerful existence outside purely socioeconomic class relations.

One charge leveled at Moynihan is that he has been the ultimate political opportunist, a man willing to change his ideas to suit his audience, willing to work for anyone in order to hold power. The charge has little substance. While in fact he grew suspicious of government's ability to effect social change in the 1960s and more confident about the potentially salutary role of private enterprise, his prescriptions for eradicating poverty and creating a more just society in the United States have remained virtually unchanged. He has consistently advocated job creation and a family allowance or a guaranteed annual income. There was little difference between the programs he recommended to the Nixon administration and those he had recommended to the Johnson and Kennedy administrations, except that he became more strongly committed to free-market capitalism after 1967. This is not to say that Moynihan's approach to a specific issue would not change upon the presentation of new evidence. On the contrary, he has tried wherever possible to structure specific policy proposals on the available research findings.

On domestic issues Moynihan has remained a rather traditional Democratic liberal—one with a specific unwillingness to engage in the social experimentation that many on the left supported. And more than many Democratic liberals, he became concerned that the stability of the social order was in question during the late 1960s. Nor were his fears the result of ideological opportunism; he genuinely believed that American democracy was in jeopardy, and he concluded that social policy had to be developed that would enhance the stability of the social order. Perhaps this concern contributed to his reluctance to support government-inspired social change, for he was worried that the indirect effects of such initiatives would aggravate—rather than alleviate—social instability.

Moynihan's foreign policy views have probably changed most in the last decade. During the Vietnam War he was concerned that the United States assess the limits of its power and reconsider the merits of pursuing

interventionism in foreign policy. But third world attacks and the sense
of malaise and defeatism that developed in American society following
the Vietnam War convinced him that the United States had to be much
more assertive than it had been in world politics. Rather than conclude
from the Vietnam disaster that American influence in the world should
recede, Moynihan drew precisely the opposite conclusion. Internationally America must show that it could still stand up forcefully for liberty
and freedom. Domestically it must counteract the sense of guilt that had
developed. A reassertion of American nationalism was in order, and
when he perceived a growth of Soviet power, he called more strongly for
American involvement in international conflicts.

Moynihan's critics generally cite his service in the Nixon administration, following his close identification with the Kennedys and the Democratic left, as a demonstration of "opportunism." Moynihan responds
that it is his duty to serve when the president asks. Certainly Moynihan
is a patriot. Yet his service in the Nixon White House went beyond both
patriotism and opportunism. By late 1968 he was angry that his approach
to race relations (and social policy in general) had been rejected by the
Johnson administration—with what he believed were calamitous consequences. He believed that he had a contribution to make toward protecting domestic tranquility and reforming the welfare system. And he saw
Nixon surrounded by hard-line conservatives when it was clear that
liberal influence was also needed. For these reasons he agreed to serve
in the Nixon administration.

Moynihan has also been charged with using his post as ambassador to
the United Nations as a means of launching a campaign for the Senate
in New York. Yet other than changing his voter registration to his
upstate New York farm on assuming his post at the United Nations (a
move that he says was occasioned by his desire to remove from office a
local road superintendent who had been cutting down oak trees around
his property), there is no real indication that he was thinking about a
political campaign during his time at Turtle Bay. In fact he was so eager
to dispel these rumors that he made that Shermanesque statement on
Face the Nation in October to try to turn attention away from such
speculation. He was simply too busy at the United Nations to think
about the Senate. When close friends brought the idea up, he invariably

refused to discuss the subject seriously. Before the Reston column appeared Moynihan had agreed to remain at the United Nations through the November election. Even after leaving the United Nations he vacillated until the last minute, deciding to enter the Senate race only after being persuaded to do so by a group of labor and political leaders. At the time of his announcement he had done so little planning that it was several weeks before his campaign got off the ground.

Moynihan's life has been busy and colorful. He has sold newspapers, tended bar, and campaigned for votes—all in Times Square; he was an advance man and doorkeeper for Governor Averell Harriman in New York; he served in the administrations of four presidents; he was a professor of government at Harvard University. Yet any assessment of Pat Moynihan's career today is necessarily incomplete. At the age of fifty-two he has at least twenty years of active service ahead of him. His career has been marked by periods of controversy, prominence, and influence followed by times of seeming defeat or virtual quiescence. But at some point Moynihan always breaks his silence and comes to center stage, attracting national and even international attention. The black family report became an issue in 1965, "benign neglect" created a storm in 1970, and his outspoken tenure at the United Nations put America back on the offensive in the fall of 1975 and early 1976. Whether or not Daniel Patrick Moynihan sticks to this five-year time frame, there is every reason to believe that the pattern will continue to keep him at the center of American politics in the years to come.

Notes

1. A Sociological Phenomenon!

1. Much of the material on Jack Moynihan's early years was derived from his obituary in the Bluffton *News Banner*, August 9, 1952.
2. Bluffton *Evening Banner*, September 15, 1937.
3. Bluffton *News Banner*, August 9, 1952.
4. Jeffersonville *News*, September 15, 1935.
5. *New York Times*, July 8, 1933.
6. *New York Times Book Review*, June 26, 1977, p. 10.
7. Thomas Meehan, "Moynihan of the Moynihan Report," *New York Times Magazine*, July 31, 1966, p. 49.
8. See for example his foreword to William F. Buckley, *United Nations Journal: A Delegate's Odyssey* (New York: Anchor Books, 1977), p. xv.

2. The College Years and London Life

1. Moynihan and Mewhinny's column appeared in the February 26, March 4, and March 11, 1948, issues of the Tufts *Weekly*. Their letter of resignation, quoted here, was published March 18, 1948.
2. See for example his "The United States in Opposition," *Commentary* 59 (March 1975), pp. 31–44.
3. G. D. H. Cole, "As a Socialist Sees It," *New Statesman and Nation*, February 3, 1951, pp. 120–121; Daniel P. Moynihan, "Correspondence," *New Statesman and Nation*, February 17, 1951, p. 186.

3. The Return to New York

1. Daniel P. Moynihan, "Bosses and Reformers: A Profile of New York Democrats," in *Coping: On the Practice of Government* (New York: Vintage Books, 1975), p. 60.
2. Ibid., p. 55.
3. Ibid., Introduction, p. 10.
4. Daniel P. Moynihan, "Epidemic on the Highways," *The Reporter*, April 30, 1959, pp. 16–23.
5. For the "drenched in blood" image see his "Traffic Safety and the Body Politics," in *Coping*, p. 83.
6. Daniel P. Moynihan, "New Roads and Urban Chaos," *The Reporter*, April 14, 1960, pp. 13–20.
7. Richard Meryman, "Playboy Interview: Pat Moynihan," *Playboy* 24 (March 1977), p. 64.
8. *New York Times*, March 16, 1959.
9. Daniel P. Moynihan, "Officers and Gentlemen," *The Reporter*, July 9, 1959, p. 39.
10. Daniel P. Moynihan, "Second Look at the School Panic," *The Reporter*, June 11, 1959, pp. 17, 18.
11. Daniel P. Moynihan, "Showdown on the Wall," *The Reporter*, February 4, 1960, pp. 43–45.

4. We'll Never Be Young Again

1. Daniel P. Moynihan, "The Private Government of Crime," *The Reporter*, July 6, 1961, pp. 14–20.
2. "A Policy for Employee-Management Cooperation in the Federal Service: Report of the President's Task Force on Employee-Management Relations in the Federal Service," November 30, 1961. See also the U.S. Civil Service Commission, "The Role of the Civil Service Commission in Federal Labor Relations," May 1971, pp. 9–16.
3. See his "Bosses and Reformers," in *Coping*, pp. 53–68, for his views on the Democratic party in New York during the early 1960s.
4. See the department's mimeographed document, "Policy Planning and Research in the Department of Labor, 1965," for a statement of how they viewed the office's developments.

5. See "Proceedings of a Conference on Research, Passenger Car Design and Highway Safety," May 17, 1961, The Association for the Aid of Crippled Children and Consumers Union of the United States, pp. 265–281.

6. See "Traffic Safety and the Body Politics," in *Coping,* pp. 89–93.

7. See Charles McGarry, *Citizen Nader* (New York: Signet, 1973), pp. 67–74.

8. *New York Times,* October 25, 1963.

9. William Manchester, *The Death of a President* (New York: Harper & Row, 1967), p. 252.

10. Ibid., pp. 424–425.

11. Ibid.

12. Meryman, "Playboy Interview: Pat Moynihan," p. 72.

13. Manchester, *The Death of a President,* p. 506.

14. Ibid., p. 527n.

15. Meryman, "Playboy Interview: Pat Moynihan," p. 72.

16. Moynihan, Introduction, *Coping,* p. 5.

17. United States Department of Labor, *One Third of a Nation,* January 1, 1964.

18. On the evolution of the poverty program, see Robert A. Levine, *The Poor Ye Need Not Have with You: Lessons from the War on Poverty* (Cambridge, Mass.: MIT Press, 1970), pp. 44–52; James L. Sundquist, "Origins of the War on Poverty," in *On Fighting Poverty* (New York: Basic Books, 1969), pp. 6–33; Sar A. Levitan, *The Great Society's Poor Law* (Baltimore: Johns Hopkins Press, 1969), pp. 3–48; Daniel P. Moynihan, *Maximum Feasible Misunderstanding* (New York: Free Press, 1970), pp. 75–101; and Richard Blumenthal, "Community Action: The Origins of a Government Program," Harvard College Senior Honors Thesis, Cambridge, Mass., 1967.

19. Blumenthal, "Community Action," p. 63.

20. Moynihan, *Maximum Feasible Misunderstanding,* p. 100.

21. The statement, by James L. Sundquist, appears in Lillian Rubin, "Maximum Feasible Participation: The Origins, Implications and Present Status," *Poverty and Human Resources Abstracts* (November–December, 1967), p. 6.

22. *New York Times,* October 16, 1964.

23. Nathan Glazer and Daniel P. Moynihan, *Beyond the Melting Pot* (Cam-

bridge, Mass.: MIT Press, 1963), p. 310. Moynihan's participation in the study grew out of his earlier article," When the Irish Ran New York," *The Reporter,* June 8, 1961, pp. 32–34.

5. Moynihan for Mayor

1. *New York Times,* June 19, 1965; William Shannon, *The Heir Apparent: Robert F. Kennedy and the Struggle for Power* (New York: Macmillan, 1967), pp. 160–167.
2. *New York Times,* June 19, 1965.
3. Washington *Post,* June 22, 1965.
4. *New York Times,* June 22, 1965.
5. *New York Times,* June 25, 1965.
6. *New York Times,* June 19, 1965.
7. *New York Times,* July 20, 1965.
8. Ibid.
9. Ibid.
10. *New York Times,* August 26, 1965.
11. *New York Times,* August 9, 1965.
12. *New York Times,* August 10, 1965.
13. Oliver Pilat, *Lindsay's Campaign* (Boston: Beacon Press, 1968), p. 183.
14. *New York Times,* September 16, 1965.

6. The Family

1. Daniel P. Moynihan, Introduction to Alva Myrdal, *Nation and Family* (Cambridge, Mass.: MIT Press, 1968) p. x.
2. Daniel P. Moynihan, Address to the Pacem in Terris IV Convocation, Washington, D.C., December 2, 1975 (United States Mission to the United Nations, Press Release, USUN-169 [75]), p. 2.
3. Lee Rainwater and William L. Yancey, *The Moynihan Report and the Politics of Controversy* (Cambridge, Mass.: MIT Press, 1967), is devoted to the black family controversy.
4. See Harry McPherson, *A Political Education* (Boston: Atlantic-Little, Brown, 1972), pp. 334–357.
5. Office of Policy Planning and Research, United States Department of Labor, "The Negro Family: The Case for National Action," March

1965 (introduction, unpaginated). See also Daniel P. Moynihan, "Employment, Income and the Ordeal of the Negro Family," *Daedalus* 94 (Fall 1966), pp. 745–770.

6. Department of Labor, "The Negro Family," p. 29.

7. Moynihan, "Employment, Income and the Ordeal of the Negro Family," pp. 747–748.

8. McPherson, *A Political Education*, p. 342.

9. Reprinted in Rainwater and Yancey, *The Moynihan Report*, pp. 457–466.

10. Ibid., p. 458.

11. Reprinted in Rainwater and Yancey, *The Moynihan Report*, pp. 233–244, 395–402.

12. Reprinted in Rainwater and Yancey, *The Moynihan Report*, pp. 314–341.

13. White House Conference, "To Fulfill These Rights," June 1–2, 1966, Washington, D.C.

14. Daniel P. Moynihan, "The President and the Negro: The Moment Lost," *Commentary* 43 (February 1967), p. 32.

15. Ibid., p. 44.

7. Fulfilling a Dream: A Harvard Professorship

1. James Q. Wilson and Daniel P. Moynihan, "Patronage in New York, 1955–1959," *American Political Science Review* 63 (June 1964), pp. 286–301.

2. *New York Times*, December 12, 1965.

3. Frederick Mosteller and Daniel P. Moynihan, "A Pathbreaking Report," in Mosteller and Moynihan (eds.), *On Equality of Educational Opportunity* (New York: Random House, 1972), pp. 3–66.

4. Ibid., p. 56.

5. Ibid., p. 43.

6. Daniel P. Moynihan, "The Education of the Urban Poor," in *Coping*, p. 184.

7. "Cities: Light in the Frightening Corners," *Time*, July 28, 1967, pp. 10–13; Fred Powledge, "Idea Broker in the Race Crisis," *Life*, November 3, 1967, pp. 72–82.

8. *New York Times*, February 5, 1967.

9. Daniel P. Moynihan, "The President and the Negro: The Moment Lost," *Commentary* 43 (February 1967), p. 42.

10. Daniel P. Moynihan, "The Crisis in Welfare," in *Coping,* pp. 134–166.

11. Ibid., p. 160.

12. Quoted in Franklin D. Raines, "Policy Advocacy: The Case of the Family Assistance Program," unpublished third-year paper, Harvard Law School, 1976, p. 59.

13. Daniel P. Moynihan, *Maximum Feasible Misunderstanding* (New York: Free Press, 1970), pp. 185–187.

14. *New York Times,* July 25, 1967.

15. Powledge, "Idea Broker in the Race Crisis," p. 72b.

16. *New York Times,* August 3, 1967.

17. Powledge, "Idea Broker in the Race Crisis," pp. 77–78.

18. Daniel P. Moynihan, "Nirvana Now," in *Coping,* p. 131.

19. Ibid., pp. 132–133.

20. Daniel P. Moynihan, "The Politics of Stability," in *Coping,* p. 191.

21. Ibid., pp. 193–194.

22. Ibid. p. 194.

23. Melvin Laird, Introduction, *Republican Papers* (New York: Praeger, 1968), p. xi.

24. *New York Times,* February 17, 1968.

25. Moynihan, "Nirvana Now," p. 128.

26. Daniel P. Moynihan, "Speaking Out," *Saturday Evening Post,* May 4, 1968, p. 16.

27. Ibid., p. 12.

28. Daniel P. Moynihan, "The Democrats, Kennedy & the Murder of Dr. King," *Commentary* 45 (May 1968), pp. 18–20.

29. Moynihan, "Speaking Out," p. 12.

30. Moynihan, "The Politics of Stability," p. 193.

31. Moynihan, "The Democrats, Kennedy & the Murder of Dr. King," p. 16.

32. Moynihan, "Speaking Out," p. 16.

33. *New York Times,* February 18, 1968.

34. Moynihan, "The Democrats, Kennedy & the Murder of Dr. King," p. 16.

35. Ibid., p. 15.

36. Ira Mothner, "The Odd Alliance: Moynihan and 'The Robber Barons'," *Look,* April 7, 1970, p. 20.

37. Moynihan, "The Democrats, Kennedy & the Murder of Dr. King," p. 26.

38. Quoted in George Plimpton (ed.), *An American Journey: The Times of Robert Kennedy* (New York: Harcourt Brace Jovanovich, 1970), p. 185.

39. Ibid., p. 300.

40. Moynihan, Preface, *Maximum Feasible Misunderstanding,* p. lxi.

41. Moynihan, Introduction to paperback edition, *Maximum Feasible Misunderstanding,* p. vi.

8. Switching Sides

1. *New York Times,* December 11, 1968.

2. Ibid.

3. "Pat Moynihan on Welfare," *Newsweek,* February 8, 1971, p. 26.

4. William Safire, *Before the Fall* (New York: Tower, 1975), p. 115.

5. *New York Times,* December 19, 1968.

6. *New York Times,* January 13, 1969.

7. The memo was leaked to the *New York Times* in March 1970. See the *New York Times,* March 11, 1970.

8. Daniel P. Moynihan, Preface to Ada Louise Huxtable, *Will They Ever Finish Bruckner Boulevard?* (New York: New York Times Books, 1970), pp. xviii–xix; *New York Times,* February 1, 13, 14, 1969.

9. Roland Evans and Robert Novak, *Nixon in the White House: The Frustration of Power* (New York: Vintage Books, 1972), pp. 41–43.

10. This section draws heavily on three works: Franklin D. Raines, "Policy Advocacy: The Case of the Family Assistance Program," unpublished third-year paper, Harvard Law School, 1976; Daniel P. Moynihan, *The Politics of a Guaranteed Annual Income: The Nixon Administration and the Family Assistance Plan* (New York: Vintage Books, 1973); Vincent J. and Vee Burke, *Nixon's Good Deed* (New York: Columbia University Press, 1974); and also on interviews with many of the participants.

11. Quoted in Raines, "Policy Advocacy," p. 106.

12. Quoted in Burke and Burke, *Nixon's Good Deed,* p. 64.

13. Daniel P. Moynihan, Memorandum to the President, March 26, 1969.

14. Raines, "Policy Advocacy," pp. 153–154.
15. Daniel P. Moynihan, "One Step We Must Take," *Saturday Review,* May 23, 1970, p. 22.
16. *New York Times,* July 15, 1969.
17. Raines, "Policy Advocacy," p. 177.
18. Burke and Burke, *Nixon's Good Deed,* p. 102.
19. Ibid., p. 128.
20. Lawrence Spivak, "The Proceedings of 'Meet the Press,' August 10, 1969" (Washington, D.C.: Merkle Press, 1969).
21. Ibid., p. 3.
22. *New York Times,* August 26, 1969.
23. "The White House Idea Man For Urban Problems," *Business Week,* September 27, 1969, p. 72.
24. See Stephen Hess, *Organizing the Presidency* (Washington, D.C.: Brookings, 1976), pp. 121–123.
25. Evans and Novak, *Nixon in the White House,* pp. 223–237.
26. See Daniel P. Moynihan, *Toward a National Urban Policy* (New York: Basic Books, 1970), pp. 3–25, for a statement of the policy. See also Daniel P. Moynihan, "Policy v. Programs in the 1970s," in *Coping,* p. 274.
27. *New York Times,* March 6, 1970.
28. *New York Times,* March 1, 1970, contains the text of the memo.
29. *New York Times,* March 3, 1970.
30. Daniel Patrick Moynihan with Suzanne Weaver, *A Dangerous Place* (Boston: Atlantic-Little, Brown, 1978), p. 91.
31. Ibid., p. 60.
32. *New York Times,* July 2, 1970. See also Daniel P. Moynihan, "Remarks to Urban Coalition Action Council," Statler Hilton Hotel, New York City, July 1, 1970, p. 1.
33. *New York Times,* October 16, 1970.
34. Evans and Novak, *Nixon in the White House,* pp. 360–362; *New York Times,* November 25, 1970.
35. Daniel P. Moynihan, "Address to the President, Vice President and Cabinet," December 21, 1970, Mimeograph, p. 5.
36. Ibid., p. 3.
37. Ibid., p. 4.
38. Ibid., p. 5.
39. Ibid.

40. *New York Times,* December 22, 1970.

41. *New York Times,* January 5, 1971.

42. "A Case for the President's Plan," *Time,* February 8, 1971, p. 23; "Pat Moynihan on Welfare," *Newsweek,* February 8, 1971, p. 26.

43. "Moynihan Writes Again," *Time,* April 19, 1971, p. 16.

44. Daniel P. Moynihan, "The Presidency and the Press," in *Coping,* pp. 314–343.

45. Max Frankel, "Letter to the Editor," *Commentary* 55 (July 1971), pp. 6–20.

46. Daniel P. Moynihan, "The United States in Opposition," *Commentary* 59 (March 1975), p. 35.

47. An excerpt from the speech appears in *New York Times,* October 28, 1971, p. 41.

48. *New York Times,* November 10, 1971.

49. Ibid.

50. *New York Times,* November 23, 1971.

51. Daniel P. Moynihan, "Emerging Consensus," *Newsweek,* July 10, 1972, pp. 22–23.

52. Daniel P. Moynihan, "How the President Sees His Second Term," *Life,* September 1, 1972, pp. 26–29.

53. *New York Times,* September 27, 1972.

9. A Retreat to India

1. *Newsweek,* December 25, 1972, p. 20.

2. *Times* of India, January 15, 1973.

3. *Times* of India, February 7, 1973.

4. *New York Times,* February 8 and 10, 1973; *Times* of India, February 10, 1973.

5. *Times* of India, February 10, 1973.

6. *Times* of India, February 14, 1973; *New York Times,* February 10, 1973.

7. *Times* of India, February 21, 1973.

8. *New York Times,* February 22, 1973.

9. President's Secretariat, Staff Instructions for the Presentation of Letter of Credence by the Ambassador Designate of the United States of America on 28 February 1973.

10. *New York Times,* March 1, 1973; *Times* of India, March 5, 1973.

11. *New York Times,* March 16, 1973; *Times* of India, March 16, 1973.
12. *New York Times,* March 24, 1973.
13. *Times* of India, April 10, 1973.
14. *Times* of India, April 17, 1973.
15. Richard Meryman, "Playboy Interview: Pat Moynihan," *Playboy* 24 (March 1977), p. 78.
16. *Times* of India, July 18, 24, and 27, 1973.
17. *New York Times,* July 23, 1977.
18. Ibid.
19. Washington *Post,* August 19, 1973.
20. *New York Times,* September 3, 1973.
21. *Times* of India, December 13, 1973, and January 30, 1974.
22. *Newsweek,* March 18, 1974, p. 60.
23. *New York Times,* March 6, 1974.
24. *Times* of India, March 5, 1974.
25. *New York Times,* March 7, 1974.
26. *New York Times,* April 5, 1974.
27. *New York Times,* April 10, 1974.
28. *New York Times,* September 13, 1974.
29. *New York Times,* September 20, 1974.
30. Washington *Post,* December 15, 1974; *New York Times,* December 15, 1974.
31. *New York Times,* December 16, 1974; Washington *Post,* December 15 and 30, 1974.
32. *New York Times,* February 13, 1975.
33. Washington *Post,* December 18, 1973. For two interviews that reveal Moynihan's mood during his last year in India see the *New York Times Magazine,* March 31, 1974, and the *New York Times,* December 15, 1974.
34. C. L. Sulzberger, *Seven Continents and Forty Years* (New York: Quadrangle Books, 1977), p. 602.
35. Meryman, "Playboy Interview: Pat Moynihan," p. 76.

10. Turtle Bay

1. *New York Times,* December 15, 1974.
2. Bernard Weinraub, "Daniel Moynihan's Passage to India," *New York Times Magazine,* March 31, 1974.

3. Ibid.

4. Daniel P. Moynihan, "The United States in Opposition," *Commentary* 59 (March 1975), pp. 31–44.

5. Moynihan, "Nirvana Now," in *Coping*, pp. 127–128.

6. Daniel P. Moynihan, *A Dangerous Place*, p. 38.

7. *New York Times*, February 26, 1975.

8. *New York Times*, April 13, 1975.

9. Moynihan, *A Dangerous Place*, pp. 3, 60.

10. Ibid., p. 72.

11. *New York Times*, May 3, 1975.

12. The discussion of Moynihan's foreign policy views is drawn principally from his "The United States in Opposition"; his "Was Woodrow Wilson Right? Morality and American Foreign Policy," *Commentary* 57 (May 1974), pp. 25–31; his "How Much Does Freedom Matter?" *The Atlantic* 236 (July 1975), pp. 19–26; and his Address to the Pacem in Terris IV Convocation, Washington, D.C., December 2, 1975.

13. Moynihan, "Was Woodrow Wilson Right?" p. 27.

14. Ibid., pp. 30–31.

15. Henry Kissinger, "The Process of Détente," Statement delivered to the Senate Foreign Relations Committee, September 19, 1974, reprinted in Kissinger, *American Foreign Policy* (3rd ed.) (New York: Norton, 1977), p. 145.

16. Henry Kissinger, "The Moral Foundations of Foreign Policy," Address delivered at meeting sponsored by the Upper Midwest Council, Bloomington, Minnesota, July 15, 1975, reprinted in Kissinger, *American Foreign Policy*, p. 205.

17. Henry Kissinger, "The Nature of the National Dialogue," Address to the Pacem in Terris III Convocation, Washington, D.C., October 8, 1973, reprinted in Kissinger, *American Foreign Policy*, p. 121.

18. Henry Kissinger, "The Permanent Challenge of Peace: U.S. Policy Toward the Soviet Union," Address to the Commonwealth Club and the World Affairs Council of Northern California, San Francisco, February 3, 1976, reprinted in Kissinger, *American Foreign Policy*, p. 309.

19. Michael Berlin, "Pat Moynihan: Our New Voice at the UN," New York *Post*, June 14, 1975.

20. Nomination of Daniel P. Moynihan, of New York, to be United

States Representative to the United Nations with the Rank of Ambassador, United States Senate, Committee on Foreign Relations, June 4, 1975, pp. 370–372, 377.

21. Ibid., p. 373.
22. *New York Times,* July 1, 1975.
23. Moynihan, *A Dangerous Place,* p. 145.
24. Washington *Post,* September 15, 1977.
25. See *Public Reaction to Seventh Special Session of the 30th General Assembly,* Associated Press account of Compromise Reached on Economic Cooperation, September 17, 1977, United States Mission to the United Nations.
26. The account of the debate over the Zionism resolution and the controversy surrounding Moynihan's speech on Amin is drawn from three principal sources: interviews with participants; Michael J. Berlin, "The U.N. and Zionism: Background to the Vote," New York *Post,* November 15, 1975; and *The Sunday Times* of London, November 30, 1975.
27. Daniel P. Moynihan, Address at the AFL-CIO Constitutional Convention, San Francisco, October 3, 1975, United States Mission to the United Nations, Press Release USUN-108 (75).
28. *New York Times,* October 9, 1975.
29. Leonard Garment, Statement in Committee III, October 17, 1975, United States Mission to the United Nations, Press Release USUN-108 (75).
30. Transcript of a Press Conference Held by Ambassador Daniel P. Moynihan, United States Representative to the United Nations, and Mr. Leonard Garment, at United Nations Headquarters, October 17, 1975, United States Mission to the United Nations, Press Release USUN-120 (75).
31. Daniel P. Moynihan, Address to the Appeal of Conscience Foundation, Annual Award Dinner, New York, October 21, 1975, United States Mission to the United Nations, Press Release USUN-123(75).
32. *Face the Nation,* CBS News, October 26, 1975 (Metuchen, N.J.: Scarecrow Press, 1976).
33. Daniel P. Moynihan, Statement to the General Assembly on Resolution Equating Zionism with Racism, November 10, 1975, United States Mission to the United Nations, Press Release USUN-141(75).
34. Daniel P. Moynihan, Statement in Committee III on the U.S. Pro-

posal for a World Wide Amnesty for Political Prisoners, November 12, 1975, United States Mission to the United Nations, Press Release USUN-144(75).

35. Department of State Bulletin, December 1, 1975, p. 771; see also George Miller, "Sound and Fury at Turtle Bay: Daniel P. Moynihan at the United Nations," Harvard graduate seminar paper, January 13, 1977.

36. *Newsweek*, November 24, 1975, p. 31.

37. Ivor Richard, Speech delivered to the Board of Directors of the United Nations Association of the USA, November 17, 1975, United Kingdom Mission to the United Nations.

38. Moynihan, *A Dangerous Place*, p. 221.

39. *New York Times*, November 25, 1975.

40. *New York Times*, December 3, 1975.

41. *New York Times*, December 11, 1975; Daniel P. Moynihan, Statement in Plenary on Angola, December 8, 1975, United States Mission to the United Nations, Press Release USUN-180(75); Moynihan, *A Dangerous Place*, pp. 247-253.

42. Daniel P. Moynihan, Statement in Plenary in Explanation of Vote on the Resolutions Dealing with the Report of the Special Committee on Decolonization, December 11, 1975, United States Mission to the United Nations, Press Release USUN-184(75).

43. United States Mission to the United Nations, Press Release, USUN-136(75), October 31, 1975; *New York Times*, November 29, 1975.

44. Daniel P. Moynihan, Statement in Plenary at the Close of the 30th Session of the United Nations General Assembly, December 17, 1975, United States Mission to the United Nations, Press Release USUN-190(75).

45. Transcript of Interview with Ambassador Daniel P. Moynihan by Richard C. Hottelett and Hughes Rudd, on the CBS Morning News, December 17, 1975, United States Mission to the United Nations, Press Release USUN-189(75).

46. Transcript of Press Conference Held by Ambassador Daniel P. Moynihan at the Conclusion of the 30th Session of the United Nations General Assembly, December 18, 1975, United States Mission to the United Nations, Press Release USUN-191(75).

47. Daniel P. Moynihan, "Abiotrophy at Turtle Bay," *Harvard International Law Journal* 17 (Summer 1976), pp. 494-502.

48. See the *New York Times*, December 20, 1975; January 4 and 7, 1976.
49. *New York Times*, January 9, 1976.
50. Daniel P. Moynihan, Interventions in the Security Council on the Proposal to Invite the Palestine Liberation Organization to Participate in the Security Council Debate on the Middle East, January 12, 1976, United States Mission to the United Nations, Press Release USUN-4(76).
51. *New York Times*, January 28 and 29, 1976.
52. *New York Times*, January 30, 1976.
53. *New York Times*, February 3, 1976.
54. Ibid.

11. The Big Gamble

1. Daniel P. Moynihan, Statement in the Security Council in Exercise of the Right of Reply to the Statement by Ambassador Malik, USSR Representative, February 6, 1976, United States Mission to the United Nations, Press Release USUN-18(76).
2. Harvard *Crimson*, February 13, 1976.
3. *New York Times*, February 13, 1976.
4. *New York Times*, February 18, 1976.
5. *New York Times*, March 18, 24, and April 7, 1976.
6. Richard Meryman, "Playboy Interview: Pat Moynihan," *Playboy* 24 (March 1977), pp. 65–66.
7. *New York Times*, June 16, 1976.
8. *New York Times*, August 3, 1976.
9. *New York Times*, August 21, 29, and September 1, 1976.
10. *New York Times*, September 1, 1976.
11. *New York Times*, September 4, 1976.
12. *New York Times*, September 16, 1976.
13. *New York Times*, October 31, 1976.
14. *New York Times*, October 4, 17, and 26, 1976.
15. *New York Times*, October 29, 1976.
16. *New York Times*, November 5, 1976.

12. A New Year in the Senate

1. Michael Daly, "The Senator from Benign Neglect," *Village Voice*, October 31, 1977, pp. 12–14.

2. Daniel P. Moynihan, "The Federal Government and the Economy of New York State," July 15, 1977, mimeographed.

3. President Jimmy Carter to Senator Daniel P. Moynihan, September 14, 1977; Statement of Senator Daniel P. Moynihan in reply, September 17, 1977; Statement of Daniel P. Moynihan, January 17, 1978; *New York Times*, January 18, 1978.

4. Senator Daniel P. Moynihan to President Jimmy Carter, January 4, 1978.

5. Daniel P. Moynihan, Address to the New York State Bankers' Association, New York, February 9, 1978.

6. *New York Times*, April 26, 1977.

7. *New York Times*, May 13, 1977.

8. *New York Times*, June 12, 1978.

9. Washington *Post*, March 7, 1978.

10. Statement of Senator Daniel P. Moynihan, March 21, 1978.

11. Statement of Senator Daniel P. Moynihan, April 5, 1978.

12. Daniel P. Moynihan, Commencement Address, Baruch College, June 9, 1977.

13. Daniel P. Moynihan, "The Politics of Human Rights," *Commentary* 64 (August 1977), pp. 19–26.

14. Daniel P. Moynihan, Address Before the American Council for Emigrés in the Professions, New York, October 9, 1977.

15. Daniel P. Moynihan, Address to Temple Israel, New York, April 7, 1978.

16. *New York Times*, July 11, 1978.

17. *New York Times*, November 7, 1977.

13. Moynihan in Opposition?

1. *Congressional Record*, United States Senate, December 15, 1977, S19827–19828.

2. Ayn Rand, *The Fountainhead* (Indianapolis, Ind.: Bobbs-Merrill, 1968), esp. pp. 405–442.

3. Richard Meryman, "Playboy Interview: Pat Moynihan," p. 72.

4. Here Moynihan's thought appears to have been influenced by two books: Robert Nisbet, *The Quest for Community* (New York: Oxford University Press, 1953), and Milton Gordon, *Assimilation in American Life* (New York: Oxford University Press, 1971).

5. Moynihan's Address to the Pacem in Terris IV Convocation, Washington, D.C., December 2, 1975.
6. Moynihan, "The Politics of Stability," in *Coping*, p. 193.
7. Moynihan, "Politics as the Art of the Impossible," in *Coping*, pp. 255–256.
8. Moynihan, *Maximum Feasible Misunderstanding*, pp. 167–205.
9. Moynihan, "The Rocky Road to Welfare Reform," *Journal for Socio-economic Studies* 3 (Spring 1978) pp. 9–10.
10. Moynihan, "The Deepening Schism," in *Coping*, pp. 344–369.
11. Washington *Post*, March 20, 1977; see also Daniel P. Moynihan, "The Automobile and the Courts," in *Coping*, pp. 100–115.

Index

Abzug, Bella, 248, 251, 255–258, 261, 287
AFL-CIO, 77, 90, 219, 224, 229, 250, 251, 271, 275
Africa, 238, 239, 241, 242, 246, 290
African nations, 230, 231
Agnew, Spiro, 159, 166, 168, 169, 172, 174, 286
Agriculture Department, 85, 146
Ahmad, Shri Mahboob, 191
AID, 198
Aid to Families with Dependent Children Program, 155
Air India, 191
Algeria, 211
Alinsky, Saul, 129
Amalgamated Clothing Workers of America, 72
America, 40
American Jewish Community, 223
American Newspaper Publishers Association, 171
American Political Science Review, 119
Americans for Democratic Action, 131–139, 145
Amin, Idi, 223–225, 233, 235

Amnesty International, 232, 292
Amsterdam News, 114
Anderson, Martin, 155
Andrea Doria, 49
Andrews Air Force Base, 79
Angola, 238, 239, 241
Anti-Semitism, 226, 231, 233
Anti-war activists, danger of, 138
Appeal of Conscience Foundation, 227
Arab states, 228, 231, 243
Architectural planning, 73
Arista, 17
Armstrong, Neil, 158
Arnow, Phil, 75
Ash, Roy, 198
Astoria, 27
Atomic Energy Commission, 57
Austria, 49
Auto safety, 61, 62, 76, 77, 291. *See also* Traffic safety
Avellina, Tony, 7, 12, 14
Avelina, Winnie Winckler, 7, 12, 14, 47

Bailey, Stephen, 66, 67
Ball, George, 79, 80

Banfield, Edward, 125
Bangladesh, 187
Barkan, Al, 250
Barry, John, 40, 41, 43, 45, 46
Barton, Paul, 75, 104
Bateman, Worth, 154, 155
Beame, Abraham, 94, 95, 97, 99, 101
Belgium, 229, 230
Bell, Daniel, 125
Bell, David, 69, 70
"Benign neglect" memorandum, 128, 165–168, 175–178, 186, 188, 209, 247, 285–287, 295
Benjamin Franklin High School, 14–17, 23, 277
Bermuda, 34
Beyond the Melting Pot (Moynihan and Glazer), 91, 92, 98, 119
Bhutto, Zulfikar Ali, 205
Bickell, Margaret. *See* Phipps, Margaret Bickell
Bingham, Jonathan, 51, 52, 56, 249
Birth control, 108, 114
Black families, 103–117, 120
stable middle class, 105, 106
Black Family Stability Report, 102, 104–117, 285–287, 291, 295
Black Panther Party, 178
Blitzer, Charles, 134
Blumenthal, Richard, 149, 172, 250, 252, 253
Boaten, Francis, 228
Bok, Derek, 243, 244, 260
Bolivia, 227
Boone, Richard, 87
Boston *Globe*, 173
Bowdler, William, 35
Bowles, Chester, 188
Brazil, 231, 238
Brennan, Elizabeth, 53. *See also* Moynihan, Elizabeth Brennan (Mrs. Daniel P.)
Brickett, Margaret, 75
Britain, 214, 231, 288, 290
Brittain, Cathy, 26
Broderick, Ellen, 75, 104
Brooke, Edward, 267
Brown University, 27
Buckley, Charles, 65, 94
Buckley, James, 229, 247, 257, 258, 260, 261, 287
Buckley, William, 101, 157
Budget Bureau, 69, 70, 84–87, 158, 164
Buffum, William, 237
Bundy, McGeorge, 78
Bureau of Labor Statistics, 75, 115
Burke, Adrian, 50, 51
Burns, Arthur, 146–148, 154–159, 162, 163

Bush, George, 205
Byrd, Robert, 264, 275

Califano, Joseph, 121, 269, 270, 285
Callaghan, James, 235, 236
Cambodia, 169, 170, 212
Campbell, Colonel and Mrs., 41
Cannon, William, 84
Capitalism, 21, 22
free market, 293
Carey, Hugh, 248, 258
Carnegie Corporation, 122
Carter, Jimmy, 260, 261, 265–267, 270–274, 285, 292
Carter administration, 261, 264, 265, 268, 270, 292
Cavanagh, Jerome, 126
CBS, 42, 229
Center for Advanced Studies, 101, 118
Center for International Affairs, 182
Chavan, Y. B., 198, 200
Cheney, Richard, 236, 245
Cherne, Leo, 52
Chile, 203, 205, 232, 233
China, 44, 184, 189, 204, 205, 288
CIA, 192, 194, 203–205
City College (CCNY), 17, 19, 20, 24, 211, 250, 259
City Planning Commission, 91
Civil rights, 77, 104, 105, 108–115, 121, 142, 165, 166, 286. *See also* Human rights
Civil Rights Act of 1964, 103, 121
Civil Service Commission, 69, 70, 81
Clark, Kenneth, 166, 258, 286
Clark, Ramsey, 248, 251
Cleveland, Harlan, 59, 65
Cloward, Richard, 86
Cohen, Wilbur, 87
Cole, G. D. H., 43, 44
Coleman, James, 121, 122, 123
Colombia, 226
Colonialism, 211, 239, 240
Commentary, 116, 126, 166, 178, 180, 205, 209–211, 222, 241, 271
Commerce Department, 85, 146, 222
Commission on Juvenile Delinquency and Youth Crime, 84, 85
Committee on Traffic Safety, 76
Communism, 35, 43, 46, 62, 209, 216, 228, 271, 275, 288, 290
Community Action Programs, Title II, 86–89
Community Services Administration, 267
Conference of Major American Jewish Organizations, 223
Conference on Food and Nutrition, 164, 165
Conway, Jack, 89

Cooke, Cardinal, 157
Cooper, John Sherman, 189, 190
Corbett, Ray, 251
CORE, 111
Cornell University, 177
Costikyan, Edward, 258
Council of Economic Advisers, 84, 85, 156, 266
Crangle, Joe, 249, 252, 254, 256–258
Crime, 166, 167
Cuba, 211, 218–220, 223, 235, 238, 239, 290
Cuomo, Mario, 249
Cyprus, 231

Daily News, 255, 257
Daily Worker, 46
Dallas *Morning News*, 72
Das Kapital, 15
Day, Edward, 69, 71
Dean, John, 197
Decade Against Racism, 225–227
Decision making, decentralized, 292
Decter, Midge, 248
Defense budget, 255
Defense Department, 69, 70, 83
Deming, Angus, 23, 24, 27, 29, 161
Democratic Party, 49–51, 56, 58, 64, 77, 140, 275, 278, 281
Democrats for Nixon, 183
DeMuth, Chris, 149, 153
DeSapio, Carmine, 50, 53, 56, 58, 94
Détente, 215, 217, 220, 280
Diego Garcia Island, 202
District of Columbia, 151, 152
Domestic Council, 163, 164
Domestic policy, 35, 71, 108, 109, 139, 145, 147, 183, 185, 187, 208, 209, 288, 290
Driver Research Center, 60
Dungan, Ralph, 78
Dunlop, John T., 177
Dutton, Fred, 142

Eastman Kodak, 129, 130, 134, 149
Eberstadt, Nick, 259
Economic Opportunity Act of 1964, 97, 103
Edelman, Peter, 141
Egypt, 231
Ehrlichman, John, 156, 162–164, 168, 188
Eisenhower, Dwight D., 62
Eizenstat, Stuart, 266
Elkins, Stanley, 106
Employment, 82, 83, 87, 88, 91, 103, 104, 108, 111, 126
Enders, Thomas, 221
Energy legislation, 274

Environment Committee, 264
Epstein, Edward J., 199
Estes, Billie Sol, 74
European Economic Community, 232

Face the Nation, 228, 229, 294
Family allowance, 127, 128, 153, 280, 281, 291
Family Assistance Program (FAP), 159–165, 170–172, 175, 178, 182–184, 255, 278, 291. *See also* Family Security System
Family policy, 120, 121, 126–128, 280, 282
Family Security System, 155–158
Farley, James A., 50
Farmer, James, 114
FBI, 68, 69, 136, 142, 150
Federal expenditures, 266, 267
Federal loans, 267
Federal Reserve Bank, 266
Federal Reserve Board, 147, 162
Fenton, Frank, 46
FIGHT, 129, 130
Fiji, 226
Finch, Robert, 145, 146, 151, 153, 155, 156, 159, 170
Finletter, Thomas, 57, 58
Finn, Chester (Checker), Jr., 149, 150, 164, 194
Fisher, Robert, 36, 37
Flanagan, Peter, 164
Fletcher School, 34–36, 59, 60
Ford, Gerald A., 153, 210, 219, 225, 234, 236, 237, 243–245, 261
Ford Foundation, 84, 124
Foreign policy, 136–139, 173, 185, 186, 190, 195, 196, 209, 213–216, 253, 260, 270–273, 288–293
Foreign service, 194, 238, 243
Frankel, Max, 178
Frazier, E. Franklin, 106
Freiden, Bernard, 169
Frelinghuysen, Peter, 201
Friedman, Milton, 127
Frucher, Meyer (Sandy), 252–255, 258

Galbraith, John Kenneth, 188, 189
Garment, Leonard, 144, 145, 149, 164, 212, 221, 227, 229, 234, 236, 245, 252, 258
General Services Administration, 73
Geneva Conference, 272
George VI, king of England, 46
Germany, 49
Ghana, 228
GI Bill, 28, 32, 40

Gifford, Bernard, 251, 254
Ginzburg, Aleksandr, 273
Giri, V. V., 191, 192
Glazer, Nathan, 91, 119, 125, 149, 199, 293
Golan Heights, 238, 242
Goldberg, Arthur, 66–76, 118, 218
Gollogly, Mary, 42–47
Goodwin, Richard, 109, 120
Gordon, Kermit, 83
Graham, Fred, 69
Greenley, Gloria, 26–29
Gross, H. R., 201
Guatemala, 231
Gutheim, Frederick, 73

Haar, Charles, 169
Haddon, Dr. William, Jr., 60, 77
Haldeman, H. R., 150, 163, 164, 168, 188
Hall, Harry, 13, 16, 18, 19, 22, 23, 28, 35, 39, 47
Harlow, Bryce, 146, 153, 163, 165, 170, 172
Harriman, Averell, 52–59, 64–67, 74, 112, 276, 281, 295
Harrington, Michael, 84, 143
Harris, Fred, 141
Harvard Crimson, 247, 287
Harvard Law School, 169
Harvard Medical School, 112
Harvard University, 115, 118–126, 135, 136, 169, 173, 176, 188, 203, 205, 243–247, 259–262, 278, 279, 295
Head Start, 153
Health, Education and Welfare Department, 85, 87, 106, 146, 151, 154, 168, 269, 270
Hebrew University, 253
Heinz, John, 265
Heller, Walter, 83–85
Hendrix College, 170
Henning, Jack, 90
Herman, George, 229
Herzog, Chaim, 223
Hess, Stephen, 149
Higgins, Monsignor George, 120
Hirschfeld, Abraham, 248
Hogan, Frank, 57, 58, 64, 65, 74, 94
Holborn, Fred, 81
Hollemen, Jerry, 74
Holy Name School, 11
Hoover, J. Edgar, 69, 150
Horgan, Paul, 101, 120
Horsky, Charles, 73, 78
House Foreign Affairs Committee, 191, 200, 202
House Ways and Means Committee, 170, 171
Housing and Urban Development Department, 146

Howard University, 109, 112, 114, 285
Human rights, 52, 211, 224, 232, 245, 270–272, 292. See also Civil rights
Hume, Cameron, 225, 226
Humphrey, Hubert H., 78, 143, 144, 263, 264

Income tax, negative, 153, 155
India, 134, 187, 188, 190–195, 210, 260, 278
aid to, 202, 203
rupee debt, 189, 196–204
Indian Press, 198, 200, 202, 204
Indo-American Chamber of Commerce, 195
Inouye, Daniel, 264
Insurance Institute for Highway Safety, 291
Intelligence Committee, 264
Interior Department, 146
International Labor Organization, 38, 59, 229
International Ladies' Garment Workers Union, 72
International Monetary Fund, special drawing fund, 221
International Organizations Bureau, 232, 237, 242
International Rescue Committee, 51, 52
International Textile Agreement, 72
International Women's Year Conference, 228
Ireland, 45, 46
Israel, 218, 223, 224, 227, 228, 233, 237, 238, 242, 253, 272, 273
Italy, 49

Jackson, Henry, 146, 248, 249, 273, 275
Japan, 134, 226, 231
Javits, Jacob, 53, 264
Jewish organizations, 223
Jha, L. K., 189
Job Corps program, 88, 153
Job programs, 85, 88, 153, 281
John Birch Society, 77
Johns Hopkins University, 121
Johnson, Lyndon B., 84–91, 97, 103, 105, 108–110, 139, 145, 151, 157, 160, 168, 211
Johnson, Thomas, 160
Johnson administration, 90, 108, 114–116, 120, 126, 145, 148, 157, 174, 282, 285, 290–294
Joint Center for Urban Studies, 118–126, 144

Kasmire, Bob, 58
Katzman, Bob, 259
Kaul, T. N., 197, 198
Keating, Kenneth, 57, 58, 189, 190
Kennedy, David, 156, 158
Kennedy, Edward, 72, 264
Kennedy, John F., 63–66, 71, 72, 78, 82, 143, 288

Kennedy, Robert, 66, 74, 80, 90, 94–97, 101, 138–143
Kennedy administration, 70, 74, 95, 145, 293, 294
Kennedy assassination, 78–83
Kennedy Institute of Politics, 176
Kennedy School of Government, 253
Kerner Commission report, 139
Kerr, Clark, 135
Kilson, Martin, 185
King, Martin Luther, Jr., 110, 142, 152
Kirkland, Lane, 90, 249, 271
Kisburg, Nicholas, 96
Kissinger, Henry, 146, 150, 163, 169, 170, 189, 197, 199, 203, 211, 212, 218–228, 232–238, 242–248, 288
  ideological differences with Moynihan, 213–216
Klebanoff, Arthur, 149, 169, 248, 252, 258
Koch, Edward, 250
Korea, 40, 43, 44
Korean War, 209
Kristol, Bill, 259
Kristol, Irving, 62, 125

Labor, 38, 41, 75, 77, 90, 115, 219, 224, 229, 250, 271, 275
Labor Department, 66–69, 73–79, 83–92, 101, 104, 278
Laird, Melvin, 129, 132, 134, 164
Latin American nations, 199, 226, 230, 231
Lawford, Pat Kennedy, 65
Leadership Conference on Civil Rights, 166
League of Nations, 213
Lehman, Orin, 96
Levin, Bernard, 241
Levitt, Arthur, 94
Lewis, Hylan, 112–114
Lewis, Samuel, 237, 243
Liberal Party, 258
Libya, 223
Life, 126, 184, 187
Lincoln, Mrs. Evelyn, 79
Lindsay, John, 95, 96, 98, 101, 124, 157, 258
Lipset, Seymour Martin, 121, 135
London School of Economics, 39–46, 136, 193, 214
London Times, 241
Long, Russell, 170–172, 264, 275
Lowenstein, Allard, 141
Lubin, Isidor, 56
Luxembourg, 234

Macy, John, 69–71, 81
Malik, Yakov, 242, 246, 255
Marshall, Burke, 142

Marshall, Ray, 268
Martin, William McChesney, 147
Marxist Popular Movement for the Liberation of Angola (MPLA), 239, 242
Maximum Feasible Misunderstanding (Moynihan), 143, 148, 153, 177
Maxwell, Bill, 19
Maxwell School of Citizenship and Public Affairs, 59
Mayer, Dr. Jean, 164, 165
Mayo, Robert, 158
McCarthy, Eugene, 138, 139, 146, 183
McCloskey, Mark, 56, 276, 277
McCracken, Paul, 156, 158
McCrae, Bernice, 53, 58
McCrory, Mary, 81, 100, 110
McGovern, George, 183, 184
McHugh, Matthew, 250
McKenzie, Robert, 43
McKissick, Floyd, 111
McManus, Bob, 58
McNamara, Robert, 69, 78, 199
McPhee, Dr. Alan, 41
McPherson, Harry, 105, 138
Meet the Press, 115, 160, 183
Merrick, Sam, 87
Meryman, Dick, 28–30, 32, 36–38
Mewhinny, Larsh, 32, 33
Mexico, 227, 231
Middlebury College, 22–27, 29
Middle East, 202, 211, 212, 237, 238, 242, 272–274
Mills, Wilbur, 170
MIT, 118, 169
Mitchell, Clarence, 111, 223, 225, 239, 240
Mitchell, John, 151–153, 167, 168, 178
Model Cities program, 153, 283
Mondale, Walter, 260
Monroe, Mike, 149
Morgenthau, Robert, 74
Moses, Robert, 124
Mosteller, Frederick, 122, 123, 125
Moyers, Bill, 105, 148
Moynihan, Cornelius, 2, 45
Moynihan, Dan Conn, 46
Moynihan, Daniel Patrick
  ambassador to India, 187–207, 210, 260, 278
  ambassador to the United Nations, 211–245, 278, 288, 292, 294, 295
  attitude toward blacks, 127, 284–286
  Averell Harriman and, 52–58
  "benign neglect" memorandum, 128, 165–168, 175–178, 186, 188, 209, 247
  Beyond the Melting Pot, 91, 92, 98, 119
  "blocs are breaking up" cable, 243

Moynihan, Daniel Patrick (*cont'd*)
childhood, 7–10, 276, 279
children of, 58, 192, 212, 276
City College (CCNY), 17–20, 23, 211
comments on American foreign policy, 209–211
Communism and, 35, 43, 51, 62, 209, 216, 228, 271, 275, 288
Doctorate of Philosophy, 59, 65, 66
domestic policy and, 35, 71, 108, 109, 139, 145, 147, 183, 185, 187, 208, 209, 288, 290
family background, 2–10
foreign policy and, 35, 40, 43, 44, 62, 63, 136–139, 173, 185, 186, 190, 195, 196, 209, 213–216, 253, 260, 270–273, 288–293
Fulbright scholarship, 39
Harvard University, 1, 112, 118–126, 135, 136, 176, 177, 181, 188, 203, 205, 243, 244, 245, 247, 259–262, 278, 279, 295
health, 28, 34, 36, 38, 39
honors, 17, 39, 253
ideological differences with Kissinger, 213–216
International Rescue Committee, 51, 52
John F. Kennedy and, 64–66, 71, 72, 78, 82, 143, 288
Labor Department, 68–92, 101, 104, 278
Librarian of Congress, 205
London School of Economics, 39–46, 186, 193, 276
magazine articles, 11, 60–63, 68, 77, 116, 119, 121, 180, 184–187, 209–211, 222, 253, 271
marriage, 54, 59
Maximum Feasible Misunderstanding, 143, 148, 153, 177
mayoral campaign, 93–102
Middlebury College, 22–27, 29, 277
military service, 19, 20, 22, 24, 27–29
Nixon administration and, 144–186, 206, 207, 278
personal vulnerability, 279, 280
poverty programs, 83–91, 103–117, 148, 149, 175
presidential candidacy consideration, 274, 275
speeches on American Society, 131–134
student demonstrations and, 21, 131, 182
Syracuse University, 59, 60, 63–67
Tufts University, 27–29, 32–38, 277, 278
United Nations and, 179–181, 186, 246, 247, 252
U.S. Senate campaign, 247–262, 265, 279, 287, 294, 295

U.S. Senator, 264–275, 278
Vietnam War and, 135–139
welfare reform and, 153–161, 163, 165, 170–172, 253, 264, 268, 269, 274, 280, 291, 294
Wesleyan University, 102, 118
youth, 11–55
Moynihan, Elizabeth Brennan (Mrs. Daniel P.), 54, 58, 65, 66, 81, 95, 97, 100, 119, 134, 146, 150, 173, 188, 192, 193, 204, 205, 212, 252, 254. *See also* Brennan, Elizabeth
Moynihan, Elizabeth Effinger (2nd Mrs. John C.), 2
Moynihan, Ellen (sister), 8, 11, 16, 31, 39. *See also* Parris, Ellen Moynihan
Moynihan, Hannah, 17
Moynihan, John (cousin), 17, 31
Moynihan, John (father), 2, 3, 13, 47
abandoned family, 10
boyhood and youth, 3–5
finances, 10
jobs, 7, 8
in journalism, 5, 9
Moynihan, John C. (Jack) (grandfather), 2, 10, 11, 29, 46
death of, 3
early years in American, 2, 3
marriage, 2
reputation, 3
Moynihan, John McCloskey (son), 192, 276
Moynihan, Margaret Phipps (Mrs. John; mother), 6, 9. *See also* Stapelfeld, Margaret P. M. (Mrs. Henry)
defense plant job, 16, 31
to England, 47
finances, 11, 12, 31, 35
Hell's Kitchen saloon, 30
homes, 7, 8, 10, 11, 13, 14, 16
marriages, 7, 10, 12–14, 32
Moynihan's Bar, 32, 34, 39
Rockaways bar, 31, 32
welfare, 11
Moynihan, Mary, 2
Moynihan, Mary Fitzpatrick (1st Mrs. John C.), 2
Moynihan, Maura (daughter), 58, 192
Moynihan, Michael (brother), 7, 10, 11, 13–17, 31, 35, 39, 47
Moynihan, Timothy (son), 58, 212
Moynihan-Amin controversy, 223–226
Murray, Emmett Van Allen, III, 23
Murray, Thomas, 57
Myerson, Bess, 254
Myerson, Jacob, 221

NAACP, 111
Nader, Ralph, 77, 133, 291
Nation, 112
National Defense Education Act of 1958, 63
National District Attorneys' Association, 64
National Governors Conference, 162
National Herald, 201
National Liberation Front, 136, 288
National Security Council, 146, 150, 163, 236
NATO, 162, 170, 172, 239
NBC-TV, 126, 160
Negotiations Now, 135, 136, 288, 289
Nepal, 226
Nessen, Ron, 160, 225
Neustadt, Richard, 177
New Nigerian, 241
New School for Social Research, 143
New Statesman, 44, 288
Newsweek, 145, 177, 184, 188, 234
New York, 253
New York City, fiscal affairs of, 253, 265–268
New York City Loan Guarantee Act, 268
New York State, fiscal affairs of, 265–267
New York State Bankers' Association, 267
New York State Court of Appeals, 50
New York State Department of Health, 60
New York Times, 9, 62, 95, 96, 121, 134, 143,
        148, 160, 167, 168, 173, 178, 185, 191,
        206, 213, 224, 235, 243, 244, 249, 252,
        255, 256, 269, 274
New York University, 19
Niven, Paul, 43, 49
Nixon, Richard M., 117, 128, 134, 143–188,
        190, 195, 197, 199, 206, 207, 211, 243,
        248, 251, 286, 288, 289, 291
Nixon administration, 62, 144–148, 157, 163,
        165, 172–174, 177, 179, 183, 188, 190,
        194, 205, 264, 278, 287, 291, 293, 294
"Nixon White House" tape, 255
Noe, Courtland, 14
Noe, Julia (Mrs. Courtland), 8, 10–12
No-fault auto insurance, 291
Northern Indiana Public Service Company, 2,
        3
North Vietnam, 218–220. *See also* Vietnam
Notre Dame University, 5
Nuclear war, 215, 217
Nuclear weapons, 203, 204

Oakes, John B., 256
Oakeshott, Michael, 136
O'Brien, Lawrence, 68
O'Connor, Frank, 97, 99, 100
O'Donnell, Kenneth, 64, 66
O'Dwyer, Paul, 95, 248, 250, 251, 256
Office of Economic Opportunity, 87, 88, 148,
        153

Office of Management and Budget, 197, 198,
        266
Office of Policy Planning and Research, 74
Ohlin, Lloyd, 86
One Third of a Nation, 83, 89
Ordway, Ellen, 20, 27
Organization of African Unity, 224, 225, 233
O'Riordan, Dan, 32
Oswald, Lee Harvey, 79–81, 280
Other American, The, 84
Owen, Roberts B., 36
Owings, Nathaniel, 73

Packwood, Robert, 270
Pakistan, 187–189, 194, 195, 204, 205,
        231
Palestine, 232, 272, 274
Palestine Liberation Organization, 238, 242,
        243, 272, 274
Panama Canal Treaty, 274
Parris, Addison, 53
Parris, Ellen Moynihan (Mrs. Addison), 53.
        See also Moynihan, Ellen
Payton, Dr. Benjamin, 112–114
Pei, I. M., 73
Peru, 227
Pettigrew, Thomas, 122, 123, 144, 286
Phipps, Daniel, 6
Phipps, H. Willard (Harry), 6, 11
Phipps, Julia, 6, 8. *See also* Noe, Julia (Mrs.
        Courtland)
Phipps, Julia Grayson, 6
Phipps, Lucille, 6
Phipps, Margaret, 5, 6. *See also* Moynihan,
        Margaret Phipps
Phipps, Margaret Bickell, 6, 29
Pickles, William, 43
Playboy, 72
Plumb, J. H., 46, 156
Podhoretz, Norman, 125, 234, 252, 258
Political prisoners resolution, 232, 233, 236
Politics, 1
        ethnic, 92, 247
        expansion of realm of, 284
        international, 189, 190, 211, 213, 215, 216,
                223, 281, 289
        national, 64–66, 246, 275
        New York City, 49–51, 93–102, 278
        New York State, 52, 58
Pope John XXIII, 104, 280
Poverty programs, 83–91, 103–117, 148, 149,
        175
Powell, Jody, 274
Powledge, Fred, 126
Price, John, 149, 157, 162
Price, Raymond, 145, 164

Protestant Council of the City of New York, 112
Proxmire, William, 267
Public Assistance subcommittee, 264, 268
Public Interest, The, 121
Public Works Committee, 264
Public works legislation, 265
Puerto Rico, 235

Race riots, 152, 280, 285. See also Urban riots
Racism, 223–227, 231, 284, 285
Rainwater, Lee, 169
Randolph, Jennings, 264, 265
Rao, Paul, Jr., 98, 99
Ravitch, Richard, 250
Ray, Sidhartha Sanker, 196
Rayburn, Sam, 264
Reagan, Ronald, 236
Red Cross, 232
Reisler, Joe, 23, 24, 46, 47, 161
Reporter, The, 60, 62, 63, 68, 77
Report on Black Family Stability. See Black Family Stability Report
Report on Equality of Educational Opportunity, 121–123
Report on the World Social Situation, 289
Reserve Bank of India, 200
Reserve Officers Training Corps, 27–29, 34, 62
Reston, James, 244, 245, 295
Reynolds, Dean, 4, 7, 9, 99
Rhodesia, 239
Ribicoff, Abraham, 171, 172
Richard, Ivor, 228, 234–236
Richardson, Elliot, 243
Rickman, Herbert, 254
Riley, Paul, 49, 50
RKO, 7–9
Rockefeller, David, 157
Rockefeller, Nelson A., 58, 63, 74, 77, 127, 134, 211
Rogers, William, 191, 194, 197, 199, 211
Romney, George, 159
Roosevelt, Franklin D., 10, 23, 281
Roosevelt, Franklin D., Jr., 52
Rosovsky, Henry, 244
Rosow, Jerome, 159
Ruby, Jack, 81
Rumania, 227
Rumsfeld, Donald, 153, 172, 236
Rupee debt, 189, 196–204
Rush, Kenneth, 197
Rusk, Dean, 80
Rustin, Bayard, 251
Ryan, William, 112
Ryan, William F., 94, 95

Sadat, Anwar el-, 272
Safire, William, 145, 235
St. Louis University, 142
Sakharov, Andrei, 240
Saltzman, Dick, 52
Sayre, Joel, 9
Scali, John, 210
Schlesinger, Arthur, Jr., 259
Schlesinger, James, 236
Schneider, David, 194
Schultze, Charles, 87, 266
Scranton, William, 210
Screvane, Paul, 91, 94–101
Senate Banking Committee, 267
Senate Finance Committee, 170–172, 175, 184, 264, 266, 269, 291
Senate Foreign Relations Committee, 190, 201, 203, 218
Senate Watergate Committee, 197. See also Watergate
Shcharansky, Anatoly, 273
Sheldon, Courtney, 225
Shriver, Sargent, 86–88, 97
Shultz, George, 158, 198
Sierra Leone, 226, 227
Sinai, 219
Singh, Kewal, 200, 202
Singh, Swaran, 195
Sisco, Joseph, 189, 197, 242
Sizer, Theodore, 119, 121, 122
Slaner, Al, 250
Smith, Cloethill Woodward, 73
Smith, H. Allen, 5, 7, 9
Smith, Howard K., 42
Smith, Nell (Mrs. H. Allen), 9, 10
Smith, Stephen, 96
Socialism, 21
Social policy, 153, 281–284, 289, 293
Solzhenitsyn, Aleksandr, 219, 220
Somalia, 223
Some American People (Caldwell), 15
Sonnenfeldt, Helmut, 212
Sorensen, Theodore, 69, 78, 142
South Africa, 218, 232, 234, 239, 240
Southeast Asia, 188, 195, 288
Southern Christian Leadership Conference, 142
Southern Yemen, 223
South Korea, 220
South Vietnam, 218–220, 288. See also Vietnam
Soviet Union. See U.S.S.R.
Spain, 227
Sputnik, 62, 63
Stafford, Robert, 265
Stapelfeld, Henry, 12–14

Stapelfeld, Margaret P. M. (Mrs. Henry). *See* Moynihan, Margaret Phipps (Mrs. John)
Stapelfeld, Thomas, 14
State Board of Elections, 55
State Department, 188, 190, 196–199, 202, 210, 219–225, 228, 232–237, 243–245, 271, 278
Stein, Andrew, 248
Steingut, Stanley, 94, 99
Stevenson, Adlai, 64, 281
Stewart, Milton, 53, 54
Strategic Arms Limitation Treaty (SALT), 271, 273
Student League for World Government, 29
Student protest demonstrations, 21, 131, 182, 280
Students for a Democratic Society, 182
Sulzberger, Arthur Ochs, 256
Sulzberger, C. L., 206
Sweeney, Jack, 6
Syracuse University, 58, 59, 63–65
Syria, 223

Tammany Hall, 50, 57, 94
Task Force on Community Action Programs, 86–88
Task Force on Employee-Management Relations, 69–72
Task Force on Manpower Conservation, 82–88
Tass news agency, 241
Television, 91, 98
Tenenbaum, Robert, 14, 16, 18, 23, 28
Third Committee, 179, 223, 225–228, 230
Third World, 209–223, 228, 230–235, 241, 294
Thorn, Gaston, 234
Time, 9, 117, 126, 177
Times of India, 191
Today, 231
Totalitarianism, 242, 288
Totalitarian nations, 233, 290
Traffic safety, 60, 61, 65, 76, 291. *See also* Auto safety
Traffic Safety Policy Coordinating Committee, 56, 60
Transportation Department, 146
Treasury Department, 197, 222
Truman, Harry S., 34, 35, 281
Tufts University, 27–29
Tufts *Weekly,* 32, 33

Uganda, 223, 224, 253
Unemployment, 71, 106, 107, 112, 127, 166, 265
UNESCO, 95

United Nations, 44, 118, 132, 153, 172, 173, 181, 207, 213, 229, 230, 235, 236, 241–246, 248, 264, 278, 288
Colonialism committee, 211, 239, 240
General Assembly, 210, 218–224, 227, 228, 230, 237, 239, 240, 272
Group of 77, 221, 222
nonaligned nations, 218, 219
Report on the World Social Situation, 180
Security Council, 238, 242, 245, 246, 255
Seventh Special Session, 225
Third Committee (on Social, Humanitarian and Cultural Affairs), 179, 223, 225–228, 230, 289
U.S. Mission, 219, 244
United Nations Association, 234
University of California, 135
Unsafe at Any Speed (Nader), 77
Urban affairs, 145, 146, 165, 282
Urban Affairs Council, 146, 150, 151, 154, 155, 157, 162, 164, 169
Urban riots, 130, 131. *See also* Race riots
Urban studies, 124
U.S. Employment Service, 19
U.S. Navy, V-12 program, 19, 20, 22, 24, 25, 27
U.S. Senate, 190, 219, 229, 264, 265, 273, 275, 278
U.S.S. *McDougall,* 34
U.S.S. *Quirinus,* 29, 30
U.S.S.R., 179, 180, 184, 188, 189, 203, 204, 209, 214–217, 220, 238–243, 246, 270–275, 280, 290, 294

Vance, Cyrus, 271, 273
Vanocur, Sander, 42, 44, 45, 66, 69
Veneman, Jack, 154
Vest, George, 202
Vietnam, 52, 212. *See also* North Vietnam; South Vietnam
Vietnam War, 21, 135–139, 149, 173, 184, 190, 191, 199, 210, 211, 214, 288–290, 293, 294
VISTA, 172
Vogt, Peter, 161
Vorster, John, 239–241

Wagner, Robert F., Jr., 50, 51, 91, 93, 94, 96
Wagner, Robert F., Sr., 50
Waldheim, Kurt, 219, 223
Walinsky, Adam, 141
Wallace, Bob, 80
Wallace, Henry, 35
Wallis, George, 35
Wall Street Journal, 269
Walters, Barbara, 231

NOV 0 8 2001	DATE DUE	

1996